Debbie

Dear Reader:

The book you are about to read is the latest bestseller from St. Martin's True Crime Library, the imprint the *New York Times* calls "the leader in true crime!" Each month, we offer you a fascinating account of the latest, most sensational crime that has captured the national attention. St. Martin's is the publisher of perennial bestselling true crime author Jack Olsen (SON and DOC) whose SALT OF THE EARTH is the true story of how one woman fought and triumphed over life-shattering violence; Joseph Wambaugh called it "powerful and absorbing." DEATH OF A LITTLE PRINCESS recounts the investigation into the horrifying murder of child beauty queen JonBenét Ramsey. FALLEN HERO is the *New York Times* bestselling account of the O.J. Simpson case. Fannie Weinstein and Melinda Wilson tell the story of a beautiful honors student who was lured into the dark world of sex for hire in THE COED CALL GIRL MURDER.

St. Martin's True Crime Library gives you the stories *behind* the headlines. Our authors take you right to the scene of the crime and into the minds of the most notorious murderers to show you what really makes them tick. St. Martin's True Crime Library paperbacks are better than the most terrifying thriller, because it's all true! The next time you want a crackling good read, make sure it's got the St. Martin's True Crime Library logo on the spine—you'll be up all night!

Charles E. Spicer, Jr.

Charles E. Spicer, Jr.
Senior Editor, St. Martin's True Crime Library

D0925629

San Angelo, TX 76901
(325) 942-0845

Extraordinary Acclaim for the Work of Ken Englade

"HOT BLOOD is Kenneth Englade at the top of his craft—impeccable reporting, solid writing, and a surgeon's eye for the vivid detail."
—Jack Olsen, author of *Salt of the Earth* and *Hastened to the Grave*

"Excellent . . . Insightful . . . Both a sensational murder investigation and a psychological thriller."
—Maury Terry, author of *The Ultimate Evil*, on BEYOND REASON

"A grim and fascinating story skillfully told."
—Tony Hillerman on BEYOND REASON

"Chilling . . . May be the most engrossing true crime book of the year."
—Leslie Walker, author of *Sudden Fury*, on BEYOND REASON

"A powerful account of the slaying of a wealthy Virginia couple by their college-age daughter and her teenage lover."
—*Kirkus Reviews* on BEYOND REASON

"Englade ably narrates a complex case."
—*Publishers Weekly* on BEYOND REASON

"Spiced with the stuff that rolls out of tabloids and soap operas—affairs, fast living, fancy cars, money, famous attorneys and courtroom drama."
—*Birmingham News* on BLOOD SISTER

Other St. Martin's titles by Ken Englade

EVERYBODY'S BEST FRIEND

KEN ENGLADE

St. Martin's Paperbacks

EVERYBODY'S BEST FRIEND

Copyright © 1999 by Ken Englade.

Cover photographs courtesy AP/Wide World Photos.

ISBN: 0-312-96917-1

Printed in the United States of America

St. Martin's Paperbacks edition / January 1999

10 9 8 7 6 5 4 3 2 1

For Robert Krell. One of the best.

ACKNOWLEDGMENTS

For their assistance in helping me put this book together I am especially indebted to the following people: Detectives Rich Peffall, Charlie Craig, Tim Woodward, and John Fallon, Sergeant Mark Keenan, Lieutenant Peter Hertzog, Montgomery County First Assistant District Attorney Bruce Castor and ADA Risa Ferman, Neil Epstein, Marilyn Phister of WPVI–TV, Robin Warshaw, and the members of the American Society of Journalists and Authors, who offered counsel and support. If I've neglected to mention anyone, it's completely unintentional. This expression of gratitude is woefully inadequate to express my appreciation, but I hope it helps.

K.E.

AUTHOR'S NOTE

The dialogue represented in this book was constructed from available documents, court filings, and police reports, or was reconstructed from the memory of the participants. Some of the scenes depicted were reconstructed from interviews and accessible documentation.

In order to protect their privacy, a few of the characters have been given fictitious names. Such names have been put in italics the first time they appear.

EVERYBODY'S
BEST FRIEND

ONE

"Isn't it beautiful?" Anne Newman gushed, cupping the tiny, gold baby shoe in her palm. "I can see just it on a gold chain. What grandmother wouldn't love to have something like this?"

She turned with anticipation to her daughter, expecting to see her familiar grin. "Stef?"

Stefanie Rabinowitz blinked. "What was that, Mom? What did you say?"

"Oh, Stef," Anne said in mild exasperation. "I was asking you what you thought about this charm."

"My, that is pretty," Stefanie said, leaning closer. "How much is it?"

Apprehensively, Anne turned over the attached tag, uttering a quiet gasp when she saw the figures written precisely in stark, black ink. "Oh, my goodness," she sighed. "Two hundred and seventy dollars. That is *definitely* out of my price range."

Returning it politely to the clerk, she and Stefanie left the store, exiting onto Lancaster Avenue, the narrow old street that ran through the heart of downtown Ardmore.

"What is it?" Anne asked with concern. "You've hardly said two sentences all afternoon. This is a holiday, for goodness' sakes. We're supposed to be enjoying ourselves."

It was the last day of Passover, the time when conscientious Jews around the world commemorated their deliverance from enslavement in Egypt more than 3,200 years ago. That morning, Anne and Stefanie had decided to celebrate by not doing much of anything. "Let's just wander among the shops," Stefanie suggested.

Normally, both women enjoyed their excursions together. Although they lived within a twenty-minute drive of each other, neither of them had much time during the normal work week for casual mother/daughter conversation. In the mornings, Anne did secretarial work for a rabbi in Elkins Park, where she and her husband, Lou, a quiet, serious-minded accountant, had lived since before Stefanie was born. Stefanie, too, was usually harried, what with a baby not yet a year old and a high-pressure job as a litigator with a prestigious Center City law firm.

"I'm sorry, Mom," Stefanie apologized. "I guess my mind was somewhere else."

"Is something wrong?" Anne asked, concerned.

"Goodness, no," Stefanie replied quickly. "Everything's fine. I was just thinking about work."

"Everything's all right, isn't it?"

"Sure. It's just that I have a new client coming in tomorrow for our first meeting. The firm decided to represent him and assigned me the case. He's a very valuable client and I want to make sure everything is handled correctly."

"If that's all it is," Anne said breezily, "I'm sure it is nothing to worry about. You're a wonderful lawyer. You'll do fine."

Ever since she had been a little girl, Anne recalled, Stefanie had been intense. When she made up her mind to do something, she let nothing stand in her way. There had been the time nineteen years before when Stefanie, then only eleven, had announced that she was going to learn to "Read Torah."

When she made the pronouncement, Anne and Lou had

been mildly shocked, wondering for a time if their daughter was biting off more than she could chew. Not that she wasn't bright enough. They had no doubt that Stefanie, an honor student who, in the first and second grades, used to come home from school sobbing because her advanced books were different from those of her classmates, was intellectually capable. Still, it was an ultra-ambitious goal. The Torah was a collection of the first five books of the Judaic Scriptures, the entire body of Jewish law and learning. It was written in Hebrew. "Reading Torah" meant chanting from the scripture in the original language. It was not easy, mastering the intonations required to give meaning to the words.

On her own, Stefanie had called the cantor and arranged for lessons, then had applied herself to learning the task with diligence. By the time Stefanie became a *bas mitzva* at age thirteen, she was an accomplished Torah reader, one qualified not only to "read" but to help teach younger, would-be readers as well. It was typical of her daughter, Anne thought, that the passage she liked the most was called "The Curses" since it required a Reader of particular skill, one who could intone the rising and falling cadences of the difficult text in the way in which it was meant to be delivered, chanting some sentences rapidly, then dropping her voice and switching to a deliberate slow pace in others. Done correctly, it could be an impressive service. And Stefanie always strove to do it correctly, just as she did everything else.

When she was a student at Cheltenham High School, which was generally regarded as possibly the best in all of Montgomery County, she had pushed herself to a National Merit Scholarship. And then she selected Bryn Mawr to do her undergraduate work, intending at first to be a physician. But in her freshman year she discovered that she had a phobia about needles, so she switched her major to political science, graduating with honors in 1989. The following fall, she was accepted into law school at Temple University, from which she graduated, again with honors, in 1992. After passing the bar, she took a much-coveted job with one of Center City's more respected firms.

Now, it seemed to Anne, her daughter was equally determined to be both a good mother and a good lawyer, balancing the difficulties of two major tasks with her usual ease and finesse. After the baby, Haley Sarah, had been born in May 1996, Stefanie asked the partners in her firm if she could work three days a week until she felt comfortable leaving her daughter with a nanny full-time. Unwilling to lose her, they readily agreed. So on Mondays, Wednesdays, and Thursdays she commuted to Philadelphia; the rest of the week she was home with Haley.

"Should we go in here?" Anne asked as they approached a boutique.

Stefanie glanced at her watch. "Oh, no! Look at the time."

Anne smiled to herself. It was typical of Stefanie that she wore an inexpensive watch when many of the other female lawyers she knew would be sporting the newest and most conspicuous models they could find. In that regard, Stefanie had not changed since high school. Although she dressed impeccably for the job, when she wasn't working she was perfectly content to parade around in baggy sweat clothes with very little makeup. If anyone ever asked her for a definition of the word "unpretentious," Anne thought, she would quickly say, "Stefanie Rabinowitz."

"I'd better get home," Stefanie said. "Craig will be going crazy with Haley."

"That's not true and you know it," Anne chuckled. "He absolutely dotes on her."

"Yes, he does," Stefanie replied, laughing. "And you don't know how happy that makes me."

"Oh, I might have some idea," Anne said, returning the smile. "How's Craig's business doing?" she asked somewhat nervously, not wanting to seem as though she were prying. The downside to the arrangement Stefanie had worked out with her firm to work only part-time meant she was getting only part-time pay as well. It was $30,000 a year, which wasn't bad at all, but it wasn't sufficient to support the lifestyle she and her husband, Craig, wanted to maintain. Especially not with the baby.

"I think it's getting ready to really take off," Stefanie said. "He's made a terrific connection with a guy in New York. Craig thinks it's going to result in a huge upswing in sales. Come on, Mom," she added ardently, "we'd better hurry."

Striding briskly to her blue Volvo, she unlocked the passenger-side door, holding it for her mother while she got in. "What would you like to do for dinner tomorrow?" she asked, settling behind the wheel.

"Oh, it doesn't matter. Did you have anyplace special in mind?"

"No, but we can decide tomorrow."

"That sounds good," Anne nodded. "You're working tomorrow, aren't you? Because today was a holiday."

"Yeah," Stefanie nodded. "But I'll be home about six. Then we can make up our minds. Do you want us to pick you up?"

"No. Your father and I will meet you at your place and we can go from there."

"Good. Then we can come back for coffee afterwards. How's Dad feeling?"

"Much better. This new treatment seems to be working. He's going to beat this cancer," she said with determination.

"Oh, I hope so," Stefanie sighed. "It's so scary."

"Yes," Anne nodded solemnly. "It is that."

Turning her attention to her driving, Stefanie swung the Volvo right on Lancaster Avenue, then headed east. Neither woman paid much attention as they drove down the familiar row of shops and restaurants, past the Lower Merion Police

Department, then left, toward Merion, where Craig and Stefanie lived.

While Stefanie concentrated on the traffic, Anne let her thoughts drift to Craig, the son-in-law she got without having the opportunity to decide if he was the one she wanted. Stefanie had focused with a single-minded intensity on everything else in her life, and it was just as true when it came to her relationship with Craig.

Anne recalled how happy her daughter had been that summer in 1983 when she returned from Camp Wohclo, a facility for girls near Gettysburg. A vivacious sixteen-year-old with large, expressive brown eyes and thick, dark-brown hair that fell in loose waves to her shoulders, Stefanie explained what it had been like to be a counselor-in-training, in effect a Big Sister to the younger girls, many of whom had been away from home for the first time. But there had been something else to brighten her spirits, too. She had become friendly with a boy who was a counselor at a neighboring facility, Camp Comet Trails. The boy's name was Craig Rabinowitz.

Anne remembered meeting him the previous year when Stefanie's younger brother, Ira, attended the camp. As well as she could recall, he seemed like a nice enough boy. Four years older than Stefanie, he was an undergraduate student at Temple University, a well-respected, ninety-nine-year-old state school that was an easy commute away.

At the time, Stefanie herself had been interested in another Philadelphia college, the University of Pennsylvania, a member of the venerable Ivy League, along with Brown, Columbia, Cornell, Dartmouth, Harvard, Princeton, and Yale. Stefanie remembered Craig saying that he had a friend at Penn, so she called him to get the friend's name in hopes that she could learn more about the school. Craig gave it to her, then asked her if she would go with him to a movie. Soon afterwards, he asked her out again, this time to an ice hockey game. He was, Stefanie explained, an avid fan of the Philadelphia Flyers. He liked them so much that he even held expensive season tickets.

But on the night she was supposed to attend the Flyers game, while waiting for Craig to pick her up, she began having second thoughts about the date, wondering if she wanted to continue seeing Craig.

"I don't think I'm going to go," she told her mother.

"Oh, no," Anne replied quickly. "You made a commitment. You have to go."

Stefanie went. And from that day onward she was never seriously interested in anyone but Craig. Not that Anne didn't encourage her to date others. But Stefanie's reaction was always the same. Whenever Anne mentioned that she should date someone besides Craig, just to be able to compare him to others, Stefanie rolled her eyes and tried her best to ignore her. On June 17, 1990, almost exactly seven years after that fateful summer at Camp Wohelo, and two weeks after her twenty-third birthday, Stefanie and Craig were married.

As in most new marriages, the years since had not been trouble-free. In many ways, Anne felt, Craig and Stefanie were complete opposites.

Where Stefanie had been determined to get the best education possible, Craig cared little about schooling. Growing up in Penn Wynne, the son of an executive with BVD, the huge clothing manufacturer, Craig had graduated without distinction from Lower Merion High School. He dropped out of Temple after a brief period and never went back. Education was secondary to his interest in sports. Craig was a jock wannabe, a faithful fan with a lifelong interest in baseball and hockey, dual fascinations that he carried deep into adulthood. Well after he and Stefanie were married, he continued to play a rough-and-tumble game called deck hockey—essentially ice hockey without the ice, as Stefanie had described it—and first base on a softball team sponsored by the Jewish Community Center.

Where Stefanie was unpretentious to a fault, Craig wanted the best of everything. After Craig and Stefanie had set their wedding date they went to the major stores to register for gifts. Although most of their friends were either still in college or had only recently graduated and could hardly afford expensive wedding presents, Craig had insisted on listing them for the most costly merchandise he could think of: Waterford crystal, Haviland china, and Ralph Lauren towels. While Stefanie did most of her shopping from catalogs, Craig bought his clothes from expensive men's stores.

Unlike Stefanie, status, too, was important to Craig. Whenever they went to a wedding, if he and Stefanie weren't seated among the top echelon of guests, he got grumpy and pouted.

But the main difference between Stefanie and Craig, from what Anne could see, was their opinion on work. While Stefanie had always been a hard worker, Craig was indolent and ambitionless. For much of the time that Anne had known him, he had drifted from one undemanding job to another. At one time he had planned to open a summer camp for kids, but that had fallen through years before. After that, he worked for a while at a women's spa; then for a short time as a real-estate appraiser.

In 1990, the year Craig and Stefanie were married, he and a friend, Craig Yusem, started a business called C&C Vending, which evolved into a two-man company that sold latex gloves to health care practitioners. The partnership broke up rather quickly and Craig branched out on his own, starting a new company called C&C Supplies Inc.

The way he explained it to Anne and Lou, he bought containers of latex gloves from Malaysia and re-sold them to Philadelphia area retailers. According to him, he made a neat thirty-three percent profit on the sale of every container of gloves, or $11,000 per sale. It was almost pure profit, since his only major expense was for rental of warehouse space on Delaware Avenue in Center City, not far from the Port of Philadelphia.

He had made the venture sound so promising that Anne and Lou, and even their son, Ira, had been willing to invest when Craig had come to them the previous February asking if they would be willing to back a loan he needed to make a big sale. He needed $88,000, he said, to buy four containers of gloves. The terms of the loan were steep, he explained: nineteen percent interest for six months. That meant he had to pay back the original amount plus $8,500 in interest, for a total of $96,500. But he was sure he could sell the gloves for $132,000, thereby clearing $35,500, making the high interest worthwhile. He would put up his and Stefanie's house as security, Craig said, but the $230,000 residence already had two mortgages totaling $204,000 and he couldn't borrow any more against it. Would the Newmans be willing to help him out? Anne and Lou talked it over and agreed to offer their own home in Elkins Park as collateral.

It was not the first time the Newmans had put themselves out for Stefanie and Craig. Anne still laughed about how they had agreed to let their daughter and son-in-law come live with them four years before, only a little more than three years after the young couple had been married.

One night when they were having dinner together, Anne recalled with a smile, Craig had cavalierly announced that he and Stefanie were moving in. "We want to save some money," he said with a big smile.

Anne and Lou discussed it and the next day told their daughter and son-in-law that they were welcome. "But you have to pay us rent," Anne said sternly.

"Rent!" said Stefanie, surprised. "You mean you're going to take money from *us*!"

"Yes," Anne replied adamantly. "Fifty dollars a month."

Every month for the next year and a half she and Craig

paid the Newmans. When they bought the house in Merion and moved out, Anne gleefully handed them a check representing what they had given the Newmans in "rent"— $900, which they used toward the down payment on the house.

What Lou and Anne did not discover until later was that Stefanie and Craig had moved in because they were deeply in debt at the apartment in which they had been living. The owner was suing them for almost $6,000 in unpaid fees, and their joint bank account at the time had contained only ninety-eight dollars. They promptly repaid the debt. Anne had every confidence that Craig also would pay off the loan for the gloves and she and Lou would get their house deed back along with a substantial interest payment.

Merion, Pennsylvania
5:43 p.m.

"Here we are," Stefanie chirped happily, pulling into the long driveway that led to the back of their home on Winding Way, a twisting, pleasant street shaded by oaks, elms, and maples and lined with handsome houses set off by neatly manicured lawns. The Rabinowitzes' house, while not extraordinary, was pretty enough in its own right, its fieldstone-and-brick front melding tastefully with the surrounding shrubbery. Bright flowers lined the front of the small porch and the grass was neatly trimmed. Anne smiled inwardly every time she noticed the landscaping, taking pride in the fact that it was the product of many an afternoon's labor by her husband, Lou. Craig was spectacularly inept at gardening, demonstrating neither an inclination nor a talent for the task, so Lou Newman came over periodically to cut the grass and tend the shrubs.

Stefanie continued down the drive, making the bend to the rear and stopping in front of what used to be a two-car garage before a previous owner converted it into a family room.

"Hey!" Craig called, rushing enthusiastically to greet his wife and mother-in-law.

"Hi," Stefanie replied cheerfully, giving her husband a quick kiss. "Where's Haley?"

"Just finishing her dinner. Why don't you go tell her hello?"

At just under six feet and 210 pounds, Craig gave the impression of bulk but not strength. Despite his membership in an expensive health club and his preoccupation with sports, he had a round, pudgy face and a stomach that bulged over his belt. Combined with his receding hair and sagging jaw line, he looked older than thirty-three. While he was not particularly handsome, he was warm and open. Most of those who knew him would describe him as a born salesman.

Anne walked in and glanced casually around the room. Scattered here and there was evidence of her daughter and son-in-law's eclectic choice of reading material: *Vanity Fair* next to *Gourmet*; *Bon Appetit* thrown casually atop *Parents*. A copy of *Newsweek* and one of *People* were open by a chair that Anne and Lou had given them. A new issue of *Philadelphia Magazine* sat on a nearby table.

"Did you have a good time?" Craig asked, following the two women into the other room where Haley was still in her high chair.

"Oh, we just wandered around," Stefanie said, hugging her daughter, who cooed and laughed with delight. "We looked, but we didn't buy," she told Craig with a smile.

"That's good," Craig said, feigning relief. He opened his mouth, obviously intending to say more, but was cut off by the jangling telephone.

"I'll get it," Stefanie said, running out of the room. "It's probably for me."

"What did you want to do for dinner tomorrow?" Anne asked, turning to Craig.

"Uuuummm," he replied. "That's a good question. Let me think about it for a minute."

While he was pondering, Anne walked over to Haley, lifting her and giving her a big smack on the cheek. The baby laughed merrily and rubbed Anne's nose. It was a grandmother's prerogative, Anne said to herself, to believe that Haley was the happiest child she had ever known.

Goodness knows, Anne admitted, she had not always been Craig's biggest fan. He had some traits that really rubbed her the wrong way. Take the babysitting thing, for instance. On Wednesdays the nanny did not come to stay with Haley, so Anne and Craig shared the duties. Craig watched the baby in the morning and Anne came over in the afternoons to relieve him so he could take care of his business. But if she was late and didn't call him to say she was running behind schedule, he was very displeased. He wouldn't show his anger at her—Anne had never known Craig to lose his temper—but he would tell Stefanie that he was unhappy because Anne had been tardy. Then Stefanie would complain to Anne.

As far as Anne knew, her son-in-law had never mistreated her daughter, not once in the nearly fourteen years they had been together. Stefanie would never have put up with *that*, Anne was sure. In fact, she thought her daughter secretly wished that Craig would be a tiny bit more aggressive. "He won't ever even argue with me," Stefanie had told her mother once.

On the other hand, Anne felt that Craig didn't need to. Stefanie always went along with whatever he wanted. When things didn't go his way, Craig scowled and went into a funk. Stefanie always gave in to him, and she always defended him to others.

Whatever they had worked out between them, however, seemed to be succeeding. Anne had never seen Stefanie so happy. She practically glowed. If Craig played a large role in that, Anne certainly wasn't going to try to find fault.

Certainly, though, Haley was responsible to a large extent as well. As a semi-outsider, Anne could see subtle changes in both Craig's and Stefanie's attitudes since the baby had been born. For one thing, Stefanie had told her just recently that she and Craig were searching for a congregation to join. This pleased Anne immensely since she and Lou both were very observant. When Stefanie and her brother, Ira, were growing up, Anne had kept a kosher home. She didn't serve meat and milk at the same meal. When she shopped, she bought only kosher meat and chickens, never shellfish or pork. Stefanie and her brother were brought up thinking that was the right way, the proper way. From the time she was eleven until she married Craig, Stefanie had attended devotions nearly every Sabbath. But after she and Craig were married, Stefanie was not as outwardly devout. Although Anne was sure they both kept the Holy Days like Rosh Hashanah, which begins the Ten Days of Penitence, and Yom Kippur, which ends the ten-day period, as well as attending Seders during Passover, they had not joined a congregation. This puzzled Anne a little because Craig came from a very observant family. His grandmother had been one of the founders of Yeadon, a synagogue in Southwest Philadelphia, and Craig had become a *bar mitzva* at Temple Beth Hillel, one of the more prominent synagogues in Greater Philadelphia. It was something that she and Lou had discussed. In the end, they agreed that Craig and Stefanie's religious life was really none of their business; let them work it out for themselves in their own time.

"How about some oriental food?" Craig asked, breaking her reverie. "Are you and Lou up to spicy?"

"I guess we can do that," Anne replied less than enthusiastically. She and her husband preferred plainer food, especially Lou with his heavy medication, but she decided not to argue.

"Good," Craig said cheerily, rubbing his hands together. "Let's go to that place in Ardmore, the Thai Pepper."

"Okay," Anne said, forcing a smile. "By the way," she added, looking around quickly to make sure Stefanie was out of earshot, "how are the plans for her birthday party coming along?"

"Great! Evviva's says they're all ready for us. I've given them the deposit, but I want to thank you and Lou for taking care of the announcements."

"It isn't every day our daughter turns thirty," Anne smiled.

"That was Elaine," Stefanie said, bustling back into the room.

"Oh, gosh!" Craig said. "I forgot this was your night out. You being off today made me lose track."

"We're not going. Elaine isn't feeling well so we decided to postpone."

"Uh-oh," Craig replied, frowning. "I hope it isn't anything serious."

"No," Stefanie smiled, "just a touch of the flu or something. There's a lot of it going around."

"I'm glad you're not going then. I wouldn't want you to bring anything back to Haley. By the way," he added, pointing to the table, "that envelope came for you today from FedEx."

Stefanie ripped it open, extracting a letter and a check. "Here it is," she said, handing it to Craig. "The check for my stock portfolio."

Craig looked at the piece of paper. "Seven thousand, seven hundred and eleven dollars," he said, reading the figures aloud.

"Don't forget," Stefanie said firmly, "That's *my* money! And I want it back!"

"Sure," Craig said somberly, sticking the check in his pocket. "Don't worry, it's just a loan."

Anne looked at Stefanie, surprised by the unusual note

of resolve in her daughter's voice. "I'd better go," she said, slightly embarrassed.

"Okay, Mom," Stefanie said. "We'll see you tomorrow."

Craig clicked on the tv. "Good night," he called half-heartedly, his attention already on the newscast.

TWO

On their way back to Merion from the Thai Pepper, Anne, who was sitting with Lou in the back seat of Craig and Stefanie's Volvo, leaned over, resting her head on her husband's shoulder. "Stefanie is happy," she said softly, squeezing his hand. "Life is good. You continue to get well and they have a good life together."

Lou smiled and squeezed back.

As soon as they got inside, Anne and Stefanie bustled into the kitchen to put on a pot of coffee. But Craig, rather than settling in front of the tv and searching for a hockey game, as he normally would have done, paced nervously around the room.

"What's the matter?" Lou asked, sinking into the couch.

"I'm just a little restless," Craig replied. "Must have been the caffeine in the tea we had at dinner."

"Well, sit down," Lou urged. "Maybe we can find a good game."

"I'm too nervous to sit," Craig replied. "I think I'll take Haley for a walk. It's a nice night."

"The ladies will be back with the coffee in just a minute."

"That's just what I need," Craig laughed. "More caffeine. You guys go ahead without me. I'm going out for a bit. Come on, Haley," he said, swinging his daughter in the air, "let's go walk around the block."

Haley giggled and made bubbling sounds while Craig fastened her into her stroller. "Tell Stef I'll be back in a few minutes," he said to Lou as they headed out the door.

"What took you so long?" Stefanie asked when father and daughter returned thirty minutes later.

"It was so nice we just went farther than I'd planned. Your parents gone?"

"Yeah. You just missed them. I'll get Haley to bed," she added, unbuttoning the baby's sweater.

"Darn!" she said when the phone rang. "Can you get it?"

"It's for you," Craig called thirty seconds later.

"Who is it?" Stefanie frowned.

"One of your favorite people," Craig grinned, covering the mouthpiece. "Jeff Solomon."

"Jeff?" Stefanie asked, puzzled. "What's he want?"

"I haven't the faintest idea," Craig smiled, knowing that Stefanie was not particularly fond of his friend. "You talk to him," he said, handing her the receiver. "I'll put Haley to bed."

Ten minutes later, he came back downstairs.

"What did Jeff want?" he asked curiously. "Anything important?"

"No," Stefanie said, shaking her head. "He wanted to tease me about being a snob."

"A snob? What's he talking about?"

"Oh, he thought he saw me in my car this afternoon and he honked but I didn't wave back."

"Was it you?"

"No, but obviously he thought it was. He got his feelings hurt."

"Oh, well," Craig sighed. "He'll get over it. I think I'll have a beer. How about you?"

"I don't think so. I'm full of tea and coffee."

"Aw, come on. A beer will do you good."

"Okay," Stefanie replied somewhat reluctantly, "open one for me, too."

"I talked to Elaine," Craig called from the kitchen.

"Oh, good," Stefanie replied. "I meant to, but I didn't get a chance. I hardly stopped all day. How's she feeling?"

"Oh, she's fine today," Craig said, handing her an opened can.

"That's nice. Must have been one of those twenty-four-hour bugs. You know," Stefanie added, sipping the beer, "I really don't want this."

"You've hardly touched it."

"I took a few sips, but I don't want any more. Here, you finish it."

Todd and *Elaine Miller* were Craig and Stefanie's oldest friends. The men had met more than a decade ago playing deck hockey. After one of the games, Todd introduced Craig to Elaine, who was then his fiancée. A week or so later, Craig brought Stefanie to meet the couple. "This is the girl I'm going to marry," the twenty-two-year-old Craig had said proudly, throwing his arm across the shoulders of the eighteen-year-old Bryn Mawr freshman. Although Elaine was five years older than Stefanie, the women became close friends, with Elaine laughingly referring to Stefanie as "the child" and Stefanie jokingly calling Elaine "the old lady."

By 1997, Craig and Stefanie, after being together so long, had worked out a fairly complicated system whereby each maintained a circle of individual friends while still having a clique of mutual friends.

Stefanie was by far the best at keeping in touch with people she had been close to at various stages of her life: elementary school, high school, Bryn Mawr, and law school. These friends were not *ipso facto* Craig's friends, just as some of his buddies were not necessarily friendly with Stefanie. While it was important to Stefanie to stay connected to people she had known as long as twenty years previously, Craig did not seem bound by the same compulsion. For the most part he had drifted away from his high school companions while developing new relationships with a much smaller crowd. Craig's chief comrades were people he had met later in life, people like Jeffrey Solomon, a personal injury lawyer who had represented him in an accident claim several years earlier. There were a couple of other independent businessmen—*Robert Feldman* and *Russ Kaplan*—and another lawyer, *Matt Rosen*. But it was primarily the mutual friends they spent most of their time with as a couple.

Through the Millers they met two other couples—*Betty* and *Brian Schwartz*, and *Jennifer* and *Mark Hirtz*—and it was these eight, including the Rabinowitzes, who did almost everything together. These were the people Craig and Stefanie were closest to: people they partied with, shared confidences with, and met with on a regular basis, and communicated with often, in some cases daily.

Since Craig did not have an office to which he had to report every day, unlike Todd, Brian, and Mark, who had day jobs (Todd and Brian with growing businesses; Mark as a lawyer), he developed a special rapport with the three wives. If Elaine, Betty, or Jennifer needed someone to watch the kids while they ran errands, they could call on Craig. If they needed a fourth for tennis, Craig was available. Or if they just wanted someone to talk to, Craig invariably was handy.

"He's everybody's best friend," Elaine cracked one day to her husband after explaining how she had needed some help with a project and no one was free except Craig. "He's always there when we need him and he never says no."

"I don't think he ever works," Todd had replied, smiling.

"Of course not, silly," Elaine chuckled. "Craig has never worked a day in his life and he's getting a little old to start now."

"I'm surprised that doesn't bother Stefanie."

"That's part of what makes Stef what she is. She likes Craig that way. For her, it's part of his charm."

"Maybe she tolerates it so well because he always treats her like royalty. He makes me nervous sometimes, the way he's always so attentive. 'Can I get you a glass of water? Are you comfortable? Would you like a pillow?' It's— what can I say?—*unnatural*."

"Unnatural for you," Elaine laughed. "Maybe you should take lessons."

For years, Craig had talked on the phone almost every day to most members of the clique, both husbands and wives. For a time, Betty, a nurse, had had a job that required a daily commute of forty-five minutes each way from her home to the clinic and back. To help pass the time on the boring drive, she'd call Craig on her cell phone and the two would jabber like housewives trading tales over the back fence.

But, if possible, Craig was even closer to Elaine. A teacher, Elaine would get home in mid-afternoon and Craig would go over to the Millers', spending hours chatting about nothing.

"I spend more time with Craig than I do with my husband," Elaine commented one day to Betty. She was only half joking.

Among the wives, all of whom were Jewish, Craig was known as a *yenta*, the Yiddish word for gossip. His favorite topic was people, especially people they all knew. Among his services to the group was that of communications officer. If one of Betty's children was down with the flu, Elaine and Jennifer likely would find out about it from Craig. If Elaine's dog was having puppies, Jennifer and Betty got the word from Craig. When Stefanie found out that she was pregnant, Craig spread the news as soon as Stefanie got confirmation from her gynecologist.

With the husbands, Craig was an acknowledged "guy's

guy,'' one who would talk mainly about sports, rambling on in great detail about baseball, football, basketball, golf, and hockey. Particularly hockey. Craig could discourse for what seemed like hours about his beloved Flyers.

Although he was no gambler—indeed, on fairly frequent group excursions to Atlantic City he would shun the casinos as if they were quarantined—Craig was an avid participant in monthly small-stakes poker games in which he, Mark, Todd, and Brian often were joined by Robert Feldman and Matt Rosen. The bets were negligible and the night's big winner might go home with an extra fifty dollars in his pocket. But the games were less about gambling than they were an excuse for the males to get together to shoot the bull. Curiously, despite all his talk about sports, Craig never bet on sports events, either. His lust for taking chances seemed limited to a one-dollar raise on a pair of kings.

Early in the summer of 1996, despite his history of unprofitable financial ventures, Craig began bragging to Todd, Brian, and Mark about how rosy his situation had become, implying that his glove-import enterprise was spurting to unexpected heights. The reason this was so, he confided between hands of stud and draw, was because of a contact he had made with a man from New York. As far as the others were concerned, this new colleague of Craig's was a mystery figure. None of them had ever met him on his fleeting trips to Philadelphia or gone with Craig when he traveled to a meeting in Manhattan or Montreal. But that did not stop Craig from talking about him. This New Yorker, he boasted, had valuable contacts with retailers which dovetailed with the contacts in Asia that had enabled Craig to buy gloves at reasonable prices. Together, Craig would declare, smiling, they made a powerful team. Mark, Todd, and Brian, who were preoccupied with their own businesses and growing families, wondered why Craig had never brought this colleague around for them to meet, or why Craig had never mentioned his name.

The wives also had their equivalent of poker. Every

Monday, Elaine and Stefanie met for dinner, leaving Craig to babysit Haley, and at least once a year, Stefanie, Betty, Jennifer, and Elaine drove into Center City for a British-style tea at the tony Ritz Carlton Hotel.

While Craig basked in his reputation as one of the fellows—slightly raucous, almost totally sports-oriented—Stefanie was his antithesis. Quiet and somewhat withdrawn, Stefanie was intense where Craig was glib; pointedly ethical where Craig was faintly decadent; intrinsically religious while Craig was anything but.

Once, years before, Elaine had been entertaining a friend when Stefanie dropped in for a visit. The friend, although Jewish, seemed to go to great lengths to deny his heritage. While Elaine gently teased him about being a Gentile wannabe, Stefanie took the conversation to heart. "You should be proud to be Jewish," Stefanie lectured, though having only just met the youth. "It's *important* to be Jewish," she continued, tears starting to roll down her cheeks. But that was before she had married Craig, while she was still regularly going to the synagogue and observing Sabbath.

Stefanie's attitude, however, had made a tremendous impression on Elaine. So did Stefanie's position during a later discussion about money. Bloomingdale's had mistakenly given Stefanie credit for an extra hundred dollars on her bill. In a quandary about whether to report it, Stefanie posed the dilemma to the group. "Keep it," urged Craig. "Bloomingdale's is a big company; they can afford it."

"No," said Stefanie. "It wouldn't be right to keep it. It doesn't matter whether they can afford it or not. It isn't mine." She reported the error.

Although the men and women had separate identities, the group occupied a place of extreme importance in their lives. On weekends, they'd gather at one another's houses; Craig would take them to a Flyers game using his season tickets, or they would get together for dinner at an upscale, Main Line restaurant like Evviva's. Craig's parents, before his father died, had had a membership at a fancy private restaurant in Atlantic City called The Basement. Twice a year, Craig and Stefanie would invite the other six for an evening out at the establishment. It was an occasion to look forward to, a celebration that invariably began with cocktails at Craig's parents' apartment and ended with after-dinner drinks at one of the resort city's swankier clubs.

Over the years—like most close-knit groups—the couples fell into a routine and developed their private jokes and in-group taboos.

One of the jokes revolved around an incident that occurred before one of the Basement dinners. While the eight were having cocktails at the elder Rabinowitzes' place, Betty and Elaine complained of headaches and asked Stefanie if she might be able to find some Tylenol in her mother-in-law's medicine cabinet. Stefanie, who never took pills unless she was really sick, returned a few minutes later with four tablets. Betty and Elaine each swallowed two of the pills and, soon afterwards, they all left for the restaurant. Three-fourths of the way through the meal, Elaine and Betty fell asleep at the table. Later, they discovered that Stefanie had brought them Tylenol P.M. rather than regular Tylenol. After that, it was an in-group joke about how Stefanie had drugged her friends, causing them to go face-down in their pasta.

There also was a running gag about Craig. It blossomed after he let slip one evening about how he had been required to take his New York colleague to a local "gentlemen's club" called Delilah's Den.

In Philadelphia, gentlemen's clubs are major attractions for lonesome men. Essentially, they are expensive strip joints that feature scantily clad dancers performing on runways or, if the price is right, at tables or—if the price is even better—in more secluded areas. Some of the city's more than two dozen clubs are undeniably seedy, serving basically as places where men can meet prostitutes or semi-professional women looking to bring in a little extra income. Delilah's Den, however, was more than a step above the run-of-the-mill Center City strip joint. Advertising on billboards and through blurbs in local tourist publications, even on the Internet, Delilah's Den referred to itself as an elegant cabaret where men could come for a superb gourmet dinner and good entertainment. As far as such clubs went, Delilah's enjoyed a surprisingly good reputation. Some of the city's elite, including leading businessmen, prominent politicians, well-known judges, and readily recognizable sports figures, were among the regulars.

But a strip club is a strip club and Craig's pronouncement that he had visited the place at least once drew slight gasps from the group of friends. Craig moved quickly to cover his gaffe, adding that the only reason he would be seen in such a place was because it was his duty to keep his colleague entertained. "I hated it," he explained, with feeling. "It's so stupid. I have to sit there and nurse a drink while my client ogles these near-naked women. I only went because I had to."

From then on, Craig's adventure at Delilah's Den became part of the group's lexicon of humor, an occasion for some gentle ribbing.

Instead of being angry about her husband's taste in entertainment, Stefanie laughed and made a joke. Later, on the occasions when Delilah's came up, she would just roll her eyes and accept the remarks in the same good humor in which she took kidding about the Tylenol PM. It was all part of the price one paid for being a member of a circle in which everyone knew, or thought they knew, everyone else's secrets.

But all this *bonhomie* had a negative side as well. Occasionally, jealousies erupted that threatened the welfare of the group. Not the romantic sort, but another type that could be just as injurious. Usually, they revolved around Craig.

Proud of his position as the group's chief confidant, especially to the women, Craig reacted strongly if he thought his role was being challenged, or if he thought he was not being shown the proper respect. In such a situation, he might quit speaking to the offending party for weeks, sulking like a five-year-old.

At one point, when Betty and Elaine began growing closer, Craig took it personally and pouted whenever he was around the two. When they confronted him, he cooled considerably toward Elaine, treating her more as a stranger than as a friend of more than ten years. It was weeks before she felt she was back in his good graces. He seemed to enjoy manipulating his friends. In contrast, Stefanie was the primary peacemaker in the group; the one who wanted everyone to be happy and enjoy each other's company.

Most of the group's social events were planned on the principle that everyone should be involved. If one of the couples invited another couple for dinner, for example, that was permissible. But to involve a third couple and not bring everyone in the group into the affair was dangerous to group unity, especially if Craig knew about it.

If Brian Schwartz, for instance, hosted a poker game and invited someone from outside the group but not all the regular players, Craig made a point of making sure those who were not invited knew about it. Far from being subtle, he gloried in his role as troublemaker. If anyone was embarrassed or offended, it was too bad.

On the plus side, his old-maid habits notwithstanding, Craig was almost always in good spirits, always ready with a joke or a quip. The women valued him for his willingness to drop everything to help or provide support; the men respected his encyclopedic knowledge of professional sports, his apparent business acumen, and his evenness of temper. None of them, not even those who had sweated with him on a baseball diamond, had ever seen him blow his top. Never, even in the rugged give-and-take of a spirited game of deck hockey, which could be as competitive and aggressive as the brand played by the Flyers, had Mark, Brian, or Todd ever seen Craig become violent or even react in anger.

Despite, or perhaps because of, these dynamics the group remained extremely tight. They were like a family; no single member was perfect but together they could conquer whatever came their way. Or so they believed.

THREE

James Driscoll gripped his heavy flashlight in one hand, the steering wheel in the other. It was a balmy spring night, just cool enough for a long-sleeved shirt to feel comfortable. But, God, it was dark, the police officer thought; the darkest part of the lunar cycle with a quarter-moon not due for another four days. It didn't help, either, that he was off the main streets, deep into a dimly lit residential neighborhood where the house markers were not the most readable, where everyone except him and the person who had called the emergency number minutes before was sound asleep. Straining to penetrate the deep shadows, Driscoll searched for a number, a sign, any indication that someone was awake.

Rounding a curve on aptly named Winding Way, he almost passed it: a bright rectangle of light blazing through the darkness. Sweeping his beam across the neatly trimmed lawn he picked out the numbers. 526. It was the house he was looking for. Gunning the squad car forward into the empty driveway, he screeched to a halt. The vehicle was still moving slightly when he leaped out, grabbing the portable oxygen tank as he went.

"Hello!" he called loudly, banging on the frame. "Police! Hello! Is anybody here?"

"I'm upstairs," a male voice called weakly.

Driscoll yanked the screen door open and took the stairs two at a time. At the top, on his right, was a tiny room containing a bathtub, a vanity, and a commode. A man, wearing cut-off jeans, a blue polo shirt, and white sweat socks, was kneeling in the tub, water to the middle of his thighs. In his arms was a naked woman, her head lolling limply to one side. The man's face, Driscoll noted, was as white as his socks. The woman's was blue.

"She went to take a bath," the man wailed. "I guess she fell and hit her head. I can't revive her."

The 911 call had gone to an ambulance service in nearby Narberth. "My wife!" a panicky man had screamed. "She's in the tub. I can't get her to respond. Please come."

"Do you know CPR?" the dispatcher asked calmly.

"Yes!"

"Then start using it. An ambulance is on its way."

As a matter of course in Lower Merion Township, a normally placid suburban area just north and west of Philadelphia, police officers also answer such calls, which was why Driscoll was there. Since the LMPD was closer than the ambulance service, Driscoll had beaten the paramedics to the scene.

"She was so heavy . . . ." the man moaned, staring wide-eyed at the policeman.

"Help me get her out," commanded Driscoll.

Together, they muscled the woman from the tub and stretched her on the floor. In one smooth motion, Driscoll clamped the oxygen mask over her face and flipped the switch, starting the flow of gas. Water poured out of her nose and mouth.

"She's not breathing," the man sobbed.

Driscoll began applying CPR.

"Please help her," the man begged.

Driscoll stopped, looking up. "What's that noise?" he asked sharply.

"The baby! It's the baby," the man said, his voice rising. "We've waked her up!"

"You go see to the baby," Driscoll commanded. "I'll keep trying with the CPR." He was still trying three minutes later when the paramedics arrived.

Jostling the officer aside, the paramedics carried the woman out into the hall where there was more room.

"She's not coming around," one of the men said.

"Let's get her to the hospital," said the other. Turning to Driscoll, he added: "We're taking her to Lankenau."

The EMTs lifted the woman onto a gurney and hurried down the stairs.

As the paramedics were going out the door, the man reappeared carrying a screaming baby. "What are they doing?" he asked shrilly, trying to calm the crying toddler. "Where are they taking her?"

"To the hospital," Officer Driscoll said. "They haven't been able to revive her. You should go, too."

"I can't!" the man wailed. "What about the baby?"

He had hardly spoken the words when a man and a woman, drawn by the noise and flashing lights, pounded up the stairs.

"I'll take Haley," *Jane Rothstein* said, holding out her arms. "You go to the hospital."

"You'd better change clothes," Driscoll told the man, pointing at his sopping shorts and shirt. "But answer a few quick questions first," he said, whipping out a pad and pen. "What's your name?"

The man looked confused. "Cr . . . Cr . . . Craig. Craig Rabinowitz."

"And the woman's your wife?"

"Yeah. Her name is Steffi. Stefanie. We call her Steffi."

"What happened tonight?"

"Steffi . . . my wife . . . was having trouble sleeping. She went to take a bath . . ."

"Where were you?" Driscoll asked.

"I was in the master bedroom, watching a hockey game. When she didn't come out I went to check on her and found her in the tub. Her head was under water. I don't know how it happened.''

"You didn't see anything? Hear anything?"

"I heard a thump. I thought it was the shampoo bottle falling. It always does that. I should have gone to help her when I heard the thump. . . .''

"Was there anyone else in the house?" Driscoll asked.

"No," Craig said, shaking his head. "Just me and Stef and the baby. I had closed up for the night, like I usually do. I locked the doors and then I went upstairs.''

"You'd better get changed and go to the hospital," the officer prompted.

The man covered his face with his hands. "I was trying to hold and comfort her. . . . I'm so sorry," he sobbed. "What are me and the baby going to do without her?"

While the man was changing, Driscoll walked back into the bathroom where the woman had been found. He was surprised to see the water still slowly draining from the tub. Reflexively responding to training that told him *everything* was evidence and therefore valuable until it was determined otherwise, he quickly replaced the rubber plug which must have come dislodged when they took her out. As he did, he remembered there had been no water on the floor when he had entered; until he and the man had removed the woman and thoroughly splashed the area, the floor had been as dry as the Sahara. He scribbled a note on his pad.

Driscoll looked around. In a neat pile on the floor, just inside the door, were a pair of dark sweatpants, a tee shirt with the word GAP on the front, and a pair of off-white printed panties with a feminine napkin resting on top. Driscoll wrote it down.

Pausing, he stared at the wall, struggling with his memory. There had been something unusual, he recalled. Something about the woman. Of course, he said half aloud, remembering. Hurriedly, he jotted something else in his notebook. When he and the man had pulled the woman from the tub, Driscoll noted that she had been wearing several pieces of jewelry. He wanted to make a note of it before he forgot: an inexpensive gold-colored watch, a gold wedding ring, and a couple of bracelets, one on each wrist.

In the master bedroom, Rabinowitz slipped into a fresh polo shirt and neatly pressed jeans, then wiggled his sock-less feet into a pair of loafers. As he ran out the door, he turned to his neighbors. "Call Elaine," he pleaded. "She'll need to know."

Elaine Miller was asleep. Her husband, Todd, was still getting ready for bed after a long, late day at the office. When the phone jangled, Elaine rolled over and glanced at the clock. It was 12:52.

"I've got it," Todd said, snatching the receiver off the hook.

"Who is it?" Elaine asked groggily.

Todd covered the mouthpiece. "It's *Joe Rothstein*," he said.

"Joe! Craig's neighbor?" Elaine said, popping up in bed. "What's wrong?"

Again Todd covered the mouthpiece. "He says there's been an accident and Steffi has been hurt. She hit her head in the bathtub. He wants to know if I can come over."

Elaine was angry. Craig had done the same thing once before, roused all his friends to respond to an alleged emergency only for them to discover there was nothing to it. Friend or no friend, someone could cry wolf only so many times.

"You go," Elaine said grumpily. "They probably need someone to house-sit for a couple of hours."

"Okay," Todd said, starting to put his clothes back on.

"Wait a minute!" Elaine said, throwing back the light blanket and jumping to her feet. "Why didn't Craig call instead of Joe? I'd better call over there."

Her hands shaking, she dialed the Rabinowitzes' number. Joe Rothstein answered.

"They've taken Stef away," he said calmly. "I think you need to talk to my wife."

Jane came on the line. In contrast to her husband, she sounded half hysterical. "Oh, my God," she screamed. "I think she's dead."

Elaine slammed down the phone. Sleep forgotten, she pulled on a pair of sweats and ran into the garage, catching Todd just as he was starting the car. "I'll go," she said, pulling him by the arm. "You stay with the kids. I'll call you when I know something."

During the six minutes it took her to drive to Merion, Elaine chewed her lip and prayed. When she arrived, she found the scene chaotic. There were several police cars there, their lights flashing. Inside, Haley was still screaming, upset by the commotion and unhappy with being held by Jane rather than her mother or father.

"What happened?" Elaine barked.

Jane told her that Stefanie apparently had slipped in the bathtub, striking her head. "They couldn't revive her. I think she's dead," she repeated.

Elaine yelled at her. "How can you say that! Don't say that! Don't you *dare* say that! Where's Craig?"

"He just left."

"Left? For where?"

"Lankenau," Jane said, bouncing the screaming Haley on her arm.

Elaine jumped back in her car and headed south, toward the busy hospital in Overbrook, a community that straddled the border between Philadelphia and Montgomery Counties. On the five-minute drive, she tried to calm herself by remembering that Lankenau, because of its close proximity to some of Philadelphia's rougher neighborhoods, had an excellent emergency room and a top-flight, experienced staff that was accustomed to handling all sorts of trauma. Still she worried. Could Jane be right? she asked herself over and over. Could Stefanie really be dead?

Ardmore
1:13 a.m.

While middle-of-the-night calls are thankfully rare for most people, they are all too commonplace for Mark Keenan. When the phone jarred him awake early Wednesday morning he was neither surprised nor alarmed, just resigned. "Sergeant Keenan!" he growled into the mouthpiece.

"This is the night patrol supervisor," the voice on the other end said. "You need to know that a twenty-nine-year-old woman was found unresponsive in her bathtub a little more than a half-hour ago."

Just as it was standard operating procedure for an LMPD uniformed officer to respond to 911 calls, it was the duty of the patrol supervisor to keep the man in charge of detectives advised of unusual developments like major accidents, suicides, and murders. Often this was during the hours when Keenan was sleeping. But that was immaterial. When such incidents occurred, Keenan demanded that he be one of the first to know.

The sergeant ran his fingers through his bushy moustache. "Woman dead in the bathtub, huh?" he asked.

"Not dead yet. At least not officially. She's en route to Lankenau."

Although the witching hours are a prime time for crime and misfortune, the detective bureau at the Lower Merion Police Department shuts down for eight hours after midnight on the theory that common emergencies can be handled by the uniformed division. When something unusual occurs, the drill is for the night patrol supervisor to call Keenan, who then decides if it's necessary to rouse a detective and ask him to go to the scene.

Keenan yawned. "Where was it?"

"Merion."

That got Keenan's attention. The department didn't answer many calls from residents of the tony neighborhood. When they did, the sergeant was wary since almost everyone who lived there was rich and many had political pull. In such cases, Keenan reckoned, it was better to err on the side of caution and send a man, even if it meant extra work for the investigator. "Who's available?" he asked.

"Craig just went home," the supervisor said. "You want me to call him?"

"No," Keenan replied. "I'll do it."

Breaking off the connection, Keenan quickly punched in a number. "Charlie," he said when the investigator picked up, "this is Keenan."

"Hi, Mark," Detective Charles Craig sighed, knowing what was coming. "I was about to brush my teeth."

"You can brush 'em if you want," Keenan commented dryly, smiling to himself, "but you're going to have to go back out." He told the detective everything he knew, which was very little.

"I'll get right on it," Detective Craig promised, scribbling notes on a pad he always kept by the phone. Wearily, he descended the stairs that led to his second-floor bedroom, got in his car, and returned to the police headquarters building in Ardmore. There he transferred to an unmarked department car and cruised down the nearly empty streets to Merion, a ten-minute drive away.

A small community which, in the city, would be called a neighborhood, Merion is the heart of Lower Merion Township, an affluent suburban enclave that spreads over twenty-four square miles in Montgomery County, northwest of Philadelphia. The township has been a magnet for those wishing to escape the woes of the city since the turn of the century when the Philadelphia Railroad opened a rail link to Pittsburgh. Once the forested, rolling country of the Piedmont Plateau—formerly prime farm land settled initially by Welsh immigrants on acreage purchased from William Penn—was made readily accessible, the rich and influential began snapping up large parcels on which they built sumptuous estates. Since the rich could not survive without an army of support personnel, tradesmen, domestics, and craftsmen quickly followed. The dividing line between the classes was the railroad right-of-way. Workers settled on the south side of the tracks, in Upper Merion Township; the prosperous on the other side, in Lower Merion.

By the 1990s, the differences still were as apparent as they had been a century earlier. Lower Merion's 58,000 residents were mainly professionals—doctors, lawyers, dentists, bankers, entrepreneurs, and corporate executives—while the 26,000 people who lived in Upper Merion were predominantly blue-collar workers. The per capita income in Lower Merion was $42,000 a year, which was forty-two percent higher than that in Upper Merion. And the median value of a house in Lower Merion was $282,000, half again as much as one in Upper Merion.

But there is another distinction setting the townships apart that is perhaps as important as money, and that is religion. Upper Merion is largely Christian, a mixture of Protestant and Catholic. Lower Merion, on the other hand, is heavily Jewish. And one of the most predominantly Jewish sections in all of Lower Merion Township is Merion.

In addition to being recognized as a haven for Jewish professionals on the rise, there was something else that made Merion different. It was a Main Line community. In the early 1800s, when Montgomery County was still being settled, the legislature, recognizing that the area was ripe for development, authorized a series of improvement projects that included feeder roads, canals, and short-line railroads. The project formally was designated a "main line of public works." This, in turn, led to the coining of a term which would endure for the next two hundred years.

Originally, "Main Line" referred to settlements that sprouted in the legislature-mandated improvement area. Later, it shifted to the north and was used to designate communities along the Philadelphia-to-Pittsburgh route of the Pennsylvania Railroad. Then, it began being applied to other communities as well. What is and what is not "Main Line" can be confusing to outsiders. Merion, which is *not* along the Pennsylvania Railroad, is considered a Main Line Community. Ardmore, which is only a few miles away and *is* on the railroad line, is not. Part of the reason may be that Ardmore, which is much larger, also has a sizeable working-class population.

While the term had long been used by Philadelphians to signify wealth and social status, it sprang into national consciousness just before World War II with the release of the movie *The Philadelphia Story*, featuring Jimmy Stewart, Katharine Hepburn, and Cary Grant. It, and the stage play it is based on, proved enormously popular, although both did nothing but glorify the fatuous lives of a small group of extremely wealthy people who lived on an estate in what is presumed to be Montgomery County.

By 1997, "Main Line" was still a very active term in a Pennsylvanian's vocabulary. Many, especially those in the media, regarded Main Liners with something akin to envy and awe, not dissimilar to the way Los Angelinos look upon those who live in Brentwood, or New Yorkers view those who reside in Greenwich, Connecticut. An event, like maybe a murder, would be reported much differently if it occurred in a Main Line Community than it would be if it happened in North Philadelphia, a poor, crime-ridden section of the city. No police officer or public official in Montgomery County ever forgot that.

Overbrook, Pennsylvania
Lankenau Hospital
1:18 a.m.

As soon as he got to the hospital, Craig Rabinowitz went straight to a telephone.

Betty and Brian Schwartz's five-year-old daughter had

slipped into their bed after they dozed off, so when the phone rang, Betty had to reach awkwardly over her to answer it. Still dazed, she couldn't understand what or why Craig was shouting. Craig *never* shouted; he was always calm and cool. What could be so bad that he would be this upset? It was something about Stefanie.

"Calm down," she told him, using her crispest nurse's tone. "Take it easy. Take three deep breaths and then tell me what's going on."

"There's been a terrible accident," Craig blurted. To Betty, he sounded as if he were losing his sanity. "I don't think Steffi's going to make it." He paused, then sobbed: "Please come quickly."

Her nursing training forgotten, Betty began screaming. This set off her daughter, who also started bellowing. Realizing what she was doing, Betty forced herself to be calm. Holding her daughter tightly, she turned to her husband, who was staring at them both as if they were crazy. Smoothing her daughter's hair, urging her to stop crying, Betty sobbingly told Brian what Craig had said.

As Brian hurriedly pulled on whatever clothing he could find, Betty called her mother and succinctly explained the situation. "Can you please come over and watch the kids while I go to the hospital?"

She listened for a moment. "Good," she sighed. "I'll be ready to go by the time you get here."

As soon as Betty Schwartz hung up, Craig dialed another number.

"It was an accident," he exclaimed when a woman answered. "Steffi's been hurt bad."

"What!" Jennifer Hirtz gasped, trying to clear the cobwebs from her brain. Was she having a nightmare? "Is this Craig? What, for God's sake, are you talking about?"

"It was an accident," Craig repeated. "An accident!"

A car accident? Craig and Stefanie?

"It's Steffi," Craig continued, his voice rising. "I don't think she's going to make it."

The words hit Jennifer like a bucket of ice water. She began shaking violently from head to toe, like a person with malaria. "Mark," she gulped through chattering teeth, "wake up. Wake up!"

Mark Hirtz was throwing on some clothes when the phone rang a second time. It was Betty. "Get dressed," she said brusquely. "Brian is going to be coming by to get you."

While Betty was getting dressed, she called Asha, the young woman who worked as Haley's nanny. Again, Betty explained the situation and said she'd call back as soon as she knew something. When she saw her mother pulling into her driveway, Betty jumped in her car and headed for the hospital. She knew it would be at least a twenty-minute drive.

Merion
1:40 a.m.

Detective Craig strode across the lawn at 526 Winding Way, heading for a group of uniformed officers huddled outside the house. Who had been the first on the scene? he asked. One of them pointed to Driscoll.

"Not much I can tell you," the policeman said. It took him less than five minutes to explain how he had found Craig Rabinowitz kneeling in the tub, cradling his wife. Driscoll told the detective about the unsuccessful attempts to resuscitate her, what the man had told him about the circumstances surrounding the incident, and how his preliminary check of the premises turned up nothing suspicious.

Detective Craig nodded solemnly, jotting a few notes. Thanking Driscoll, the investigator began prowling around the house on his own. He was surprised at how small it was—roughly 1,600 feet, he estimated—considering how much the owners had probably paid for it, it being in Merion and all. Although it was a two-story dwelling, it lacked any intrinsic charm and, as far as he could tell, had very little to recommend it. Unimaginatively laid out in rigid squares, there were only four rooms on the first floor: a kitchen and a family room in the back, in what at one time had been a garage, and a living room and a dining room in the front. The most attractive characteristic, as far as the investigator could tell, was the picture window in the dining room. It faced the tree-shaded street, overlooking the neatly kept lawn and the flowerbeds that lined the front porch. Between the living and dining rooms was a small foyer that opened onto the stairs to the second floor. Upstairs there were only three rooms: a master bedroom which was over the living room; an ''office'' situated at the rear of the house, above the family room; and a guest room, now a nursery, which was above the dining room. Off the baby's room, opening onto the narrow hall at the top of the stairs, was a bathroom so small that he was sure he could touch both walls if he were standing in the tub. This was the room, he knew, where the woman had been found. It was easy to tell by looking at the floor. It was a mess. There were puddles of water all over it, and large, muddy footprints made by police and paramedics who had tromped in and out.

The investigator made a few more notes, then began a second, more thorough inspection, looking this time for anything that might indicate the incident was something more than an unfortunate accident. He found nothing. Although there were some toys scattered about downstairs, that was hardly unusual in a house with a toddler in residence. There were no signs of disarray that might have evidenced a struggle. The back door was closed and bolted. All the windows were locked and none had been broken or forced. He could not find a suicide note or anything that resembled one, nor were there any pill bottles, empty or otherwise. No indication at all that anyone in the house had been using drugs or drinking.

Shoving his notebook in his pocket, Detective Craig got back in the unmarked car and drove to Lankenau. He needed to talk to the husband, and the woman, if she had survived, before he could wind things up.

Lankenau Hospital
1:42 a.m.

When Elaine arrived at the hospital, she found Craig pacing in a small area between two sets of double doors.

"What's going on?" she asked breathlessly, running up and throwing her arms around him.

"It's bad," Craig said, panic evident in his face. "It's really bad."

"What are you talking about?" Elaine asked impatiently. "What's happening?"

Before Craig could answer, three people dressed like doctors—two women and a man—walked through the back set of doors and headed straight toward Craig. "I'm afraid I don't have good news to tell you," said one of the women.

"Oh, my God!" Craig bawled, staggering. "I knew it! I knew it!"

"Why don't we go over here?" the doctor said gently, placing a hand on Craig's arm and leading him to a small office off a long corridor. Elaine followed, standing behind her friend, massaging his neck and shoulders.

"We couldn't revive her," the doctor said, her eyes filled with empathy. "There was nothing we could do."

Craig started rocking and rubbing his head. His lips were moving, but Elaine couldn't unravel the sentences. After a few minutes, he put his head down on the desk and started mumbling about his father, who had died of cancer three years previously. "I can't go through this again," he whispered. "I just can't."

Elaine looked up to see Brian and Mark hurrying into the building. Craig, spotting them as well, jumped up and ran to greet them.

Feeling exhausted, Elaine sagged in the chair. She looked at her watch. It was not yet two o'clock. Barely an hour had passed since Joe Rothstein had called. Making herself get up, she prowled the hall until she found a telephone, then dialed home to tell Todd that Stefanie was dead. "You'd better ask your mother to come stay with the kids," she added. "We need you over here."

While Craig was talking to Brian and Mark, Elaine went into the room where Stefanie's body had been moved. Bowing her head, she began reciting the *shema*, the all-purpose prayer that all observant Jews say before going to sleep and upon awakening. It is also a deathbed prayer, the last one a Jew is supposed to utter.

"*Shema Yisrael*," Elaine said softly, beginning the familiar phrases. "Hear, Oh Israel . . . *Adonai elohaynu, Adonai echod* . . . The Lord our God, the Lord is One!"

When she finished, she sat next to Stefanie, taking her hand, noticing as she did that her friend's nails, as always, were perfectly manicured, flawlessly shaped and buffed. There were so many things I wish I would have told you, Elaine thought, staring at Stefanie as if she could will her to listen. How much I admired you . . . how I envied your beautiful, expressive eyes . . . and how much I'm going to miss your laugh, which was full and rich and crammed with mirth. . . .

She was still sitting there when Betty came in. After hugging Elaine, Betty reached out and caressed Stefanie's cheek. "Oh!" she exclaimed, drawing back her hand as if it had been slapped.

"What is it?" Elaine asked, alarmed.

Betty blushed. "Nothing! It's just me. I didn't expect her

to be so cold. I thought she just died. I wasn't expecting her to be cold already.''

When the two women returned to the waiting room a few minutes later, Craig was slumped in a chair, noticeably calmer but still breaking into fits of uncontrolled, tearless sobbing. "I can't believe this happened," he said again and again. "I can't believe this happened."

"Aren't you going to go see her?" Elaine asked, puzzled and for some reason perturbed.

Craig shook his head. "I can't," he wailed. "I'm so sorry. How can I ever face her parents again? They trusted me to take care of her and I didn't."

He had hardly spoken the words before Anne and Lou Newman rushed in. When Anne heard that her daughter was dead, she threw herself into her husband's arms and began shrieking. Craig grimaced and buried his face in his hands.

Ardmore
2:05 a.m.

Keenan flopped grumpily on his side. In almost all instances in which he was awakened by the patrol supervisor, he had no difficulty in getting back to sleep. Normally, those calls had no more effect on his ability to drop off again than if he had been awakened by a slamming car door on the street outside. But now he was having problems. Wide awake and staring at the wall, he thought about what the patrol supervisor had told him.

While twenty-nine-year-old women were regularly banged up in car crashes, got beaten up by jealous husbands or boyfriends, or overdosed on drugs, there were not many who were found unconscious in their own bathtubs, especially not in a neighborhood like Merion. What if this is not an accident at all? he wondered. What if it turns out to be a murder, or an attempted murder? Despite its proximity to Philadelphia, Lower Merion was a quiet community; only one or two homicides a year on average. So why should he think this apparent bathtub accident was something special? Was his imagination working overtime? He sat up and pounded his pillow. "Dammit!" he swore. "This is stupid."

But sleep continued to elude him. His instincts, honed from twenty-five years' experience as a policeman, told him to be careful. Lying in the darkness, his curiosity blanketing him like a November fog, Keenan wished he could have gone on the call. Now he had no choice but to wait until he heard from Charlie Craig. Until then, he knew, he would not be able to sleep.

Lankenau Hospital
2:45 a.m.

Detective Craig was not surprised to find that Stefanie Rabinowitz had been declared dead on arrival. From what Officer Driscoll had told him about the lack of response to the resuscitation efforts, he would have been more amazed to learn that emergency room personnel had been able to revive her. The physician who had pronounced her dead told the investigator that he had seen nothing to indicate the woman had not died accidentally.

Nodding his thanks, Detective Craig wended his way to the room where Stefanie's body was being kept. Pulling back the sheet, he stared at the young woman, who looked as if she were peacefully sleeping. He quickly examined the body. By then all her jewelry had been removed, so he did not know that she had been wearing any when she was wheeled in. He saw no signs of violence: no bullet holes; no knife wounds; no needle punctures. Shaking his head sadly, he went in search of the family.

Lou Newman was polite but obviously grief-stricken. He had not seen his daughter since he and Anne had left the

Rabinowitzes' at about eight o'clock the previous night, so
there was little he could add to what the investigator already
knew.

Craig Rabinowitz, not surprisingly, was visibly upset but
dry-eyed and coherent when Detective Craig found him sitting silent and brooding in an uncomfortable-looking waiting room chair. In a subdued but steady voice, he gave the
detective a longer, more lucid version of the incident than
he had given Officer Driscoll, but essentially it was the
same.

Looking over his notes, the forty-year-old detective pon-
dered for a moment about all the grief he had seen in his
almost twenty years with the LMPD, beginning with a job
as a dispatcher when he was in college, followed by seven
years in uniform and, finally, for the last ten, in the detective bureau, where he had investigated everything from
theft to homicide. An average-sized man with doleful eyes
and a neatly clipped moustache—a passable double for the
actor Sean Connery—Detective Craig reckoned he had seen
a little of just about everything in his career. But there was
nothing he had seen that morning that led him to suspect
that Stefanie Rabinowitz's death was not an accident.

"I'm sorry for your loss," he told Craig gently. "I know
this is tough for you, but at some point later today I'll need
to get a formal statement from you."

"What do you mean, 'a formal statement'?" Craig
asked.

"Just a for-the-record account of what happened. We
write it down. You sign it. It won't take long. It's something we have to do in all accidental deaths."

"All right," Rabinowitz mumbled, nodding.

3:15 a.m.

It was a bedraggled-looking group that huddled in the Lankenau waiting room, unsure about what to do next. Should

they go home? they asked each other. Or should they continue to wait?

"I'll see if I can find out something," Mark Hirtz volunteered, leaving to find someone in authority. Fifteen minutes later, he was back.

"We may as well go home," he said.

Lou and Anne protested. "We have to make plans for the funeral," said Anne. Conservative Jews such as Anne and her husband tried to observe the tradition of burying the dead as quickly as possible, almost always within twenty-four hours. This was facilitated, in part, because the bodies of conservative and orthodox Jews rarely were embalmed, a process that ran counter to religious belief.

Hirtz shook his head slowly. "It won't do any good to wait. The nurse told me they're probably going to have to do an autopsy."

"What?" Anne asked sharply. "What do you mean, an autopsy?" Many Jews, especially the more traditional ones, were vehemently opposed to post mortems, claiming that they violated the body and God's law. In some places, such as Israel, autopsies were not infrequently a political issue: on one side were the religious traditionalists; on the other were scientists, who claimed that autopsies helped determine potentially inheritable fatal diseases and conditions, and law enforcement authorities, who said that they were often necessary to help track down and prosecute a killer.

"This was an unusual death," Hirtz explained as gently as he could. "The nurse said that when a twenty-nine-year-old healthy woman dies unexpectedly they want to know why."

Craig stared at the floor as if he had not heard.

The Newmans were not happy with the situation, but they realized there was nothing they could do about it until later in the day. Resignedly, the group began to break up. Hirtz said he was going home to talk to his wife, who had not been able to come to the hospital because there was no one to sit with the kids. The others said they were going to Winding Way to help get ready for the start of *shivah*, the traditional week-long Jewish period of mourning.

Exhausted, unkempt, and dispirited, they left as they had come, individually or in pairs. Elaine and Betty volunteered to detour to pick up Haley's nanny, Asha. "We'll meet you back at the house," Elaine said tiredly.

As they walked out the swinging doors and crossed the parking lot, Elaine turned to Betty. "How come Craig looked so neat?" she asked, unaware that he had had the opportunity to change before coming to the hospital. She looked down at her baggy sweats. "We look like hell."

Betty, who was still wearing remnants of the previous day's makeup, smiled weakly. "You know Craig," she said. "The original Dapper Dan."

As dejected as they were, however, they had one thought foremost in their minds: The worst was over. Stefanie was dead and their duty now was to rally around Craig and the Newmans, support them through shivah, and do their best to honor Stefanie's memory. They had no idea, though, that the situation was going to get much worse before it got better; that before they could mentally lay Stefanie to rest they would have to face days and weeks of revelations they could not possibly have anticipated. Ultimately, their loyalties would be tested in ways they could never have imagined.

Detective Craig looked at his watch. It was 3:57 a.m.; twelve and a half hours since he had started his shift the previous afternoon, and almost three and a half hours since the 911 call. Kneading the back of his neck, he hunted up a telephone to call Keenan.

"Sorry to wake you again," he said when the sergeant answered.

"You didn't wake me," Keenan replied gruffly. "I haven't been able to get to sleep all night. What'd you find out?"

"Not much. She was pronounced dead at one-thirty-five.

Never regained consciousness. Everything seems pretty straightforward. It appears to have been some kind of natural death. Maybe a heart attack; maybe a stroke. Maybe she just slipped and conked her head. In any case, the examining physician didn't see any contusion or anything else to indicate it was not an accident. I didn't see anything unusual at the house. If you don't object, I'm going home. It's been a long day. I'll file a report later.''

"That's fine with me," Keenan said. "Go to bed. I'll see you this afternoon."

After Detective Craig hung up, Keenan continued to stare at the phone. "I wish I knew what's bothering me about this," he said irritably.

FOUR

"God, am I exhausted," Elaine wheezed.

"We all are," Betty admitted. "Want some more coffee?" she asked, reaching for the pot.

"Oh, no. Not another drop."

"I'll take a splash," said Brian, proffering his cup.

"We've spent half the night cleaning up the place," Betty said wearily, pouring for her husband. "What a mess. Water. Mud. Wet, dirty clothes. Do you think everything looks nice enough?"

"I think it looks as good as it's ever going to," Brian said wearily.

"What are we forgetting?" asked Elaine. "What do we need to do now?"

"Get some sleep," suggested Todd. "We can't go forever without sleep."

"I'm still feeling fairly fresh," said Jennifer, who had arrived not long before. Since she had no one to call to watch the children while the others were at Lankenau, she had stayed home while Mark went with Brian. After he came home, they talked for about an hour, then she drove to Winding Way.

"We . . ." Betty began, stopping when she heard a feminine cry of anguish from the family room.

"Poor, poor Anne," Elaine moaned. "I wonder if she'll ever get over her hurt."

"She's in shock right now," said Betty. "It's going to take her a long time to get over losing Stefanie."

"It's going to take all of us a long time," Elaine added. "I still can't believe it."

"They've been in there forever," said Todd, nodding toward the family room where Craig had been closeted with the Newmans, his mother, Joyce, and her boyfriend.

"I'm going to go see what they're doing," Jennifer said, rising.

"I think I'm going home before I collapse," said Elaine. "Come on, Todd. Let's go get a couple of hours' sleep."

"How about you guys?" Todd asked Betty and Brian.

"I think I'm going to need some sleep, too," Brian said softly.

"You go ahead," Betty said. "I'm good for a little longer."

"We can't kill ourselves on the first day," Brian said reasonably. "This is going to be a long haul. Shivah lasts for a week."

"We'll make it," Betty said, throwing back her shoulders.

"We have to get Craig through this," Brian said, pausing on his way out the door. "It's going to come down on him like a ton of bricks. They were together for more than fourteen years."

"Are you worried about him?" Todd asked thoughtfully.

"About Craig? The thought has crossed my mind, but so far I don't see any signs that he's unduly depressed."

"He's still in shock, too," said Betty. "It's going to take a little while for what's happened to sink in."

"We're going to have to watch for that," said Todd. "We don't want to lose both of 'em."

"I agree with you," Brian concurred. "But I'm too tired to think about it right now. Betty, you sure you don't want to take a break?"

She shook her head. "Go ahead. I'll be right behind you."

"Okay," he nodded. "I have to go before I fall asleep standing up. I'll see you guys later."

They watched him through the picture window as he walked across the lawn, climbed into his car and drove off.

"You know what I think is a little strange?" Betty said quietly, breaking the silence that had settled around the table.

"What?" Elaine asked, stifling a yawn.

"Well," Betty began nervously, "Craig said he couldn't get Stefanie out of the tub . . ."

"So?" Todd said crossly.

"So, he's a strong guy," Betty replied firmly. "If that had been Brian under a *car*, I'd have been able to lift it. I know I would."

"Let's don't even start thinking that way," said Todd. "We're all pooped. We have to stick together on this."

"I wasn't suggesting we shouldn't," Betty said sharply.

"I *know* you weren't," said Todd. "But we have to concentrate on helping Craig. He needs us."

"You're right," Betty whispered. "We're all just stressed."

Jennifer strode briskly up to the table. "We have a job," she said, waving a small book in her hand.

"What's that?" Betty asked.

"Craig's address book. He asked if we could call some people. There are a lot of people that need to be notified."

"Phewwww," Betty said, blowing out her breath.

Jennifer smiled. "You want to start with the A's or the K's?"

"What has to be done, has to be done. I'll take the first half."

Bill Boegly drummed his fingers impatiently on the desk-top, mumbling softly to himself. "Come on, Doc," he whispered into the mouthpiece. "Come on. Pick up the phone."

"Fillinger here," a soft voice replied.

"Hey, Doc," Boegly sighed in relief. "Glad I caught you."

A retired detective, Boegly couldn't stand not having an office to go to, so he took a new job as assistant to Dr. Halbert E. Fillinger, Jr., the seventy-one-year-old Mont-gomery County coroner, who was working on a second career himself. In 1990, the German-educated forensic pa-thologist hung up his apron after twenty-eight years in the Philadelphia County Coroner's Office to enjoy the peace and quiet of the country. It didn't take him long to realize that he had made a mistake. When the coroner's job came up for election, he ran and won.

"What's up?" Fillinger asked.

"Never rains but it pours," Boegly replied. "Got two cases this morning."

Fillinger chuckled. "Two, huh? Hope one of them's a mystery." A perpetually curious man with intelligent, pen-etrating eyes and a fringe of white hair that circled his crown like a monk's tonsure, there was hardly anything Fillinger loved more than a good mystery, unless it was his collection of antique weapons and old fire trucks. As if he couldn't find enough enigmas in his work, he was also an avid member of a Philadelphia group that re-examined fa-mous, unsolved crimes to see if they could come up with clues that others had missed.

"One's urgent; the other's not," Boegly said.

"Tell me about the urgent one first."

"Woman in Horsham. Went to the dentist early this morning. Had a prescription filled and went back home. Then there was an explosion and fire. They found her inside. They think she was shot, too."

Fillinger sighed. Burnings were bad news. Nasty cases. But that's what he was paid to do. "What's the other one?"

"Another woman. In Lower Merion. Found dead in her tub. The emergency room guy at Lankenau figured it was an accident."

"If it was an accident, why are we involved?" Fillinger asked impatiently.

"Well, we aren't yet. Not officially. The kicker is she was only twenty-nine years old."

Boegly listened to dead air. "Twenty-nine, eh? Dead in her bathtub. Any wounds?"

"Nope."

"Drugs?"

"Not as far as anyone can tell."

"Strangulation?"

"No obvious signs."

"It sounds strange to me," Fillinger drawled. "I think we need to post her."

"That's what I thought you'd say," replied Boegly.

"I'd better get over to Horsham. Who's available to autopsy the Lower Merion woman?"

"I already checked. Hood."

"Excellent!" Fillinger replied. Dr. Ian Hood, a deputy medical examiner in Philadelphia County, was reputed to be one of the best pathologists in the area. Because Montgomery County did not have enough violent deaths to warrant two full-time pathologists, the county government had worked out an agreement with Philadelphia County whereby its physicians could be used on a contract basis if Fillinger was busy. "Hood's a good man. He'll do nicely. I'd better go."

Boegly coughed. "Uh, one more thing, Doc."

"Yes?" Fillinger said impatiently.

"A bit of a problem. Re: the woman at Lankenau. The funeral home is putting pressure on to have the body released. The family is Jewish and they want a quick burial."

Fillinger paused. "I'm sympathetic. But we can't let that influence us. Ask Hood to take a peek and if he doesn't see anything, then we can talk about releasing the body."

"Yes, sir," replied Boegly. "You want me to go down there, too?" He loved a good mystery almost as much as Fillinger.

"That's not a bad idea," Fillinger agreed. "Keep me informed."

Lankenau Hospital
11:48 a.m.

By the time Ian Hood got his first look at Stefanie Rabinowitz, it had been more than ten hours since she was pronounced dead. The passage of time was to the benefit of the pathologist, since some of the tell-tale marks of violent death do not become evident until after the blood drains from the surface of the skin. This is particularly true in strangulation deaths. Not uncommonly, it is many hours after death before petechia—tiny red marks about the size of pin holes, the result of subcutaneous hemorrhaging and a certain giveaway to strangulation—begin to appear.

"What do we have here?" Hood asked briskly. A gregarious New Zealander, the physician had started going to law school in his spare time in the hope that he could learn something to give him a better insight into the way lawyers think. In his opinion, that might give him an edge when he was preparing for cross-examination about his medical findings.

Bending over until he was only inches from Stefanie's face, he closely examined the skin around her eyes. "Ah hah!" he said exultantly. "Look here," he called to Boegly, motioning him to come closer. "You see?"

Boegly stared. "That looks like petechia to me," he said, referring to the small blood-blister–like spots at the corners of her eyes.

Hood nodded enthusiastically. "There," he confirmed. "And there," he added, putting a finger on one of her eyelids.

"And on the forehead, too," Boegly added, stepping back.

"I want to take a look," Hood said. "This tells me that this situation is more than it initially appeared."

While the pathologist began organizing the implements he would need for the autopsy, Boegly telephoned Norristown, the seat of Montgomery County and home to the county's law enforcement agencies: the probation and parole offices, the coroner's office, and the district attorney's office, which included a county-wide investigative agency and an elite homicide unit.

Scattered throughout the county, which has a population of 700,000, are some fifty municipal police departments that vary in size from the very small to the moderately large. Generally, these agencies are left on their own to handle local problems as well as they can given their individual capabilities. But if a crime that occurs within Montgomery County is a very serious one, murder for instance, it moves into a special area, becoming not just a local issue but a county one as well. When someone is murdered in Montgomery County—and there are about two dozen such incidents a year—the case is dealt with either entirely by the county homicide unit or jointly by the county and the local police department. In this case, if Stefanie's death turned out to be a murder, it would be handled jointly because the LMPD is one of the larger and more efficient ones.

Boegly's call was answered on the first ring. "Metz speaking."

"George, this is Bill Boegly. Let me speak to Tim."

"Hold on a second. I'll see if I can find him."

A slight, leprechaun-like figure, the forty-six-year-old Tim Woodward was a high school dropout who fought in Vietnam as a Marine, worked as a Montgomery County Detective while going to law school at night, then became an Assistant District Attorney *and* head of the county homicide unit, a high-morale group whose puckish, unofficial motto, emblazoned on their coffee mugs over the outline of a tombstone, is "Our Day Begins When Your Day Ends."

"He isn't here," Metz reported three minutes later. "He's at lunch. You want me to page him?"

"Yeah," Boegly said. "Tell him he'd better get somebody down to Lankenau. We might have a homicide."

Metz reached Woodward at a popular eatery about halfway between Norristown and Overbrook. He and three fellow detectives—Ed Justice, Don Rohner, and John Fallon—were just finishing their meals.

"We're on our way," Woodward said when Metz relayed what Boegly had told him. Piling into Woodward's car, it took them less than fifteen minutes to get to Lankenau.

When they arrived, Boegly greeted them with the news that a contingent from LMPD also was on the way. Dr. Hood, he said, was still in the autopsy room. A group led by a bleary-eyed Mark Keenan arrived a few minutes later. With the sergeant was Detective Rick Birkenmeier and police photographer Keith Watkinson. Detective Craig was still at home asleep.

All of the men respected Hood's ability as a pathologist. If Stefanie Rabinowitz had been murdered, the somewhat eccentric Kiwi would ferret it out. While they waited, Woodward and Keenan, in anticipation that the report would be positive, agreed that since the incident occurred in Lower Merion and Detective Craig was the first on the scene, he would be the lead investigator. Keenan also nominated Birkenmeier as the evidence man, the one who would be in charge of cataloging and keeping track of material they would later need to prosecute the case. Woodward then picked Fallon to work with Birkenmeier and a detective who was not there, Richard Peffall, to work with Charlie Craig. Actually, it was another homicide unit detective's turn in the rotation, but he was out indefinitely with an injury and Peffall had slipped into his spot. With those decisions made, they waited impatiently for Hood to finish.

The pathologist emerged an hour later. Stripping off his gloves, he looked grim as he approached the group.

"It was a murder, then," mumbled Keenan, noting the pathologist's expression.

Hood nodded. "Absolutely. No doubt about it. But I can understand how it went unnoticed by the emergency room crew. Externally, there was almost nothing. A teeny scratch here," he said, pointing to the left side of his neck. "Only about an eighth of an inch long. And a very faint bruise under the right side of the jaw. The petechia, of course, didn't show up until later."

"Is that *it*?" one of the detectives blurted when Hood seemed to have entered the end of his statement.

"Oh, no," Hood said quickly. "Once I got inside I found deep bruising in the soft tissues on both sides of the neck just below the jaw. Also here in the front," he added, pointing to his own throat.

"There's no chance those bruises were inflicted when they were trying to resuscitate her, is there?" asked Woodward.

"Very unlikely," said Hood. "There's also a bruise on the side of her head, plus other indications, too, like frothy fluid in the trachea. But that's pretty technical stuff. It'll all be in my formal report, but I thought you might want to get started."

"But you're convinced she was strangled?" asked Keenan.

"Definitely. There were some bruises on her right knee

and the sides of her arms, too. I'd say she got the bruises on her arms in the bathtub. From the types of bruises and where they are, I reckon she was strangled by hand in the tub. Whoever did it probably got her in the tub first, then grabbed her around the throat, just under her jaw like this," he said, putting his hand to his neck, "and throttled her to death."

"That's interesting," one of the detectives said. "I wonder how he got her in the tub."

Hood shrugged. "Maybe she was drugged. I'm having the lab do some toxicology tests, but that'll take awhile."

"Did she put up a fight?" one of the detectives asked.

Hood shook his head. "I don't know. I did some nail scrapings."

"When did she die?" Woodward asked.

"I can't say exactly, but probably about five hours before she came in here. At least four, judging by her stomach contents."

Keenan whistled. "She was pronounced dead at one-thirty. Her husband called 911 at twelve-thirty. So you're saying she like died about nine-thirty last night, three hours before her husband called for help."

Hood nodded. "Give or take."

"No possibility she could have drowned?" asked Keenan.

Hood smiled slightly. "No."

"No heart attack? No stroke?"

"Nope."

"What else can you tell us?"

"I've given you the gist. The lab tests may tell us more."

"You've told us a lot already," said Keenan, inwardly relieved that his instincts had not betrayed him. "Let's go to work."

En route to Norristown
2:10 p.m.

Bruce L. Castor, Jr., Montgomery County's First Assistant District Attorney, and his boss, DA Michael Marino, were on their way back to the Montgomery County courthouse, a massive, marble-fronted structure erected in 1854 on a steep hill looking down on the community's narrow main street, the Pennsylvania Railroad tracks, and the fast-flowing Schuylkill River. They were discussing the case in Horsham when Castor's pager went off.

"Urgent?" asked Marino, a sometimes controversial district attorney who had raised the ire of Montgomery County police chiefs soon after he was first elected almost a decade ago by proposing a county-wide police force.

"It's Tim Woodward. I'd better see what he wants."

A politically ambitious man who was already planning to run for the district attorney's job when the fifty-six-year-old Marino was expected to retire in 2000, Castor had spent the lunch hour delivering a speech to an association of retirees in Oreland, in eastern Montgomery County; then he and Marino had dropped in on a Republican women's meeting in Lower Frederick. They were heading back to Norristown when Woodward rang.

When he got hold of Woodward, the deputy chief briefed him on Stefanie Rabinowitz's death and what Hood had found in the autopsy. He relayed the information to Marino.

"Hood thinks it's a murder; that the woman was strangled," Castor explained.

"What do you think?" asked Marino, a former FBI agent who became a high-priced defense lawyer before he made a dark-horse run for the DA's job against a popular Republican state representative.

"I think we ought to wait until Doc Fillinger can confirm it," replied Castor, a thirty-five-year-old whiz kid who in just seven years had jumped from being only one of thirty-four assistant district attorneys in the county to the top ADA job. "That situation in Horsham is nasty. We ought to give it top priority until we know a little more about the Lower Merion case."

Marino nodded. "It's your call. In about," he looked at his watch, "three hours you're going to be in charge because I'm leaving for Gettysburg for that DA's conference."

"I'll keep an eye on developments in Lower Merion," Castor said. "Let's get Horsham settled first."

Norristown
3:30 p.m.

After the detectives adjourned to Ardmore, Bill Boegly returned to Norristown. When he walked in the office, he was surprised to find Dr. Fillinger already there.

"What did Hood say?" Fillinger asked, looking as if he already knew the answer.

"It's murder," Boegly said. "She was strangled."

Fillinger smiled. "I thought there was something fishy there. Although I have every confidence in the world in Dr. Hood, I'll run down tomorrow to see for myself."

"What about Horsham?" Boegly asked.

"That's a strange situation," Fillinger replied. "It sure looked like a murder at first, but I'm almost convinced now it was a suicide. Still doing some tests."

Boegly made a face. "Suicide? Ugh. What a hell of a way to go." He was about to add something else when the telephone rang.

"Coroner's office," he said officiously. For the next thirty seconds he stood mute, nodding quietly. "Doc," he said, covering the mouthpiece, "it's Representative Cohen. Lita Cohen."

Fillinger frowned. "I'll take it in my office. I'll bet I know what it's about."

When he emerged five minutes later, Boegly raised an eyebrow. "Well?"

Fillinger waved his hand. "It's what I thought. She wanted to see if she could persuade me to release that Lower Merion woman's body. Said the family was really anxious to get her buried."

"And what did you say?"

"I told her I couldn't do that just now, that there were indications of criminal activity and we needed to run some more tests."

"Did that satisfy her?" Boegly asked.

"Oh, yes. I don't think we're going to hear any more about it, especially after the news gets out."

Ardmore
3:40 p.m.

At police headquarters on Lancaster Avenue, the detectives stocked up on coffee and soda and filed into the large conference room, joined in the meantime by Charlie Craig and Rich Peffall, a tall, sandy-haired forty-four-year-old with twenty-three years' experience in law enforcement, six of them in homicide.

"Who's the prime suspect?" asked Peffall.

"Is there any doubt?" chimed in Fallon, a soft-spoken Navy veteran with a broad sense of humor and twenty-four years' experience beginning as a uniformed officer in Lower Merion.

"What do you mean?" asked Peffall.

"Has to be the husband," Fallon said dryly.

"What makes you so sure?"

"Hell," Fallon said, smiling. "There were three people in the house. One of them's dead, and the baby is pretty much off the hook."

Murmurs of assent echoed around the room.

"But *why* did he do it?" interjected Detective Craig. Despite his years as a policeman, Charlie Craig did not have as much experience in murder investigations as the members of the homicide unit. In his career, he had investigated nine murders, two of them as lead detective. The homicide unit handled more than that in a year.

Ordinarily, motive is not particularly relevant to investigators and prosecutors. They gather the facts and lay them out, leaving the jury to wrestle with the issue of incentive. But this was a somewhat unusual situation. If Craig Rabinowitz remained the main suspect, the detectives were going to have to show that he had very good reason to want his wife dead. The fact that it seemed unlikely that anyone else *could* have committed the crime made a compelling argument for his involvement. But there had been no witnesses, so any evidence they compiled would be totally circumstantial. And ever since O.J., the word "circumstantial" had sent chills up investigators' spines.

This case, as uncomfortable as it might make the detectives to think about it, had parallels to Simpson in its potential for media exposure. As far as they knew, Stefanie Rabinowitz and her husband were upright, respected citizens. They lived on the Main Line—magic words in Philadelphia. These were ingredients for a Media Event once reporters discovered that Stefanie had been murdered. The likelihood that this would turn into a Big Story lay like a landmine that could blow the investigation apart before investigators could build a substantial case against Rabinowitz.

Investigators knew it would be impossible to keep the circumstances of Stefanie's death quiet for very long, so time was a major factor. They felt they had to move fast, not only before the media could muddy the water, but also before her husband could cover his tracks. They were confident that Rabinowitz was unaware that he was being viewed as the prime suspect, and were sure that he was ignorant of the fact that they had just discovered that Stefanie had been murdered. But once the media got that information, the value of surprise would be lost. As soon as Rabinowitz suspected they were after *him*, he would find a good lawyer and that would be that. What they had to do, they agreed, was lock him into his version of what happened before he found out about the autopsy results. The plan they drew up for accomplishing this was simple: They wouldn't tell him what they knew until after he told them what *he* knew, or rather what he wanted them to believe.

Since Detective Craig had already laid the groundwork by telling Rabinowitz that they needed a formal statement from him before they could close the file, they would bring him to LMPD, let him say whatever he wanted, and only then tell him that they knew his wife had been murdered. If they were lucky, he would dig himself into a hole he would not be able to get himself out of.

However, that alone would not put the noose around Rabinowitz's neck; not unless he was foolish enough to confess, and they didn't think that was likely to happen. A man who could cold-bloodedly strangle his wife, in the bathtub no less, while their infant daughter was sleeping six or eight feet away, was not likely to fall apart very quickly. In the heat of passion, a man might shoot, stab, or bludgeon his spouse. But strangle her? In the blink of an eye, a man could squeeze a trigger, plunge a knife, or swing a heavy object—all methods that allowed the killer to maintain some physical distance from the victim. But choking was a hands-on, up-close operation. To throttle someone, a man had to wrap his hands around the throat, squeeze, and keep squeezing for a minimum of four minutes. During that time, the killer had to look his victim in the face, subdue the inevitable, reflexive struggle, watch dispassionately as the victim's face turned blue, and try not to hear the last, horrible, frantic gasps. Strangling was a particularly brutal form of murder. It required a special cold-bloodedness that most people, even many killers, were unable to summon.

Why would Craig Rabinowitz do this to his wife?

Although they didn't yet know Rabinowitz, they doubted that he was stupid. He would quickly tumble to the fact that they needed a lot more than an autopsy report to convict him of the crime. This put the burden back on Detectives Peffall and Craig. No matter how sure they and every investigator in Montgomery County was that Rabinowitz was the killer, they would have to find the evidence to prove it.

For openers, they started the paperwork to get a court order for an official search of the Rabinowitzes' house. Although Detective Craig had spent more than an hour at 526 Winding Way, at the time he had been wearing his tourist cap, not his deerstalker. When he went back, it wouldn't be a superficial walk-through. On the next visit, there would be a *team* of investigators accompanied by an official photographer to document what Detective Craig had observed earlier: mainly that there were no signs that the house had been broken into. That would further narrow Rabinowitz's finger-pointing options. If there was no evidence of a break-in it would be difficult for his lawyers to claim that an intruder had slipped in and killed Stefanie.

If they were *really* lucky, or if Rabinowitz was really that careless or dumb, they also might find physical evidence showing that he had motive to kill his wife.

Merion
4:20 p.m.

Elaine Miller was starting to drag again. She and Todd had slipped away for a few hours of sleep shortly after dawn, but she had been back at the Rabinowitz house by noon. There was so much to be done and she felt a deep-seated loyalty to Craig—even if he had been treating her rather coolly for the last few months—and to the memory of Stefanie.

Betty and Jennifer had done a good job of notifying people, Elaine thought, judging by the number of friends and relatives coming to pay their respects, even though shivah would not formally start until the next afternoon after a memorial service for Stefanie. A long table had been set up along one wall of the dining room, and it was covered with food, all of it brought by visitors on the assumption that the mourners were too intent on their grief to pay attention to the mundane. Nothing fancy, just everyday edibles, with sodas stacked to the side. Unlike Irish wakes, where alcohol flows freely, Jews are much more sober. Liquor is never seen at a shivah.

As is customary among the observant, the Newmans spoke in whispers about their daughter. On each of their lapels was a piece of ripped cloth symbolizing the ancient expression of grief, the rending of garments. Lou Newman's chin, Elaine noticed, was covered with stubble. It would remain that way for a week. By custom, Jewish men did not shave during shivah.

Indeed, shivah—the name is derived from the Hebrew word for "seven," the number of days it would last—was a time when the mourners concentrated only on their grief to the exclusion of virtually everything else. All the mirrors in the house were draped with pillowcases so that there would be no temptation for vanity to distract anyone from the purpose of mourning the dead. For a week, for the conservative Newmans, there would be no tv, no radio, no newspapers.

Under normal circumstances, Stefanie would have been buried quickly. But Stefanie's death had not been normal. The fact that the hospital, apparently on orders from the coroner's office, was continuing to refuse to release the body had thrown everything into disarray. If the body had been released that morning, as they had hoped, Stefanie would have been buried on Thursday, May 1. But since the body had not been released, a memorial service rather than a funeral was scheduled.

No one knew for sure exactly when the funeral itself would be. There were other variables involved besides the release of Stefanie's body. Friday, May 2, was Haley's first birthday, and not an appropriate date. Under Jewish tradition, the date of someone's burial is considered that person's *yortzeit*, the date on which the death is mourned in the future. It would not be fair to Haley for her mother's yortzeit to be the same as her birthday. Since Saturday was *Shabbes*, the Jewish Sabbath, that day was definitely out of the question. Sunday was not opportune because a birthday party for Haley had been scheduled. As a result, it looked as though the first possible day for the funeral would be Monday, May 5.

To have to postpone the funeral was upsetting to some family members, especially since the cause of the delay was the need to perform an autopsy. Unlike the more observant Jews, Betty, a nurse, was inwardly thankful for the post mortem. At the time, the family and friends still believed that Stefanie had died a natural death, so an autopsy would determine if the cause was something that could be inherited by Haley.

Elaine occupied herself with busy-work, automatic, repetitive tasks that left her mind free to wonder what had come over Craig earlier when he had suggested that Stefanie be buried with her jewelry. The fact that conservative Jews *never* buried the dead with jewelry was more or less immaterial since Craig certainly wasn't conservative. But when he had blurted out his proposal while she and Jennifer and Betty were trying to pick out Stefanie's burial garments, they had all been shocked. "Think of Haley," they had said almost in unison. The jewelry belonged to Haley.

Craig—reluctantly it seemed—had concurred. While he had tried to pretend that it had been a comment caused by his grief, Elaine nevertheless considered it very strange.

In fact, several things Craig had done were strange, but then again, grief affected people differently. She considered it a plus that he no longer seemed to be hanging on the

edge of hysteria, but at the same time she couldn't understand why he always seemed to spend quite a bit of time
huddled with Jeffrey Solomon, his lawyer friend, who had
answered his call for support. Another thing Elaine thought
was unusual was that Craig had not mentioned the fact that
an autopsy was being conducted on his wife. It probably
would have made *her* a little queasy, but maybe he figured
there was nothing he could do about it anyway.

Just as Craig did not share any possible misgivings about
the autopsy with his friends, neither did they share any
feelings they may have entertained about Craig's deport-
ment. Just because Craig did not appear to be overly distraught did not mean that he felt Stefanie's loss any less.
The possibility that he also might be harboring tremendous
guilt and fear never occurred to them. Given the circumstances, it would have been easier to convince the Millers,
Schwartzes, and Hirtzes—not to mention the Newmans—
that a Martian spacecraft had landed in Rittenhouse Square
than it would have been to ask them to believe that Craig
very likely had murdered Stefanie.

FIVE

He's cool, Rich Peffall thought, openly sizing up Craig Rabinowitz; I have to give him that.

Unhurriedly arranging a pad and pen on the table in front of him, the detective used the opportunity to get a leisurely look at the man whom the detectives suspected of strangling his wife less than twenty-four hours before. Twenty minutes earlier, anxious to implement the first phase of their plan for a quick conclusion to the investigation into Stefanie's murder, Detectives Peffall and Craig had gone to Merion to ask Rabinowitz to come back with them to police headquarters.

"We need to get that statement from you," Detective Craig had explained. "We'd like to get this wrapped up."

"Can't we do it here?" Rabinowitz had asked amiably. "It's been a long day."

"I'm afraid not," Charlie Craig responded, "but you'll be back in an hour."

Rabinowitz motioned to a man behind him. "This is Jeffrey Solomon. He's my friend and he's also my lawyer. Can he come along, too?"

"Sure," said Detective Craig. "No problem."

Rabinowitz and Solomon had followed the two detectives up the enclosed stairs that ran along the outside wall of the yellow brick police headquarters building and into one of the department's two identical interview rooms. Tiny to the point of being claustrophobic, the room was furnished sparsely with a battered table and four chairs. Peffall took a seat at one end; Detective Craig at the other.

"Can I get you anything?" Charlie Craig asked affably. "Soda? Coffee?"

The two shook their heads. "Nothing, thanks," said Rabinowitz. "If it's all the same with you, I'd just as soon get on with it."

Until he came to the door at Winding Way, Peffall, unlike his colleague, had never seen the suspect in the flesh. The exchange at the house had been fleeting; the light in the car dim. But in the bright glare of the interview room's overhead fluorescent lights, he stood out in full, three-dimensional Technicolor. Peffall was not impressed.

He's dressed like he's going to a Flyers game, the detective thought. Neatly pressed jeans, long-sleeved blue shirt with the cuffs rolled to the elbows, brown loafers, no socks; hair combed straight back, exposing a high forehead and a receding hairline. The detective sniffed, sure that he could catch a whiff of expensive aftershave wafting through the room. Immediately, he was suspicious of Rabinowitz's apparent aplomb. He doesn't appear to be a bit nervous, the investigator observed, but that, in itself, meant little. Everyone reacts differently to sudden death; he might still be in shock. On the other hand, in the one hundred–plus murder investigations he had been involved in over the years, Peffall had found that a surprising number of cold-blooded killers were capable of putting up a good front right up to the time they confessed or got nailed with incontrovertible evidence. While neither detective expected Craig Rabinowitz to throw himself at their feet and beg forgiveness for choking his wife to death, especially with his lawyer at his side, Peffall reckoned that *whatever* he had to say would be interesting. And—he hoped—damning.

Rabinowitz stared at him expectantly.

"You understand," the detective explained for the record, "that you're not under arrest and you're free to leave?"

"Yes," Rabinowitz nodded.

"All right," said Peffall, picking up his pen. "Let's get started."

His first questions were simple stage-setting queries: How long had he and Stefanie lived on Winding Way? . . . What time had they gotten home the night before? . . . Did they leave the house after that? . . . What time did they go to bed?

"We went upstairs about eleven p.m. or so, but we didn't get into bed," Rabinowitz said congenially. "Stefanie was thinking about what she was going to wear to work the next day. She brushed her teeth. I was sitting on the end of the bed watching the hockey game."

What was it, Peffall asked, the preliminaries out of the way, that made him call 911?

"I saw my wife submerged in the tub," Rabinowitz replied, his voice flat.

Between the time Stefanie had gone into the guest bathroom and the time that he found her submerged, had he had any conversation with her?

Rabinowitz shook his head, explaining that he had been reading the newspaper and halfway watching a game between Phoenix and Anaheim, waiting to see if Buffalo was going to go into overtime.

When he first saw Stefanie, Peffall asked, what had been his reaction?

Rabinowitz took a deep breath. "I kind of froze. I couldn't believe what I was seeing. I got into the tub. I don't know why. I just couldn't get her out. I sat down behind her. She was so blue and pale," he said haltingly, his voice breaking. "I just couldn't get her out." He shook his head slowly, looking down at the table. "I'm kind of ashamed about that. I don't think I helped her very much. I had my arms around her . . ." his voice trailed off.

Amazing, Peffall thought. This guy's good. "Did you make any efforts to use first aid or CPR?"

"No," Rabinowitz replied, explaining that that was when he called 911. He got out of the tub, went into his office, and dialed the emergency number. Then he hurried downstairs to unlock the door so the paramedics could get in. Running back upstairs, he climbed into the tub for a second time. "I was sitting behind her again, trying to lift her, when the policeman came up and helped me."

Peffall paused, doodling on the border of the pad, collecting his thoughts. About how long, he asked Rabinowitz, had it been from the time that he first found Stefanie until he called 911?

"I was in the bedroom and this feeling came over me that something was wrong," Rabinowitz said evasively. "It was a couple of minutes. I think I was so sorry that I didn't do anything when I heard the thump. I just wanted to tell her I was sorry."

What about that "thump"? Peffall asked. What was it?

Rabinowitz laughed hollowly. "I heard it when I was in the bedroom. It was something I'd heard a thousand times. It was the shampoo bottle falling off the holder."

And how long had it been from the time that he heard the "thump" until he went to check on his wife?

Rabinowitz shrugged. "Thirty-five minutes."

Peffall decided to change directions; see if he could catch him off guard. When, he asked abruptly, had he last had sex with his wife?

If Rabinowitz was offended by the question, he didn't show it. A smile flickered at the corner of his mouth. "I was trying last night in the den," he replied lightly. "Just playing. Kissing and hugging and playing around a little. We were both really tired. But that's why I was waiting up. I thought maybe after her bath. I think we would have last night, but I can't say for sure." He paused, shaking his head slightly. "But to answer your question, two Sundays ago. When my in-laws had the baby."

Remembering the pathologist's comment about how Stefanie may have been drugged before she was killed, the detective asked Rabinowitz if his wife had been taking any medication.

He bobbed his head. Both of them had been taking an over-the-counter drug to help them sleep. It wasn't too effective, Rabinowitz said, so he had gone to his doctor and asked for something stronger. The physician had prescribed a sedative called Ambien. "I took it Monday," he added. "It really works."

In response to Peffall's next question—had Stefanie taken any of the sedative?—Rabinowitz frowned. "I don't know," he said slowly. He had not actually seen her ingest any of the medication, although he believed that she may have taken some before she took her bath. When he took a single pill—the recommended dose—on Monday, he had fumbled with the bottle, almost dropping it. The lid and perhaps some of the pills had fallen into the toilet. He noticed that there had been three pills left in the bottle, but when he checked earlier on Wednesday, it was empty. "I don't know if she took them or threw them away," he said evenly. "I have no idea."

Detective Craig cocked his head. He hadn't seen any empty bottle when he went through the house, he thought. He opened his mouth, ready to ask Rabinowitz about that, then thought better of it, deciding to wait and see if it turned up in the search which they had scheduled for later that evening. He jotted a reminder on his pad.

Peffall flipped through his notes; he was nearing the end of his list of questions.

What kind of relationship did he have with his wife? Were there any problems?

"Oh, no!" Rabinowitz said emphatically. "Never! We never had an argument. We never had any problems. Everyone has disagreements, but we had less than most. We were best friends."

Although both detectives felt sure that Rabinowitz had

killed his wife—and were becoming more convinced by the minute—Peffall continued to be mildly troubled by their inability to uncover a motive. It would move things along a lot faster if they could discern a plausible reason for such a deliberate, merciless act. If the couple's marriage was as solid as Rabinowitz wanted them to believe, maybe it was money. Before he had joined the homicide unit, Peffall had been a specialist in white-collar crime, which mainly involved financial issues. "How much life insurance did you and your wife have on each other?" he asked.

Rabinowitz replied quickly, without hesitation. There was $1.6 million on him and $1.5 million on Stefanie, most of which had been taken out after Haley was born. Plus, he added, there were two policies through the law firm where Stefanie worked: a $500,000 policy on her and one on him for $150,000.

Peffall made a note of the figures. One more question, he said. Who was Stefanie's best friend?

"Besides me," Rabinowitz replied, "there were three: Elaine Miller, Betty Schwartz, and Jennifer Hirtz."

Peffall looked at Charlie Craig and nodded.

Although Rabinowitz had told both Officer Driscoll and Detective Craig that the house had been locked at the time of the incident, the investigator was anxious to get the admission as part of the formal statement. Had he locked up the house before going to bed? Charlie Craig asked.

Rabinowitz nodded. "I go through the same routine every night. Back door, lock and chain . . . front door, lock and chain. I don't remember about the sliders, but I was in the den, so I'm sure I would have shut them."

When Stefanie had gone to take her bath, had she closed the door?

"No," Rabinowitz answered. It squeaked loudly, so they usually left it open to keep from waking Haley.

Had he and his wife been drinking that night?

He had had one beer, Rabinowitz replied. At about nine o'clock, after the Newmans had gone. He had opened one for Stefanie as well, but she took only a few swallows before giving it to him to finish.

Remembering what he had read in Driscoll's report about Stefanie having been wearing a ring, bracelets, and a watch when he pulled her out of the tub, Detective Craig asked if there was any jewelry that Stefanie habitually wore.

Rabinowitz looked thoughtful. "A gold wedding band with diamonds," he replied. "Two stackable rings, and a junky watch that gave her a rash."

Did she wear the watch all the time? Did she ever take it off?

"Maybe to shower, but she slept in it."

Detective Craig, too, was nearing the end of his list. After determining that the Rabinowitzes' home had an alarm system that they never used, he asked what position Stefanie had been in when he found her.

Rabinowitz's eyes grew moist. She had been on her right side, he said, with her face turned to the right. Her legs were slightly bent and her head was entirely under water. "I just picked her whole body up out of the water," he said slowly. "I couldn't believe how heavy she was. I was trying to hold and comfort her. I was so sorry. Thinking about it now, I am so embarrassed."

The detectives exchanged glances. "Okay," Peffall said briskly, "I think we're finished." Turning to Solomon, he asked if there was anything he would like to add.

The lawyer shook his head.

"Good," Peffall said. He had been typing the whole time Craig had been talking. Taking the last page out of the machine, he handed the entire document to Rabinowitz. "You and your attorney can review this." Peffall and Detective Craig stood, intending to leave the room so that Rabinowitz and Solomon could read through the material.

There was a knock on the door. It was Matt Rosen, another lawyer friend of Rabinowitz's.

*   *   *

Late that afternoon, after Craig and the Newmans left for the funeral home to pick out a casket for Stefanie, Mark Hirtz figured he could slip away to his office to take care of some paperwork. As a corporate lawyer in a well-respected Center City firm, he knew there would be a stack of documents on his desk that needed to be taken care of before the end of the day. Hurrying through the tasks as quickly as he could, he jumped in his car and drove back to the Rabinowitzes'.

When he arrived, he found the downstairs section of the house deserted. Figuring they were discussing personal business upstairs, Hirtz found a quiet place where he could make some notes about the eulogy he planned to deliver at the memorial service the next afternoon. Some thirty minutes later he was interrupted by Lou Newman.

"I didn't hear you come in," Newman said, surprised to see Hirtz.

"I didn't want to interfere. How's Craig doing?"

"You just missed him."

"What do you mean, I missed him?" asked Hirtz, puzzled. "Where did he go?"

"He and Jeffrey Solomon went to Ardmore. The police wanted him to make a formal statement so they could clear up their records."

"A statement! Why did they want him to make a statement now?"

"I don't know," said Newman. "Two officers came here and he and Jeffrey left with them. They said they wouldn't be long."

"I'm going to go see what's happening," Hirtz said, gathering his notes.

"Is anything wrong?" Newman asked, frowning.

"I don't think so," said Hirtz. "But I'd feel better if I knew what this is all about."

As Hirtz was leaving, Matt Rosen came in. "Where are you going in such a hurry?" he asked.

Hirtz filled him in.

"I'd better go with you," Rosen replied.

"I don't like the sound of this," Hirtz said as he turned onto Meeting House Lane. "I don't know why they had to do this right now. What's the big hurry? Don't they realize this guy has been through a terrible, traumatic experience?"

"It worries me, too," replied Rosen, a general practitioner who handled both criminal and civil cases. "I wish one of us had been there when the cops showed up."

"I hope we're not too late," said Hirtz. "I'd feel better if it were one of us with him. Especially you, since you've had some experience in this field. Solomon's a personal injury lawyer. I don't know how much he knows about dealing with the police in a situation like this."

"Craig shouldn't be making a statement right now under *any* circumstances," Rosen said emphatically.

Hirtz nodded. "Damn right."

From the reception desk in the LMPD lobby they called upstairs to the detective division, speaking to Sergeant Keenan, who served as gatekeeper to the locked second-floor inner sanctum. They said they wanted to come up.

"Not right now," Keenan replied. Rabinowitz and Solomon already were in the interview room making a statement to detectives and couldn't be disturbed. "Why don't you wait in the lobby?" he suggested. "I'll let you know when."

Rosen and Hirtz passed the next twenty minutes pacing impatiently, agitated because they felt they were being separated from their friend at a time when he might need them the most. Every four or five minutes they called Keenan.

"I just don't understand it," Hirtz groaned. "They're treating this like a criminal investigation."

After a half-dozen or so calls from the fidgety attorneys, Keenan relented. The interview was finished, he said, and was being transcribed. If they still wanted to, one of them could come up.

"You go," Hirtz said quickly. "You're the one with criminal experience."

"Okay," said Rosen, punching the button on the elevator at the far end of the reception area.

"Let me know what's happening," Hirtz added anxiously as the elevator door closed.

Upstairs, Rosen was buzzed through the door leading into the squad room. Keenan met him and took him to the interview room, where Rabinowitz and Solomon were waiting to review the typed statement.

"After we sign, we can get out of here," Solomon explained.

Five minutes later, Peffall returned with the document. "Read it and make sure it's correct," he said, handing it over.

It was Peffall's practice always to include one or more deliberate factual errors in the statements that he typed. This forced the interviewee to make initialed corrections—a good defense, Peffall had found, against a possible later claim from the interviewee that he had not read the document before signing it. Anticipating that Rabinowitz, as soon as he found out that he was the major suspect in his wife's murder, would hire a good lawyer, one who likely would immediately make such a claim, Peffall had included a single deliberate mistake.

"This is wrong," Rabinowitz said, catching it quickly.

Peffall smiled to himself. "What is it?"

"Here," Rabinowitz said, pointing to the question about Stefanie's best friends. Peffall had purposely typed "Jane" when it should have been "Jennifer." Taking the proffered pen, Rabinowitz made the correction and scribbled "CR" above it.

"Anything else?" Detective Craig asked.

Rabinowitz shook his head.

"Then please sign it here," the investigator said, pointing to a line at the bottom.

Rabinowitz affixed his signature and handed it back, watching without comment as the two detectives signed it as well.

Detective Craig took his time squaring the twelve-page document. Once all the pages were even, he set it carefully on the table in front of him. Looking up, he locked eyes with Rabinowitz. "We have a little problem," he said ominously.

Rabinowitz looked puzzled. "Oh?" he replied matter-of-factly. "What's that?"

Detective Craig paused, continuing to hold Rabinowitz's gaze. "The autopsy report indicates that Stefanie didn't have a stroke or a heart attack," the investigator said evenly. "She was strangled."

The three—Rabinowitz, Solomon, and Rosen—gaped at the detective, unsure they had heard correctly. For what seemed a long time no one said anything. Finally, Rosen broke the silence. "Oh, my God," he blurted, vocalizing the first thought that came into his mind. "Stefanie strangled herself."

Peffall rolled his eyes. "I don't think so, Counselor," he said coolly. "It's impossible for someone to strangle himself." Turning to Rabinowitz, he leaned forward. "Craig," he asked, his eyes boring into Rabinowitz's, "did *you* strangle Stefanie?"

The color drained from Rabinowitz's face. He looked ill, and when he opened his mouth, the detective wondered whether he was going to throw up or make a reply. But before he could say anything, Solomon jumped to his feet.

"That's it!" the lawyer bellowed, making an aggressive chopping motion with his right hand. "Don't answer!" he barked at his friend. "Don't answer anything!"

Peffall, whose eyes had never left Rabinowitz's face, marveled at the speed with which the suspect regained his composure. The color flooded back into his cheeks and the expression on his face changed totally. To Peffall, he now appeared completely unperturbed.

Turning slightly in his chair, Rabinowitz gave Solomon a what-now? glance.

"Can we use a phone?" the lawyer asked. "We're going to need some help on this."

Detective Craig ducked out of the room, returning almost immediately with a copy of the Philadelphia yellow pages. Handing it to Solomon without comment, he and Peffall left the room so the lawyers could make their calls in private.

Mark Hirtz, who was still downstairs, was getting more peeved by the minute. What the hell's going on? he asked himself. What's happening up there?

He was about to call upstairs again when the elevator door opened and a plainclothes detective emerged. "I'm Sergeant Keenan," the man said briskly. Without preamble, he launched into a series of pointed questions about Rabinowitz: How well did Hirtz know him? . . . Where and when had they met? . . . How did he and his wife get along? . . .

"What *is* this?" Hirtz interrupted angrily. "Why do you want to know this?"

"It has to do with Stefanie Rabinowitz," Keenan said. "She didn't die accidentally. The autopsy shows she died of manual strangulation."

Hirtz felt as if he had been blind-sided. "No!" he said. "No, no, no. It can't be. The medical examiner must have screwed up."

"He didn't screw up," Keenan replied evenly. "She was choked to death. That's a fact. And we think her husband did it."

Hirtz stared, dumbfounded. "That's impossible!" he exclaimed. "There's no way. No way. Craig could *never* do that. I'd stake my life on it."

Keenan shook his head slowly. "Don't say that," he said, not unkindly. "I've been doing this for twenty-five years and one thing I've learned is never to say you'd stake your life on anything. No one knows what happens behind closed doors."

*   *   *

As Detectives Craig and Peffall headed down the corridor toward the squad room, they passed the other interview room. Out of curiosity, Peffall peeked through the small window. Tim Woodward was inside, taking a statement from the paramedics who had answered Rabinowitz's 911 call.

"I think we've got our man," Detective Craig said, smiling broadly. "I don't think we have to look any further."

"Me, either," agreed Peffall. "After what he said about making sure the house was locked up tight, I think we can eliminate any possibility of a one-armed man," he added, referring to *The Fugitive*, an old tv series in which the title character was blamed for a murder committed by an intruder who was missing a limb.

"But we still don't know why," Detective Craig replied, sobering.

"We'll find out," Peffall added confidently. "Don't worry, we'll find out."

It was a little after seven p.m., only eighteen and a half hours since Stefanie had been found in the bathtub. But both officers knew better than to get too elated about the progress they had made. From now on, they both knew, it was going to get tougher. Rabinowitz had access to valuable resources; influential and knowledgeable friends; the money to hire a good lawyer. Although they were confident that they had the right man in their sights, they were still a long way from completing their investigation, a long way from feeling that they had a solid case.

"While we have the time, let's go get something to eat," Peffall suggested. "We still have a search to conduct."

526 Winding Way
9:30 p.m.

Before Rabinowitz and his friends left to return to Merion, Sergeant Keenan had given them an unusual preview of police plans. While officers were not unsympathetic to the family's grieving process, he said, the fact that Stefanie had been murdered put things in a different light. It was the police department's responsibility to bring a quick resolution to the matter, and that included taking whatever action they felt was necessary. "We're going to be coming to your house in a little while with a search warrant," he said. "To save embarrassment and inconvenience you might want to ask your family and friends to leave temporarily."

Rabinowitz ignored the advice. When he and the three others arrived at Winding Way, he went straight upstairs and closeted himself in the master bedroom. The other three, sworn to secrecy, were left to awkwardly ignore questions from the others. At Rabinowitz's insistence, they told no one about the autopsy results, or that Rabinowitz was the prime suspect. This was particularly frustrating to Hirtz, who could not even tell his wife, Jennifer.

When the search team arrived an hour later, Detectives Craig and Peffall were mildly irritated, but not surprised, to find about a dozen people in the house. They had hoped that Rabinowitz would have explained the circumstances and asked them to come back later.

Although he deliberately did not reveal that police knew that Stefanie had been strangled or the reason why the search was necessary, Deputy Chief Tim Woodward, who had come along to supervise the operation, explained that officers were there to conduct a court-approved procedure and that it would be better if the group gathered in one place so as not to hinder their efforts.

Peffall could feel the antagonism rise like a cloud of steam. As the mourners filed into the den, they glared hostilely at the detectives, their eyes openly challenging the interlopers' authority to wilfully interrupt an innocent gathering for no apparent reason. Peffall thought he understood. If the group had been Catholics or Methodists, the reaction may have been much the same, but because they were Jews, there was a subtle difference. It was not that many years ago that European Jews went through the Nazi terror and the memories of that experience still lingered vividly. To Stefanie Rabinowitz's family and friends, the investigators, at that moment, appeared as little more than Brown Shirts out to do Hitler's evil duty.

Hating what he had to do, Peffall sought out Lou and Anne Newman. Steering them into a quiet corner where they would not be disturbed, Peffall urged them to sit. "I don't want to have to tell you this," he said softly, taking Anne's hand, "but your daughter was murdered."

"Oh, no!" Anne Newman gasped, collapsing on her husband's shoulder. "No!" she moaned, shaking her head. "That can't be! There's been a mistake."

"I'm afraid not," Peffall continued. "There's no mistake. Stefanie was strangled. There's no doubt about it. And," he added, swallowing hard, "we believe your son-in-law was responsible."

The news was too painful for the Newmans to absorb. "No! No!" Anne wailed. "There's a mistake. There must be a mistake."

From past experience Peffall knew it would be futile to argue or continue to press the issue. She needed time for the shock to wear off. He patted her hand, saying nothing.

"It's a mistake," Anne repeated, pulling her hand away. "It has to be a mistake."

Painfully, she and her husband rose and returned to rejoin the others.

Peffall looked around the room. In a corner, as far from the police as he could get, Rabinowitz stood and watched.

While Peffall had been talking to the Newmans, the other members of the team had fanned out throughout the house. Detective Craig started in the master bedroom, digging into drawers and closets. At the same time, a photographer followed John Fallon around from window to door, recording their pristine condition on film to deflect possible later claims that someone had broken into the dwelling.

Seeing the house for a second time, Detective Craig again noted its compactness. The guest bathroom where Stefanie had been found was no more than sixteen feet from the master bedroom, where Craig said he had been sitting reading the newspaper and watching hockey on tv. If he later tried to lay the blame on an intruder, Charlie Craig thought, how could he explain why he was so close and heard or saw absolutely nothing, especially with the door to the guest bath open?

As Fallon and the photographer were working their way through the house, they passed a bookcase containing a couple of dozen hardcover books and a collection of paperbacks. One title jumped out. Pausing, Fallon pulled the book off the shelf. Entitled *How We Die*, it was a lengthy, detailed description of the process the body goes through before and at the time of death. What a strange book, Fallon thought, for young people. Flipping through it, it was apparent that it had been read.

Upstairs, Detectives Craig and Peffall scooped up whatever looked as if it might be pertinent—checkbooks, loose papers, correspondence—and tossed it in a bag to take back to headquarters so they could examine it more closely later.

Detective Craig interrupted his search of the master bedroom to go downstairs to find Rabinowitz. Where, he asked, were the clothes that had been found in the bathroom? No longer as amiable as he had been earlier, Rabinowitz replied that they were in the laundry. At the investigator's request he collected them and grudgingly turned them over.

It was a few minutes after midnight, almost three hours after the search began, when Woodward finally called a halt. Signaling the detectives, he instructed them to pack up the material they had collected and head back to Ardmore.

On the way out the door, Charlie Craig paused, staring at his pad, seeing the reminder he had written to himself earlier. "Did you find an empty pill bottle?" he asked Peffall. "The one Rabinowitz mentioned that contained that sedative?"

Peffall shook his head. "Not me. But maybe someone else collected it. We'll see if it's there when we get back to Ardmore."

Once they were back at headquarters, the investigators went straight to the conference room, where they spread the material they had collected onto the large table and began going through it. Prominent among the items were stacks of papers that looked business-related, as well as two checkbooks: one on an account called C&C Supplies and one on a joint account for Craig and Stefanie Rabinowitz. There was no pill bottle, Detective Craig noticed.

At first, they could make no sense of what they were looking at. Admittedly, the insurance policies were larger than most people in Montgomery County would have had, but Rabinowitz and his wife were Main Liners, rising young professionals with bright futures. As such, they probably would have carried more insurance that the average county resident. Additionally, the detectives had no idea what the Rabinowitzes made in a year. They knew that Stefanie was a lawyer, but they did not know she was working only part-time and that her annual salary was only $30,000. A first glance at the papers from Rabinowitz's office indicated that he was an entrepreneur who ran a business having something to do with imports.

A quick glance through the checkbooks seemed to confirm that Craig and Stefanie were prosperous young professionals. Tim Woodward, however, spoke up, cautioning them not to jump to conclusions about their financial state. "This is Lower Merion," he admonished the group. "I've seen too many people here who seem on the surface to have large incomes. They live in million-dollar houses, drive Benzes and Jags, send their children to private schools, and take long vacations abroad. But they have less in the bank than I do. Let's be careful. My intuition tells me money is going to play a major role in what happened to Stefanie Rabinowitz.''

Peffall, the white-collar crime expert, nodded enthusiastically. ''Money's always a good motive for murder,'' he commented.

As it developed later, the observations were remarkably prophetic. However, the investigation itself had barely begun. Granted, the investigators had a strong suspect, but, unless he confessed, they still had a mountain of work ahead, not the least of which was sorting the material they had collected in the search. Since it was after midnight, Woodward told everyone to go home. Most of them had been at work since the previous morning, hours before they learned that they had a murder investigation on their hands. ''The grind is just beginning,'' he said, tossing one of the checkbooks on the table. ''Let's go get some sleep.''

SIX

Rabinowitz tucked the *Inquirer* under his arm and retreated to the kitchen. While the Newmans and some of the more devout members of his late wife's family were willing to eschew newspapers and tv because it was part of the old tradition of shivah, he figured it wasn't a custom he needed to abide by, particularly in his situation. Pouring himself another cup of coffee, he scanned the front page. Relieved to find there was nothing there, he hurriedly flipped through the back sections. He found it on the obit page, under the headline "Deaths in the Region."

The story was only six paragraphs long, anchored by a laudatory quote from David Fineman, managing partner of the firm where Stefanie had worked, Fineman & Bach. It contained nothing about the real circumstances of her demise. "She died while taking a bath," the article said, adding that the cause of death was unknown.

Rabinowitz tossed the paper aside and drained his cup. The rest of the house was beginning to stir, but he had no time for idle chit-chat. Grabbing his car keys, he ducked out the back door. When someone called after him, asking him where he was going, he barked, "I have business to take care of." Without another word of explanation, he backed the vehicle he usually drove, a Honda, down the long drive and turned it toward Philadelphia.

His abrupt departure must have severely wounded the Newmans. For the spouse of the deceased to leave the house during shivah was considered a serious violation of Jewish tradition. To tend to business during the sacred period was even worse. But Rabinowitz was a man on a mission; custom and tradition meant nothing.

At that time, roughly thirty hours after Stefanie had been pronounced dead at Lankenau, there were only six people in the house who knew that she had been murdered: Rabinowitz himself, the three friends—Mark Hirtz, Matt Rosen, and Jeffrey Solomon—who had been with him in Ardmore when he made his statement to police, and the Newmans. Rabinowitz had specifically requested that no one else be told. Not until he decided it was necessary.

If they had been available—and if they had felt comfortable with sharing the information, which they probably would not have—Rosen, Solomon, or Hirtz would have been able to identify their friend's destination. Once they had gotten over the shock of the previous evening's disclosures, they had realized that their friend needed a good lawyer. Although they themselves were lawyers, they acknowledged that their experience and training did not equip them for the task. As soon as Detectives Peffall and Craig left the interview room, Solomon called a prominent defense lawyer he knew well: Jeffrey Miller, a fifty-four-year-old former federal prosecutor.

Admired for his superb knowledge of the law, Miller had been chief of the U.S. Attorney's Office criminal division when he decided to switch to the other side. As a defense attorney, he had represented a wide variety of headline-making clients, ranging from notorious mobsters to a man who had been fire commissioner in 1985, when authorities decided to drop a bomb on a house in West Philadelphia occupied by members of an aggressive radical organization known as MOVE. The bomb had set off a huge fire in which eleven people, including five children, had died. Miller was hired by the fire commissioner to defend him against possible civil lawsuits filed by surviving MOVE members.

He'd be willing to talk to Rabinowitz about representing him, Miller told Solomon, provided he could bring in another lawyer as well. Solomon did not need to ask who that would be. It was well-known in Philadelphia legal circles that Miller often worked on celebrated cases with another former prosecutor, Frank DeSimone, who had been the top-rated prosecutor in the Philadelphia District Attorney Office's homicide division before he left to represent some of the city's more prominent mobsters. Despite markedly different personalities and contrary styles, DeSimone and Miller, each of whom had his own practice, made a formidable team. When they joined forces, they put on a fight guaranteed to give any prosecutor a battle worth remembering.

After checking with DeSimone to make sure he wasn't deeply involved in another case, Miller told Solomon to have Rabinowitz in his office first thing on Thursday so that they could discuss the situation in more detail.

Interestingly, the emergence of Miller and DeSimone as Rabinowitz's likely defenders also brought another element into the mix, one that veteran observers could only describe as "explosive." Solomon may not have realized it when he dialed Miller, but his action was the first step toward what could lead to the most intense courtroom battle in Greater Philadelphia in years. If Rabinowitz were to be charged and brought to trial, with Miller and DeSimone in his corner, there would be more than his fate at stake; enormous lawyerly egos and political futures also would be at issue. The reason was a long-standing feud between the fifty-two-year-old DeSimone and Bruce Castor, Montgomery County's boyish-looking thirty-five-year-old first assistant DA. Simply put, Castor and DeSimone couldn't stand each other. On the rare occasions when they found themselves in the same room, each pointedly ignored the other. They had not spoken socially in more than three years.

The cause of this animosity can be traced to February 2, 1994, the day a Montgomery County jury acquitted a middle-aged woman named Patricia Swinehart on charges of having arranged the murder of her husband. Castor, who at the time had been relatively new in his job as first assistant, was the prosecutor. Swinehart's lawyers were DeSimone and Miller. The particulars of the case were this:

In 1982, David Swinehart, a flamboyant, ostensibly wealthy realtor, and his wife had been in the middle of a divorce. David had been visiting his children. When he left, crossing the snow-packed driveway, heading for his bright red Cadillac with the Rolls Royce trim, he was jumped by four men. They cracked his head with a baseball bat, then stabbed him—and kept stabbing him—until he died.

It took investigators three years but they found the men they thought had committed the crime, and brought them to trial. Three of them were subsequently convicted, two of them by Castor. A fourth man, a career criminal named Terry Lee Maute, was acquitted.

Fast-forward to 1993, more than eleven years after David Swinehart's murder. Maute, who had long before been cleared by a jury for his alleged participation in the Swinehart murder and could not be tried again, admitted his part in the attack to authorities, telling them it had been Patricia who had arranged the murder of her soon-to-be ex-husband. She wanted him dead, Maute said, because he was going to write her out of an insurance trust agreement worth more than $500,000. Additionally, she was intent on continuing an affair she was having with one of the murderers, a man who, incidentally, also happened to be the dead man's nephew. Despite his unsavory reputation, Maute was to be Castor's main witness against Patricia.

The prosecutor's case was severely damaged when the trial judge refused to allow him to introduce evidence of Patricia Swinehart's alleged motive for wanting her husband killed. This added fuel to heated courtroom debates between Castor and DeSimone over admissible testimony and issues of integrity. But what really sank Castor's case was Maute. In a fiery, five-hour closing argument, De-Simone ripped the prosecution's chief witness apart. La-beling anything Maute said unreliable, DeSimone urged jurors to let Patricia go. To Castor's chagrin, the jury agreed with DeSimone.

The decision infuriated Castor. Blaming DeSimone di-rectly, he claimed that the defense attorney—described in newspaper reports as being so pious a Catholic that he at-tended Mass every morning—had gone too far at the trial. What rankled Castor even more was the fact that *Swinehart* was the only murder case he had lost in a career spent entirely in the Montgomery County DA's office. If suspi-cion continued to be focused on Rabinowitz, and he even-tually was brought to trial for Stefanie's murder, the stage would be set for a rematch between Castor and the Miller/DeSimone team.

This possibility had to be on Castor's mind when Miller called him to tell him that he and DeSimone had been re-tained to represent Rabinowitz. Don't act precipitously, Miller urged; don't rush out to arrest him without knowing what you're up against. "He comes from an upstanding family and he has an unblemished reputation," Miller pointed out. "If you have any questions about that, go talk to his family and friends."

Although Miller didn't know it, Castor had already de-cided to move gingerly in the Rabinowitz case. Earlier, be-fore the defense attorney called, Castor had read Rabinowitz's statement, which had been sent across the street by Tim Woodward. As he studied it, the prosecutor became increasingly skeptical of what the young entrepre-neur had said. "This is bullshit," Castor whispered aloud, scanning the document. Still, he cautioned himself to be circumspect. Among other things, he had concerns about how the media would react once the strangulation story broke. It would be a major item, he knew, even though at the time he had no idea just *how* big a story it would eventually become. Before a week was out, print and broadcast reporters would jump on Stefanie Rabinowitz's murder with an alacrity that surprised even dedicated news junkies.

As he considered his options, Castor must have acknowledged the possibility that if he acted too quickly he could be leaving himself open to criticism from the media down the road. If he made a big to-do over Stefanie's death and it turned out to have been accidental after all, he would look like a fool. It would be better, he decided, to take it one step at a time, making sure of his position before he acted. Although he had no reason to question Hood's autopsy findings, Castor wanted to hear from his own man—Fillinger—on the strangulation issue. When Miller called, the county pathologist had not yet made his own examination of Stefanie's body. In fact, up until then, both Fillinger and Castor had been preoccupied with the Horsham incident and had not given Stefanie's death much more than a passing thought. But thanks to some fancy forensic work by Fillinger, it was determined that the Horsham woman had not been shot at all. In fact, she had not even been murdered. After examining the body and studying the material gathered by investigators, Dr. Fillinger had ruled her death a suicide. That effectively removed the case from Castor's plate, leaving him to concentrate on Stefanie Rabinowitz. But before making a decision on formally charging Rabinowitz, the prosecutor wanted to huddle with Fillinger, Woodward, and Detectives Peffall and Craig. He also wanted to talk it over with his boss, Marino, who wouldn't be back from the meeting in Gettysburg until Sunday. Instinctively, he knew this would not be a good case to make a mistake on.

Naturally, Castor didn't share all this with Miller. What he did tell the defense attorney, though, was that he intended to examine all facets of the situation before taking any action. "I've checked with my people and the earliest we can all get together is Monday. Until then, I'll be proceeding cautiously. I don't have any plans for an immediate arrest," he promised.

About the time that Castor was talking to Miller, Rabinowitz's hard-core group of friends was learning some of the facts of Stefanie's death.

Following a brief memorial service in a room packed with more than two hundred people at the Joseph Levine Funeral Home in Philadelphia, Rabinowitz approached Elaine and Jennifer and asked them to come outside. Standing in the driveway, he looked around to make sure no one else was near. Leaning forward, he said conspiratorially, "The coroner's report said Stefanie was strangled."

Elaine felt the blood rush from her head and she started to swoon. Reeling, she grabbed Rabinowitz's arm to steady herself. He threw her hand off and looked at her contemptuously.

"Strangled!" blurted Jennifer. "That can't be. Everyone believes it was an aneurism. You said so yourself. You said that's what a reporter told you."

Rabinowitz shook his head. "The pathologist says it was manual strangulation. *But*," he added hurriedly, "that's incorrect. The report is wrong. I'm getting an independent pathologist to do another autopsy on Sunday."

Aware that the two women were staring at him strangely, Rabinowitz quickly added, "I didn't *do* anything! I didn't have anything to do with it, but they're trying to frame me for it."

"Why would they do that?" Elaine asked reasonably, some of her color coming back.

"They're trying to pillory me. Bruce Castor is looking for a high-profile case so he can build a good reputation. He wants to run for DA and he needs a lot of publicity." He paused, again checking to make sure no one else was close. "I'm going to fight this!" he said with determination. "I can't let them frame me. I went to see a couple of lawyers this morning and they've agreed to help. But it's going to be expensive, somewhere around fifty thousand dollars. I'm going to need your help, too. Any donations you feel you can make would be greatly appreciated.''

The two women nodded solemnly; they saw no reason to doubt what Craig was telling them. Of course they would help financially, they said. What else were friends for? And of course they would continue to support him. He was like family. It was all so puzzling, Jennifer and Elaine agreed. Like a horror movie. Stefanie's sudden death had been so unbelievable that if the county autopsy report indeed turned out to be false it would not be a surprise. Things were happening too fast.

Sensing that he had cleared a hurdle, Rabinowitz appeared relieved. ''Do you remember how Stefanie used to always wear her jewelry?'' he asked anxiously. ''Her watch! Remember her watch? She always wore her watch, even in the shower. Do you remember?''

Elaine and Jennifer looked at each other and shook their heads. ''Not really,'' Elaine said. ''But we'll ask Betty.''

Friday, May 2
Morning

For Craig, Friday morning was a repeat of Thursday. Without even waiting for the rush-hour traffic to clear, he was out of the house and on the road, again without telling anyone where he was going. ''Business,'' he mumbled on his way out the door. Investigators would later learn precisely where he went, what he did, who he talked to, and about what. Once Rabinowitz's family and tight-knit group of friends had this information, they would be almost as shocked as they had been when they learned of Stefanie's death. In the meantime, independent of material unearthed by investigators, seeds of doubt were beginning to grow among the friends about Rabinowitz's possible involvement in his wife's death. Despite a deep desire to believe him when he said he was innocent, common sense and the power of deduction were making tentative inroads into grief and loyalty.

While Rabinowitz was driving to Center City, Brian and Betty were in their kitchen, lingering over coffee, discussing what Elaine and Jennifer had told them about the previous day's driveway conversation. The Schwartzes had been as appalled as the others when they learned the results of the Lankenau autopsy, but ignorant of the fact that Hood's findings had been confirmed by Fillinger the previous afternoon, even while Rabinowitz was claiming that the post mortem had been botched, they were still holding out hope that the pathologist had been wrong. They *wanted* to believe in their friend. To do otherwise would be to admit that they had been wrong about him for the whole time they had known him, some six years. They had taken Craig and Stefanie into their hearts; Craig had babysat their children; he had selflessly given up his time when the Schwartzes needed help. Now they were being told that Stefanie possibly had been murdered. And there had been no one in the house with her except Craig and the baby.

Brian, particularly, seemed disturbed by the implications of the autopsy report, presuming it was correct. Staring into his cup with the intensity of a psychic divining tea leaves, he hemmed and stuttered, searching for a way to articulate his thoughts.

"What is it?" Betty had asked with concern, seeing that her husband was troubled.

Brian hesitated. "I wonder . . ." he began. "That is, I'm worried . . . What I mean is," he said in a rush, "what if Craig did it?"

Betty was flabbergasted. "My God!" she exhaled. "Don't even think that way. Craig and Stefanie were our best friends. We can't start to doubt Craig now when he really needs us. We don't *know* for a fact that there's anything at all to these rumors, which is exactly what they are. What Craig says makes sense. There was a mistake that's going to be corrected with a second autopsy. The prosecutor wants to satisfy his own political ambitions; it's all a political game. We can't turn against Craig now. We should be ashamed we're even talking like this."

"You're right," Brian said, setting his cup in the sink. "What kind of friends are we if we can't believe Craig? It *does* look like they're trying to get him."

"Yes, it does," Betty agreed. "We have to keep sticking together. We can't abandon Craig now."

Brian hesitated once more. "You know," he said thoughtfully, "I don't think we ought to mention this conversation to the others. We don't want them to think we're so fickle that we're ready to abandon our closest friend at the time he needs us most."

"Absolutely not," said Betty. "I can't believe we even had this conversation. I feel guilty about it already."

Bruce Castor looked confident. A tall, heavyset man with light brown hair, blue eyes, and a Larry King–like penchant for suspenders, Castor was a polished public speaker who appeared at ease with whatever group he was with. A native of Montgomery County, he had joined the DA's office in 1986 after graduating from Washington and Lee University Law School and, from all indications, unlike Miller and DeSimone, who had traded prosecuting for defending, planned to remain there. He genuinely *liked* sending criminals to jail. In his prosecutorial career, he had handled the lion's share of the county's prominent trials, the most celebrated of which was that of a man named Caleb Fairley.

Late in the afternoon on September 10, 1995, the twenty-one-year-old, five-foot-six-inch, 250-pound Fairley, a man described as "reclusive" by fellow students at a community college, was working in a children's clothing store owned by his parents in the Montgomery County community of Collegeville, when Lisa Manderach came in with her nineteen-month-old daughter, Devon. Two hours later

Devon's body was found by a hiker along a park road. Although Lisa Manderach's Firebird was parked outside the Fairley store, there was no sign of the missing woman.

Suspicion quickly centered on Fairley, who earlier had been named in a series of harassment reports by local women, but had never been charged. When investigators, including county detective Rich Peffall, found Fairley the next day, he had deep scratches on his face. They took him into custody.

What happened next lifted the Fairley case from the brutally scandalous to the politically sensitive. Using a jailhouse telephone, Fairley called Castor directly. In an eight-minute conversation, with Peffall monitoring the conversation on an extension, Fairley told the prosecutor: "I really do own up to what I've done." Soon afterwards, Fairley's lawyer called DA Michael Marino with an offer. If Marino would promise not to seek the death sentence, Fairley would lead investigators to Manderach's body.

Marino hesitated not at all. Remembering the scratches on Fairley's face, the DA figured that there would be traces of his DNA under the victim's nails. If the body was found quickly, the DNA would still be fresh; if they waited, it might deteriorate to the point where it would be useless as evidence. They needed to find her body soon. So what if he couldn't get the death sentence? Pennsylvania had not executed a criminal for more than thirty years. The DNA, if they could get to it in time, probably would be enough to get a conviction on first-degree murder, which meant Fairley would spend the rest of his life in prison anyway.

"Deal!" Marino said quickly. Fairley gave police directions to the body, which was hidden in a wooded area adjacent to an industrial park miles away near King of Prussia.

He went on trial the following April before a jury brought in from a distant county, a rare move considered prudent because of the huge amount of publicity given to the case. His lawyer—not the same one who made the deal with Marino—argued that while Fairley would not contest killing the woman and her daughter, he should be facing charges of third-degree murder, not first-degree. The reason was that the killings were not premeditated. The difference to Fairley was that third-degree conviction carried a maximum sentence of forty years, while first-degree was mandatory life.

Castor, the lead prosecutor, contended that the murders indeed had been premeditated because it took a minimum of four minutes for Fairley to strangle each victim. That meant that Fairley had time to think about what he was doing and could have stopped; Manderach and her daughter were not killed in a flash of temper or passion. Castor would remember this argument later, when he was preparing his case against Craig Rabinowitz.

The jury—which quickly grasped the prosecutor's argument about strangulation—returned guilty verdicts against Fairley on two counts of first-degree murder. However, instead of being content with the knowledge that Fairley would never see the outside of a prison again, a number of people in Montgomery County attacked Marino, claiming that he had caved in on the death penalty issue. By transference, Castor, as the lead prosecutor *and* Marino's first assistant, had come in for a measure of criticism himself regarding the way the case had been handled.

Even as he debated how best to proceed on the Stefanie Rabinowitz murder, Castor was not unmindful of the lessons learned in the Fairley case, which was described by one *Inquirer* reporter as "one of the most viscerally disturbing crimes" in county history.

Castor glanced at the small group of reporters who had gathered to hear details about the burning death in Horsham and smiled quietly to himself. He felt entirely in his element.

"It was definitely a suicide," he said easily, summing up his explanation of the Horsham incident. "Dr. Fillinger can give you the gory details if you want them, but we're confident the woman took her own life."

After fielding a few follow-up questions, Castor was ready to bring the news conference to an end when an *Inquirer* reporter lobbed one more query. Is it true, the reporter asked, that the young woman lawyer found dead in her bathtub in Lower Merion had not drowned but had, indeed, been strangled?

Castor was taken slightly aback. How had the word gotten out? Recovering rapidly, he nodded. There was no sense trying to duck the issue. "It was manual strangulation," he confirmed. "And, since manual strangulation is very difficult for one to perform on oneself, we're investigating it as a homicide." He did *not* add that the woman's husband was the major suspect.

The reporters looked happy. They had a story after all. And what a story it would be! For more than half a year it would dominate the local news to a degree that, at the time, would have seemed impossible. Not even the media-savvy Castor had been able to envision what effects his plain-vanilla confirmation about Stefanie's death would have on the Philadelphia media. His affirmation that Stefanie had been murdered was a rolling pebble that started a landslide.

There were several reasons why the death of Stefanie Rabinowitz would become the hottest story in Montgomery County since Caleb Fairley. Foremost, of course, was the fact that it *was* a good story. As the layers were peeled back, it proved to be one that was extraordinarily rich in detail, taking twists and turns that both fascinated and repelled a scandal-hungry public. Before it was over, the coverage would dwarf that given to the Fairley story. Second, it was a story that wouldn't die. Every time it seemed as if the media had run out of information and the story would begin to fade, a new development would erupt that would throw it back on the front page or push it to the top of the newscast. Also—and this was very important—it was a matter of timing, particularly for Philadelphia's tv news departments.

Three times a year, in winter, spring, and autumn, tv stations go through periods of hyperactivity known as "sweeps," during which they compete ruthlessly for viewership. Each network puts its most enticing programs on the air and local news shows resort to myriad gimmicks in hopes of raising the station's "ratings," the statistics used to set advertising rates. The higher the ratings, the more the station can charge. Each sweep period lasts a month. In 1997, the spring sweeps had begun a week before Stefanie was killed. In Philadelphia, it had been a rather lackluster seven days because there had been no local news story worthy of an all-out campaign. But Stefanie's death would change that. After Castor announced that the Main Line lawyer had been murdered, local stations leaped on the story with gusto. That began a self-perpetuating cycle. The harder tv and radio covered the story, the harder the newspapers tried to outdo them. And vice-versa. Even seasoned media veterans would look back later and marvel at the story's durability and the fascination it held for so many thousands of people, not only in Eastern Pennsylvania but around the country.

Afternoon

Because of the vow of secrecy he had made to his friend, Mark Hirtz had not discussed what he had learned at Ardmore with the others in the group. He personally had not doubted Craig for a moment, and he was unwilling to get drawn into a debate on the merits of his friend's integrity versus police competence. To him, it was simple. He had known Craig for five years; known him as well as he knew anyone. Or so he thought. He liked Craig; he respected him; he was confident that his friend was honest and trustworthy. Loyalty was important to Hirtz; at the moment it was the most valuable thing he could offer his friend.

If Hirtz was troubled by anything that Friday afternoon it was the way Craig seemed to be reacting to the combined pressures of his wife's death and official suspicion. In his view, Craig was becoming more and more despondent; he seemed to be sinking into a pit of depression. That was one subject he *had* discussed with Brian and Todd. To his relief, he learned that they were worried about the same thing. Without belaboring the issue, they made a pact that one of them would be with Craig during all his waking hours, at least until after the funeral, which now appeared to be set for Monday. They had lost one dear friend; they didn't want to lose another.

Late in the afternoon, as Hirtz was considering slipping away again for a quick trip to the office, Craig came up and whispered in his ear, "Mark, it's a beautiful afternoon. Let's take a walk."

Intuiting that Craig had something he wanted to discuss with him out of earshot of the others, Hirtz did not hesitate. As they strolled down Winding Way, soaking up the warm spring sunshine under a cloudless blue sky, Hirtz remained mute. This was Craig's idea, he thought. Better to let him decide when he wants to talk about whatever's on his mind.

They had gone about a half a block when Rabinowitz broke the silence.

"Mark," he blurted, apropos of nothing, "I refuse to go to jail."

Hirtz stared at him in surprise. "What are you talking about? You're not going to go to jail, Craig. Why would they want to put you in jail?"

Craig looked at him shrewdly. "You're a lawyer, so I can tell you something."

Hirtz shook his head. "I'm not *your* lawyer, Craig. I can't claim lawyer/client privilege."

For several minutes Craig said nothing. Then: "I don't care about that. I'm not going to jail for something I didn't do. If it comes down to it, I want you to help me."

"What do you mean?" Hirtz asked, concerned by the direction the conversation was taking.

"I want to get out of the country."

Hirtz couldn't believe what he had heard. "Craig, in the first place there's no country in the world that doesn't have an extradition treaty with the United States . . ."

He looked at Craig and realized his friend wasn't listening. "We need to stop talking about this, Craig," he said firmly. "Let's go back to the house."

Merion
Saturday, May 3
Morning

In the Philadelphia newspaper world, the *Inquirer* had a clear scoop on its one-time rival, the *Daily News*. On the front page of its Saturday morning edition, the *Inquirer*'s headline screamed: "Phila. lawyer found strangled in Merion home." Although the story itself was twenty-two paragraphs long, most of the text was background on Stefanie with quotes from her employers. The subhead, however, said it all: "Stefanie Newman Rabinowitz, 29, was discovered dead in her bathtub. Authorities consider it a homicide." For a story destined to loom so large, it had jumped off to a weak start. There would be no substantive newspaper coverage for two more days.

Still, the declaration in black and white that the authorities considered it a homicide dealt a severe blow to Rabinowitz's claims that the autopsy report had been erroneous. No matter that a second examination was to be made the next day by a privately hired pathologist, the general feeling, even among Craig and Stefanie's friends, was that Castor would not risk making an assertion that Stefanie's death had been a murder without feeling confident that the second pathologist was going to come to the same conclusion.

Afternoon

For the first time since Stefanie's death early Wednesday, one of the Rabinowitzes' friends was openly voicing doubts about Craig's possible involvement.

"Have any of you stopped to think about this?" Jennifer Hirtz asked Elaine Miller and Betty Schwartz in a semi-whisper.

"What do you mean?" asked Betty, her cheeks burning with the memory of the discussion she and her husband had had the day before.

"We really need to give it some thought," Jennifer insisted.

"Give what some thought?" Betty replied, hoping her friends didn't notice that she was blushing.

Jennifer sighed. "The possibility that Craig may have been involved."

"Craig *couldn't* have been involved," argued Elaine. "I've known him for eleven years. He's the dearest man I've ever known, outside of my husband."

"That's right," Betty agreed hastily. "Craig would *never* have done anything like that."

"I guess you're right," Jennifer said hesitantly. "I guess I'm just stressed out. Forget I even brought it up."

Night

The newspaper story undoubtedly affected Rabinowitz as well. All that day he moped around the house, looking as if he was about to break into tears. Even Lou Newman, who was deep into his own grief, noticed the change in his son-in-law's demeanor. Ignoring the custom about not watching tv during shivah, Lou suggested they switch on the set that evening so they could watch the NHL playoffs, hoping it might cheer Craig up.

Although Rabinowitz sat in front of the tube, Brian

Schwartz and Mark Hirtz could see that his heart wasn't in the game. Despite the action on the screen, Craig sat slumped on the couch, his head down, saying very little. This attitude, his friends noted, was extremely rare for the usually gregarious Craig.

Hirtz and Schwartz were debating some minor point about the game when Craig unexpectedly interrupted.

"I've got a bag packed," he said, totally irrelevant to the conversation. "I've got a bag and twenty thousand dollars in cash. I'm ready to go."

Schwartz and Hirtz were stunned. "What are you talking about, Craig?" Schwartz stammered.

"This situation. This stuff about Steffi being murdered. It's eating me up. I don't know how I'm going to survive."

Hirtz swallowed hard. "You *have* to survive, Craig," he said, hoping that he sounded optimistic. "It hasn't been easy . . . it isn't *going* to be easy . . . but you have to get through it. You have to draw strength from Haley. You have responsibilities now as a father."

Normally, Craig's eyes would light up at the mention of his infant daughter. In this case, he gave no sign he had even heard. Oh, God, Hirtz thought, that *is* strange. Since Wednesday, it suddenly occurred to Hirtz, Craig had completely ignored his daughter; had not picked her up, tossed her in the air, or taken her for their customary walk. Usually the most attentive of fathers, it seemed that for the last three days Craig had tried his best to avoid having anything to do with Haley, even though there would be a party tomorrow celebrating her first birthday. For Craig to show such total disregard when someone brought up his daughter was indicative of how depressed he must be.

Hirtz and Schwartz exchanged worried glances, realizing they had come to the same conclusion at the same time. "Craig," Hirtz asked carefully, "do you have a gun?"

Craig roused himself slightly. "No," he said, slowly shaking his head. "I don't have a gun."

Hirtz sighed in relief. Nevertheless, both men refused to

leave that night until they were sure that Craig was asleep. It would be several days before they realized the full significance of what Craig had said and reported the conversation to Detectives Craig and Peffall.

SEVEN

Somewhat apprehensively, Bruce Castor opened the *Inquirer*, hoping there would be nothing there that would make him regret not having had Craig Rabinowitz picked up on Friday or Saturday. There wasn't. He breathed more easily when he saw that the Sunday story was basically just a rehash of the Saturday piece with an updated lead saying that investigators were trying to find the killer. Although he was hardly averse to publicity, he didn't want the story to get away from him before he could bring the situation under control.

Knowing that Marino was back in town and that he, too, would be reading his Sunday paper, Castor picked up his phone.

"Hey, Mike," he said cheerily. "How's it feel to be the new president of the Pennsylvania District Attorneys' Association?"

"So far, just like it felt being the vice president," Marino replied dryly. "You want to bring me up to speed on what's been going on?"

Castor told him about the Horsham case and how Fillinger had shined in finding the clues that proved it was a suicide rather than a homicide.

"Speaking of homicides," Marino added, "I see where

it's now public about the woman in Lower Merion. Has Fillinger examined the body yet?''

"Yeah," Castor replied. "He agrees with Hood."

"It still looks like the husband?"

"No other viable suspects," Castor said, briefing his boss on how Rabinowitz had hired Miller and DeSimone.

"You see any flags?"

"Not really. I suspect they're going to try to say she was killed by an intruder but Woodward tells me we have good pictures showing there was no forced entry. I wouldn't be surprised, either, if they tried to argue that she wasn't actually murdered."

"Any chance this private pathologist is going to come to that conclusion?"

"Not according to Fillinger, and he's performed something like forty thousand autopsies in his career. He says it's obvious that she was strangled."

Marino was silent for a moment. "Who are you going to have try it?"

"I don't care. Husbands have been killing their wives for a long time. This isn't going to be a big deal."

"I disagree," Marino said. "I think this is going to be a very big deal. I want you to try it. Besides, don't you want another shot at DeSimone?"

"Well . . ." Castor began.

"Bruce," Marino interrupted. "Take it over. And," he added, "pick a good second chair."

"Yes, sir," Castor said, grinning.

"Any idea yet about motive?"

"I'll know more about that after tomorrow's meeting, but so far Woodward has just said it looks like it may have had something to do with money. They found policies showing she was insured for one-point-five million dollars."

Marino whistled softly. "That's a lot of money."

"No kidding. But it might not be out of line. Woodward's trying to make some sense of it all now.''

"Okay. Let's talk about it tomorrow.''

Merion
Afternoon

By this time, the Rabinowitzes' family and friends should have been feeling some relief from tension and grief. Instead, the situation seemed to be going rapidly downhill. Most were walking around in a semi-trance, practically reeling from exhaustion because of the almost constant uproar relating to the circumstances of Stefanie's death and the allegations of Craig's involvement. After the media learned that Stefanie had been murdered, the house phone started ringing constantly, day and night, disrupting the normally solemn mourning period and setting everyone's nerves on edge. It was particularly disturbing to the Newmans and the more religiously conservative family members who wanted nothing more than to be left in peace so they could lament Stefanie's death. Among the less conservative friends, who were reading newspapers and watching tv, growing doubts about Rabinowitz added to their sorrow. On one hand, their friend was vehemently denying that he had anything to do with his wife's murder. But on the other, he was being singled out by the media as the only likely suspect. The wall of friendship that at one time seemed indestructible was beginning to fracture.

Rabinowitz himself had to take much of the blame for the confusion that reigned at 526 Winding Way. His peculiar behavior and a newly emerged passion for secrecy were causing problems that no one had anticipated. As he glided through a house still decked out for shivah—which formally would not end for four more days—he looked haunted, his once amiable disposition replaced by a feral furtiveness previously unglimpsed by those who thought they knew him. Glancing around to see who was present,

Rabinowitz would zero in on one or two individuals and pounce on them as if they were prey, pulling them off to a corner where they would whisper clandestinely for several minutes. Leaving that group, he would prowl until he found one or two others he wanted to confer with and repeat the process. Once, when Elaine innocently asked him what was going on, he spun on his heel and snapped at her: "You can't ask me for any information! I'll tell you things as I learn them!"

They all sensed something momentous was brewing; they just didn't know how to prepare for it.

That evening, Jennifer Hirtz felt that she had to speak her doubts more forcefully than she had earlier. Setting her jaw, she confronted Elaine and Betty. "Listen," she said sternly, "we *have* to start to think about the possibility that Craig had something to do with Stefanie's death."

By then, all the friends had written checks to Craig to help him pay his legal fees in fighting the accusations, which he continued to claim were unjustified. They were not prepared to believe that he might have been lying to them all along.

"No!" Betty replied emphatically. "Craig *couldn't* have been involved."

"There was no way he'd do that to Stefanie," added Elaine. "He loved her. You know how attentive he was. It used to make me jealous that Todd wasn't nearly as considerate."

"What if it was all an act?" persisted Jennifer. "What if he had been planning for some time to kill Stefanie?"

"Oh, no," Betty said, putting her hands over her ears. "I won't listen to any more of that. We *have* to support Craig."

"I agree with Betty," Elaine said angrily. "Craig *needs* us."

Jennifer had never felt so frustrated. Her intuition told her that something was dreadfully wrong. The few things Craig had told them didn't add up. But she could see that it was fruitless to try to explain that to her friends. Maybe it would be better, she thought, if she just kept her thoughts to herself.

Monday, May 5
Morning

"Okay," Mike Marino said, leaning over his desk. "What've we got?"

"She was strangled," said Woodward.

"What about motive?" Marino asked, turning to Woodward.

"We suspect money."

"Give me details," Marino insisted.

"Two recent life insurance policies on Stefanie, one for five hundred thousand and one for one million."

"That's a lot of insurance. How about their income?"

"We're still trying to figure that out. They lived on the Main Line and she was a lawyer."

"And him?"

"He had his own business. Something called C&C Supplies."

"Exactly what *is* this C&C Supplies?" asked Castor.

Woodward shrugged. "So far, we haven't been able to prove there *was* a business. That's one of the things we're looking into. *He* says it has to do with the sale of latex gloves. To doctors and dentists."

"This possible problem with his business. That's interesting," Marino mumbled. "We need to keep after that angle."

"What about you guys?" interjected Castor, turning to Detectives Craig and Peffall. "What do you have?"

"We have Rabinowitz's statement in which he admits he was alone in the house. He even told the 911 operator that he would have to go downstairs to unlock the door for the paramedics and police. Plus, there's no evidence of a break-in, and Rabinowitz says as far as he can tell there's nothing missing from the house. We have Driscoll's statement in which he says the woman was wearing a watch, a couple of bracelets, and a ring when he and Rabinowitz pulled her out of the tub. That's definitely unusual. Plus, we have the autopsy report that lists the cause of death as manual strangulation and the manner of death as homicide.''

''Toxicology report?''

Woodward shook his head. ''Not yet. We're expecting it any day.''

Castor slapped the desk. ''Sounds like there's enough already for an arrest warrant. Let's pick him up.''

''They're burying his wife this afternoon,'' Peffall added.

''Okay,'' Castor replied. ''After the funeral. He's not going anywhere before then. You know the tv stations will be at the cemetery. He's going to be on camera so we'll know where he is. I don't look at this guy particularly as a flight risk.''

''Let's give his lawyers the chance to surrender him,'' Marino suggested. ''In the meantime, we can go ahead with the paperwork.''

''On what charges?'' Charlie Craig asked.

Castor rattled them off: ''First-degree, third-degree, voluntary manslaughter, and making false reports to the police.''

''You're not going to go for the death penalty?''

''I don't see how we can,'' Castor said. ''If he strangled her, that covers premeditation. Remember Caleb Fairley? But on what I've seen so far I can't make capital murder. The crime doesn't fit any of the aggravating factors.''

''Okay,'' Detective Craig nodded. ''I'll get the documents together and take them to Narberth.''

''Let's do it,'' Marino said, indicating that the meeting was over.

*   *   *

Castor went back to his own office, his thoughts on what Marino had told him the day before about being careful in choosing an assistant to help prepare for Rabinowitz's trial and offer solid support in the courtroom. There were roughly three dozen ADAs under Castor's command, but not everyone's name would go into the pot. Many, Castor knew, would be unavailable because they were involved in other cases. And of those who were available, not just anyone would fit his criteria. This required someone with special skills.

"Marie," he said, striding briskly into his spacious sanctum, "bring me the master list." Shedding his coat, he leaned back in his executive chair and checked the ever-changing chart that showed which assistants were handling what. He had to be very picky, he reminded himself, because this could be a crucial trial. If it got screwed up, it could deal a severe, perhaps fatal, blow to his ambitions to seek the DA's job in the 1999 election. On the other hand, if he was successful in getting a conviction, it would certainly be a plus because this one had Big Case written all over it.

It wouldn't be a slam-dunk; not with what they knew. All the evidence was circumstantial, and those kinds of cases were particularly hard for prosecutors to prove. O.J. crossed his mind. For sure, Rabinowitz had not confessed, nor had he given any indication that he planned to do so. No one had seen or heard him strangle his wife. His fingerprints were not on her throat. Maybe the lab tests would show something under her fingernails and he could get DNA. But better not to count on it. Plus, there was *nothing* to show that Rabinowitz had a history of violence toward his wife. Or anyone else for that matter. No one the investigators had talked to so far had even hinted that the relationship between Craig and Stefanie was not exemplary; Rabinowitz was an ardent husband who, if anything, was extraordinarily solicitous of his wife and devoted to his daughter. Barring DNA, there probably would not be any physical evidence at all tying Rabinowitz to his wife's murder. To make things even more difficult, there was not even a clear-cut motive. In his gut, Castor agreed totally with the investigators: Rabinowitz was the killer. Proving it, however, could be a real challenge. Especially with top-notch lawyers like Jeffrey Miller and Frank DeSimone on the other side. They might be the best defense team in all of Eastern Pennsylvania: tenacious, clever, exacting, and extremely articulate. This made selection of a good assistant critical. Whoever Castor picked would have to be particularly sharp, both about the law and about trial strategy. Additionally, it would have to be someone who could operate well under pressure. The demands of getting ready for trial were bad enough, but in this situation there would be the added responsibility of performing under intense media scrutiny. It would have to be someone who didn't panic easily.

Castor studied the list. When he reached the name "Ferman" he stopped. "Perfect!" he said aloud.

Risa V. Ferman, a dark-haired, petite woman, was in her early thirties, just a little older than Stefanie Rabinowitz had been. She was the mother of two young children, which meant she could identify with the women in Stefanie's circle of friends. A graduate of the University of Pennsylvania and Widener University Law School, she was the director of the county's sex crime unit; the cold-bloodedness of Stefanie's murder wasn't going to affect her judgment. Her knowledge of the law was superb. Not many months before she had won a conviction in a case that helped change the state law dictating when a prosecutor could seek the death penalty. The case involved a Montgomery County man who had been charged with murdering his estranged wife. At the time, there had been a protective order in effect forbidding him to be in contact with her. The murder had been particularly brutal, one that fairly screamed for the death penalty against the husband. However, as in the Rabinowitz case, the conditions of the slaying were not covered by the special circumstances, called aggravating factors, which had to be met if a prosecutor wanted to ask that the defendant be executed. But, using Ferman's conviction as one of their prime examples, backers of a bill to change the existing law rammed through an amendment to it that added violation of a protective custody order to the list of fifteen aggravating factors. Castor drafted the bill. Moreover, there was another factor in Ferman's favor: She was Jewish. That, Castor felt, could be important in dealing with the families and friends.

His mind made up, Castor went searching for Ferman. When he found her, she was with a group of other ADAs. "Risa," he said, knowing she would not refuse, "how would you like to help me with this Rabinowitz murder?"

He was still briefing her about the case in his office an hour later when his phone rang. It was Jeffrey Miller. "I'd like you to further delay any action against our client," Miller said. "We have reports of an unidentified male knocking on the door at the house adjacent to the Rabinowitzes' that night. Also witnesses report seeing muddy footprints in the bathroom."

"Of course there were muddy footprints," Castor replied. "Every cop and paramedic in Lower Merion must have been through there. We'll check out the unidentified male, but I have to tell you this: We've decided to arrest Rabinowitz after the funeral today. You can have him in Ardmore by four o'clock or the cops will come pick him up."

"Did you see the papers?" Jennifer asked Elaine and Betty. The *Inquirer* had quoted unidentified sources "familiar with the investigation" as saying that Stefanie "knew her killer," but offered no other specifics. It predicted an arrest "within the next few days," but did not say who it might be. The *Daily News* learned that police had interviewed Craig and had searched his house, but it said nothing about an arrest.

· "I don't like the tone," said Jennifer. "It's almost as if the newspapers are saying they know something that we don't. We have to be prepared for learning that Craig is going to be charged."

"That isn't what the newspapers say at all," insisted Betty. "Look. Right here in the *Inquirer*. Jeffrey Miller says, 'There is no evidence at all—none—that points to Craig.' "

"What else could he say?" Jennifer pointed out. "He's Craig's lawyer."

They were still discussing the likelihood of Craig being arrested when an exhausted-looking Anne Newman interrupted. "You need to know," she said solemnly, "that Craig's just told me that he's going to surrender this afternoon after the funeral."

The women gaped at Anne; their nightmare had come true.

"Oh, no," Betty said, sinking into a chair. "It can't be."

"Craig is pretty upset," Anne said. "He asked me to tell you that you also could possibly be involved because you cleaned up the house and destroyed possible evidence."

"Oh, my God," sighed Jennifer.

"How long is he going to have to be in jail?" asked Elaine. "Can't he get out on bail or something?"

Anne nodded. "His lawyers are going to try to get him out as quickly as possible. Would you all be willing to sign a note of some kind guaranteeing that he won't run away?"

Elaine thought she must be hearing things. Four days ago she could never have envisioned that a man she had known for more than a decade, a man who had been like a second father to her son, was going to run from police like a common criminal.

"Brian and I will sign whatever needs to be signed," Betty said, looking at her friends.

"Us, too," added Jennifer.

"You know we will," said Elaine, who could not shake the feeling that it was all a horrible dream.

"Are you going to continue to support him?" Jennifer asked Anne.

"Of course. He swears he didn't have anything to do with it."

The one p.m. ceremony at Stefanie's grave site in Mount Lebanon Cemetery, in keeping with Jewish tradition, was brief, particularly since a memorial service had already been held. Rabinowitz went back to Merion from the cemetery, then, wearing the same dark suit he had donned for the funeral, he and his lawyers drove to LMPD headquarters in Ardmore. He was booked, fingerprinted, and taken to nearby Eagleville Prison, where police put him in a cell by himself.

Norristown
Afternoon

Although he had already decided to charge Rabinowitz with Stefanie's murder, Castor still wanted to meet in-person with the two pathologists. Crossing the street, he took the elevator up to Fillinger's office. Hood was already there.

"You agree she was murdered?" the prosecutor asked.

"Absolutely!" Hood said firmly.

"No doubt about it. Here're the pictures to prove it," Fillinger added, handing over a stack of autopsy photos.

"That's good enough for me," Castor said, passing the photos back. He was about to walk out the door when the coroner's assistant, Bill Boegly, knocked on the door.

"Phone call for you," he told Castor.

"Uh-huh," Castor said into the mouthpiece. "That's right. Oh, really! That's interesting. Thanks a lot for calling. I'll be back to you," he promised, hanging up.

"That was an attorney for the First Colony insurance company," he explained to the two pathologists. "Listen to this. According to him, a million-dollar policy on Ste-

fanie Rabinowitz just went into effect three weeks before
she was killed."

Two floors down, Rich Peffall was at his desk going over
some of the financial data they had recovered from Winding
Way when his phone jangled.

"Is this the detective investigating the Stefanie Rabinowitz murder?" a man asked.

"I'm one of them," Peffall replied. "Who's this?"

For several seconds the caller did not reply; Peffall
thought he had hung up.

"I'd rather not give my name right now," the man said
nervously.

Peffall sighed. Anonymous calls were not uncommon,
particularly in high-profile cases. "Why do you want to talk
to a detective?"

Again the man hesitated. "I have some information you
may be interested in. It's about the Rabinowitz woman's
husband. Craig."

Peffall grabbed a pen and a pad. "Why don't you tell
me what you know?"

"The guy, Craig," the man said slowly. "He was a frequent customer at a place on Spring Garden. A gentlemen's
club called Delilah's Den. You ever heard of it?"

"I know Delilah's Den," Peffall replied, recalling an
earlier investigation that had involved some people from
the club. "But what's the big deal?" he added, trying to
sound unconcerned. "As those places go, it's not bad."

"Rabinowitz was there a lot. And I mean a *lot*. He had
a thing going with one of the dancers."

Peffall thought quickly. So far he and Charlie Craig had
not picked up the faintest hint that Rabinowitz may have
been having an extra-marital affair. "You know for a fact
he has a girlfriend there?" Peffall asked cautiously. "It's
not just something you heard from someone else?"

"Nope. I know it."

"And you know who she is? You can name her?"

"Yep."

"Tell you what," Peffall said. "Why don't we get together and you can tell me all about it? Where are you?
We'd like to come talk to you."

"I don't know," the man said apprehensively.

"There's nothing to worry about," Peffall promised.
"You're not in any kind of trouble. My partner and I just
want to talk to you."

Reluctantly, the man agreed to meet the detectives at a
shopping mall in New Jersey, just across the Delaware
River from Philadelphia.

Breaking the connection, Peffall dialed LMPD and
quickly briefed Charlie Craig on the conversation. "I'll
come by and pick you up. I told the guy we'd meet him in
an hour."

Evening

The two detectives watched pensively as the young man
disappeared among the shoppers. Charlie Craig stared at his
cup of coffee, long gone cold. "What do you think?"

Peffall shook his head. "I think the guy's being straight
with us. His girlfriend, being one of the dancers herself,
obviously knows what's going on there—which girls spend
a lot of time with which guys and so forth. Doesn't sound
like Rabinowitz tried to keep it a big secret. Even if half
of what the guy told us is true, Rabinowitz was pretty serious about this dancer. What's her name?"

"Summer," said Charlie Craig, glancing at his notes.

"Right," Peffall smiled. "Summer. That's a hell of a
name. Wonder who thought it up?"

"This puts a new slant on things."

"It sure does," agreed Peffall. "What if his wife found
out about the stripper and made a fuss? They had a big
argument and he strangled her."

Charlie Craig nodded. "That's a possibility. But there

were no signs of a struggle at the house. She wasn't beat up or anything."

"Then there's the insurance angle," Peffall interjected. "I still think that plays a major part in all this. You don't go out and buy a bunch of insurance on your wife and then wait for her to find out about your girlfriend so you can have a fight and kill her."

"That's true. He somehow had to get her in the bathtub, too. That wouldn't be easy if she was really pissed off."

"It opens a whole new world of possibilities," Peffall grinned. "Let's wait and see what they tell us at the club tomorrow."

The lead story on all the local stations that night was Craig Rabinowitz's surrender. Bruce Castor told reporters that he felt confident the right man was in jail. After all, he added, making public for the first time Craig's claim that he had securely locked the house before he and Stefanie went upstairs, who else could it have been? The "unidentified man" that Miller had made reference to earlier turned out to be a teenage boy responding to a friend's invitation to spend the night who had gone to the wrong house by mistake. Castor also hinted that Craig Rabinowitz was having financial problems, but refused to go into detail. "That factor hasn't been nailed down," he said. Marino revealed the two new insurance policies totaling $1.5 million on Stefanie, hinting that that in itself made a strong motive. Also, conspicuous by its absence, was a claim from Jeffrey Miller that the second autopsy had indicated that Stefanie had not been murdered at all. The second autopsy was never mentioned again.

These details, none of which Rabinowitz's friends had known, had a grenade-like impact on at least one member of the group. Betty Schwartz called Jennifer in near panic. "I was wrong," she wailed, sobbing so hard that Jennifer could barely understand her. "Craig may have done it after all." It took Jennifer two and a half hours to get her friend calmed down. Elaine, however, continued to profess her faith in Craig's innocence. So, too, to a limited degree, did Todd, Mark, and Brian, although Brian had grown increasingly disturbed about the remarks that Craig had made the previous Saturday night concerning a packed suitcase and a substantial amount of cash. ''When I heard some of the things that came out on Monday, after Craig's arrest, I began thinking he had not been making an idle comment,'' he told his wife later.

EIGHT

It began slowly, as little more than a faint hint that there might be considerably more to the story of Stefanie Rabinowitz's death than had been reported so far. Although media coverage had increased steadily since it was announced that Stefanie had been murdered, it was not yet a Big Story. That was about to change.

In the beginning, the media accepted two givens. The first was that Rabinowitz was a small businessman selling latex products out of an upstairs office at 526 Winding Way. The other was that Craig and Stefanie had lived a "story book" life, one described by Rabinowitz attorney Jeffrey Miller as "tranquil, almost Utopian." Both contentions were about to be proved false; utopia would soon fade into the mist.

The initial media challenge was to Rabinowitz's business claims. According to a story in the regional edition of the *Inquirer*, Rabinowitz was listed with the Pennsylvania State Incorporation Bureau as the sole officer, CEO, and treasurer of C&C Supplies Inc., an organization said to have been founded in 1992 as a successor to Craig Vending Inc. The *Inquirer* pointed out that the local telephone directory did not contain a listing for C&C, that telephone information had no number for the business, and that the company was not recognized among the more than 2,000 members of the

Latex Advisors Association, the industry's trade organization. The *Daily News*, usually the more aggressive of the two newspapers, approached the issue more gingerly, saying rather evasively that "little is known about his work" and that there were no records of bankruptcies, liens, or judgments against him.

The major shock was going to come as an attack on the second given: that Craig and Stefanie led a paradisiacal life and shared a fairy-tale marriage. The first step toward shattering this fantasy came shortly after mid-morning when Rich Peffall slid behind the wheel of his light blue county sedan and pointed it south, toward Ardmore, to pick up Charlie Craig for an expedition to Delilah's Den. Their mission: check out what they had been told the night before by the man who claimed that Rabinowitz was having an affair with one of the club's employees.

When Peffall arrived at LMPD, Sergeant Mark Keenan was waiting with Charlie Craig.

"I'm coming with you guys," Keenan announced. "You don't mind, do you?"

"What's the matter?" Peffall smiled. "Don't you trust us alone with this group of glamorous, sexy, exotic dancers?"

"Not on your life," Keenan replied soberly.

As they barreled down I-95 toward Center City, Peffall, speaking from his previous experience at Delilah's, explained the basics. "The girls prefer to be called 'dancers' rather than 'strippers.' Some of them are college kids working their way through school. Some of 'em, too, are pretty good dancers. As gentlemen's clubs go, Delilah's ain't bad. But let me tell you how it works." While the dancers perform on the runway for everyone sitting at the bar or the tables, they make their real money on what they call "special dances," Peffall explained. "A 'couch dance,' where the girl performs for a single customer, costs twenty-five dollars. A 'lap dance,' where the dancer sits on the cus-

tomer's lap and wiggles to the music, costs a hundred dollars."

"And what's the customer doing during this 'lap
dance'?" Charlie Craig asked.

"Absolutely nothing!" Peffall replied emphatically.
"Customer contact is strictly prohibited. He touches and
he's out on his ass."

"At twenty-five to a hundred bucks a pop, I can see
where it might get expensive."

"That's only the beginning," Peffall said. "Delilah's has
a special section called the Champagne Room. That's
where the top customers go to relax, a place where they
can get away from the bar crowd for a little private conversation with the dancers or some exclusive entertainment.
The room's furnished entirely with small couches so the
money boys don't have to straddle bar stools or sit all
cramped up at those tiny tables, which are jammed together
like subway riders at rush hour."

"I assume this costs extra?"

Peffall nodded. "To get in the Champagne Room you
have to have a special card proving you're a good customer.
Also, you have to order champagne. It starts at eighty bucks
a bottle."

"Phew!" Detective Craig whistled. "That's not Bud."

"That's for sure," Peffall chuckled. "The guys who frequent the Champagne Room spend a lot of money. To save
them from worrying about carrying wads of cash, the club
issues its own scrip, called 'Delilah's Dollars.' The way
that works is this: A customer uses his credit card to purchase 'dollars,' which he then can use instead of cash. Of
course, there's a charge. Fifteen percent. For every 'dollar'
the customer buys, his credit card is charged a dollar fifteen.
Dancers turn the 'dollars' in and get the face value of the
scrip minus fifteen percent. In other words, Delilah's makes
fifteen cents for every 'dollar' they *sell*, and another fifteen
cents on every 'dollar' they *buy*. The club pockets thirty
cents on each 'dollar' transaction."

Charlie Craig shook his head in admiration. ''Not a bad profit, thirty percent.''

''It's pretty clever,'' Peffall agreed. ''But there's another little twist that's nifty, too.''

''What's that?'' Detective Craig asked, raising an eyebrow.

''Say you don't want your wife to be flipping through the credit card statements and see a bunch of charges at a place called Delilah's Den, which obviously isn't a McDonald's. Well, Delilah's takes care of that, too. When you use your card, the receipt says 'D&D Restaurant.' ''

Charlie Craig laughed. ''I can't wait to see the place.''

Norristown

While the three policemen were en route to Delilah's, a Norristown lawyer acting as local counsel for Frank DeSimone and Jeffrey Miller fiiled a request with Judge Samuel W. Salus II of the Montgomery County Court of Common Pleas asking that Craig Rabinowitz be released on bail pending trial. Under Pennsylvania law, there is only one non-bailable offense: capital murder. Therefore, since the district attorney could not seek the death penalty against Rabinowitz, not having charged him with capital murder, Craig was technically eligible to be freed. But the decision on whether to let him out was up to Salus. Before making that decision, the judge would want to hear from lawyers from both sides on issues regarding the defendant's character, his social stability, and whether he was likely to flee once he got out of his cell, particularly his character.

The previous morning, while law enforcement officials were making plans to get Craig behind bars, Brian, Todd, and Mark were scurrying to raise money so that their friend would not have to spend any more time than necessary behind bars. Eventually, some two dozen friends and family members, including the Newmans, the Schwartzes, the Millers, and the Hirtzes, agreed to sign promissory notes for $75,000 each, hoping that would be enough to insure his freedom. As additional collateral, Rabinowitz also said that he would put up the house at Winding Way, and the Newmans agreed to pledge their home in Elkins Park.

The bail petition itself, drawn up by Miller and De-Simone, and based on information given them by Rabinowitz, cited—as reasons for Rabinowitz's release— his clean criminal record, his ties to the community, his reputation as a doting father, and his high standing as a member of the local business community.

By then, Castor knew about the conversation that Detectives Craig and Peffall had had with the tipster the previous evening regarding Rabinowitz's connection to Delilah's Den. Once that was investigated—providing that it was proved true—it almost certainly would seriously damage Rabinowitz's squeaky-clean image. He could hardly put himself up as a paragon of fidelity and fatherhood when he had a stripper girlfriend hovering in the background.

"I think this bail request is a big mistake," Castor told the local lawyer, Bill Honig.

"I told Miller and DeSimone that," Honig replied. "But they think you're bluffing."

Castor, of course, could not tell the defense what investigators had learned. Instead, he hoped a quiet word to one of the lawyers might make DeSimone and Miller rethink their action. It didn't.

"They want to go ahead anyway," Honig added.

"Okay," Castor sighed. He had a feeling that the Delilah's Den affiliation was only the tip of the iceberg, that once investigators really began digging into Rabinowitz's background they were going to unearth information that would leave DeSimone and Miller with egg on their faces for stressing their client's good character. Obviously, Rabinowitz was not telling his lawyers any more than he was telling police.

Breaking the outside connection, Castor punched Ferman's extension. "Risa, this is Bruce," he said abruptly.

"We have work to do." If Castor could prevent it, Craig Rabinowitz was not going *anywhere* before he could be tried for killing his wife. In the meantime, he thought, let him learn to enjoy his eight-by-ten-foot cell while getting friendly with his closest neighbor, a burly convicted murderer.

Philadelphia
Afternoon

"Well, here we are," said Peffall, pulling into a nondescript shopping center on Spring Garden, just off Delaware Avenue and virtually in the shadow of the Ben Franklin Bridge that links Pennsylvania and New Jersey.

"Doesn't look like much from the outside, does it?" Peffall asked, pointing to a long warehouse-looking building that accommodated several businesses. "That's Delilah's," he explained, pointing at a doorway on the end, next to a VCR rental store. The sidewalk leading into the club was covered by an awning extending outward to the edge of the parking lot, a convenience to protect customers from rain and snow. "It's much nicer on the inside," Peffall added.

All three men recoiled slightly when they walked in and were hit by a blast of recorded rock being played at jet-engine volume. Directly in front of them was a large wood-and-brass bar with a raised platform running off at an acute angle. Although it was barely noon, there were several men hunched over the bar, nursing beers and gnawing on cheeseburgers. The diners ignored the detectives; they had their eyes fixed on a svelte blonde who was grinding away on the platform, using a brass pole as a fulcrum for her dips and twists. Several bills were stuck in her G-string.

"I'm told that some of the city's finest come here," Peffall said as they stood there, waiting for their eyes to adjust to the semi-darkness. "Doctors, lawyers, politicians, athletes. It isn't exactly a working-class strip bar.''

"What'd you say?'' Charlie Craig asked, cupping a hand behind his ear.

"Huh?'' echoed Keenan. "You have to speak up.''

"Come on.'' Peffall laughed. "Let's go meet SherylAnn.''

Once they were buzzed through a locked door, they tromped up a flight of steep, narrow stairs, then through another doorway into a small, cramped office containing a couch and three desks. A slim, dark-haired woman rushed to greet them.

"Hi!'' Peffall said companionably. "Long time no see.'' Turning to his colleagues, Peffall made the introductions. "SherylAnn Bernhardt, meet Mark Keenan and Charlie Craig of the Lower Merion Police Department.''

"Hi,'' SherylAnn said sociably. "I have something to show you,'' she told them, reaching for something on the desk behind her. "It's new since you were here last.'' Grabbing three slick-paper magazines, she shoved them into the investigators' hands. "It's our own publication,'' she explained proudly, handing them copies of *Delilah*. On the cover was a long-haired, twentyish female wearing a string bikini and stiletto heels. She was lying on her stomach in the grass in front of a bright red Mustang. A forest of trees with brilliant white blossoms made up the background.

"Very impressive,'' Peffall grunted, flipping it open to a story headlined, "Delilah Meets Salome.'' According to the subhead, it was a brief history of the exotic dance industry. "Is this something you guys send out? Can I put a name on the mailing list?''

"Sure,'' said SherylAnn. "What's your address?''

"Oh, it's not for me,'' replied Peffall, renowned throughout Montgomery County law enforcement agencies as an unrelenting prankster. "It's for one of the guys I work with. He likes this place a lot.''

"Okay,'' SherylAnn said, looking dubious. "Who is it?''

Peffall provided the name and home address of one of
the other detectives in the unit. Weeks later the man
stormed through the office, demanding to know which
wise-guy was responsible for the Delilah's material appearing at his home. "My mailman loves it," he bellowed,
"but I don't think much of it."

"What can I do for you?" SherylAnn asked, filing the
address away.

"Tell us about Craig Rabinowitz," Charlie Craig said.
"And his girlfriend."

SherylAnn rolled her eyes. "What do you want to
know?"

"Everything you can tell us," Peffall interjected.

Rabinowitz, SherylAnn told the investigators, had been
coming into Delilah's regularly since early the previous
summer, about June as well as she could remember. But
beginning just after the new year, he started coming in more
often, frequently three or more times per week, usually ar-
riving in time for lunch and staying until late afternoon. He
was a big spender, she added, always ordering a substantial
lunch and tipping handsomely for service. He usually went
straight to the Champagne Room. His favorite beverage
was Perrier-Jouët bubbly, which the club sold for $206 a
bottle.

"So how much would he spend on an average visit,
roughly?" Charlie Craig asked.

SherylAnn shrugged. "Somewhere between three hundred and one thousand dollars, not including food and
drink."

The investigators looked at each other. Three times a
week! That was a hell of a lot of money.

"Was that in cash?" Charlie Craig asked.

"Oh, no," SherylAnn said, "he used a credit card most
of the time."

Later, after analyzing Rabinowitz's financial data, Detectives Peffall and Craig determined that in the nine months
that he had been visiting Delilah's, Rabinowitz had dropped

at least $56,000 at the club. That included some $29,000 he spent in a single thirteen-week period between January 7 and April 8, three weeks before Stefanie was killed. During that three-month time span, Rabinowitz made at least thirty-nine trips to the club, an average of three visits a week, at about $743.50 per visit, or $2,230 a week.

"What about his girlfriend?" Peffall asked. "Summer?"

"You guys move fast," SherylAnn smiled. "Summer's her stage name. Her real name is Shannon Reinert."

"What can you tell us about her?"

"Not a lot. She started here four or five years ago as a waitress, then moved up to dancer. She's very popular; one of our headliners. She does a number with a live snake that the customers really like."

"And Rabinowitz had something going with her?"

SherylAnn hunched her shoulders and lifted her hands, palms up. "Who knows? He spent a lot of money on her. She was the only girl he was interested in."

"Can you tell us where to reach her?" Charlie Craig asked.

"Sure," SherylAnn replied easily, reaching for her Rolodex.

"You mind if we go downstairs and talk to some of the people who knew her?" Charlie Craig asked.

SherylAnn shook her head. "Be my guest."

Charlie Craig beat Peffall to the draw. "Me and Mark'll take the dancers," he said with a smile. "You take the bouncers."

Thirty minutes later, they rendezvoused in the upstairs office.

"I would never have believed it would happen to me here, of all places," Peffall said disgustedly as they were leaving.

"What's that?" Charlie Craig asked curiously.

"I had to go take a leak and this guy gets up from one of the tables and follows me into the men's room. I'm standing there at the urinal and he's trying to start a conversation. Grinning at me like I'm his long-lost buddy. Then he asks, real friendly like, 'What brings you here?' ''

Charlie Craig guffawed. Under generally recognized rules of Men's Room Etiquette, conversation in such circumstances is permissible only if the men have known each other for at least five years or are related by blood. "So what did you tell him?"

"I gave him my shakedown glare and told him I was just here for lunch. In other words, go find somebody else to be friends with. Look," he said, pointing across the bar, "he's still here. Probably waiting for someone else to have to pee."

"Holy Christ!" Keenan exploded. "He wasn't trying to pick you up. You know who that is?"

Peffall raised an eyebrow. "Now why the hell would I know *him*?"

"That's a reporter from the *Daily News*," Keenan said. "Name's Nolan. Jim Nolan. How in hell did he learn we were here?"

"They must have gotten a tip about this place, too," Charlie Craig said. "I guess he recognized Rich from the courthouse or something and was trying to get information."

"He's going to play hell getting anything out of me," Peffall said sourly.

Despite the cool response he had gotten from Peffall, an undeterred Nolan followed the three into the parking lot, firing questions at them about Rabinowitz's ties to the club.

"Look," Keenan told him, friendly but firmly, "we can't tell you anything yet. We'd like to, but it's too early. We can't afford to screw up the investigation."

"Okay," the reporter nodded.

The next day Nolan's story about Rabinowitz's connection to Delilah's was on the *Daily News*'s front page. Under the headline, "Stay-at-home hubby had his go-go side," the story detailed how Rabinowitz had visited the club regularly and spent a considerable amount of money on an as-yet unidentified "lithesome blonde topless dancer." In addition to being the first to disclose Craig's dalliances at Delilah's, Nolan also revealed some previously unpublished details about Rabinowitz's finances, namely that his house was mortgaged to the limit; that he had recently taken out a large loan from another mortgage company—it was not yet publicly known that Rabinowitz used the Newmans' house as collateral—and that his business was "somewhat of a mystery."

Philadelphia
Evening

Peffall left Norristown a little after five o'clock, stopping in Ardmore to get Charlie Craig and Mark Keenan. The three got to Summer's house about dinnertime.

"Not bad," Charlie Craig said as Peffall pulled to the curb in front of a ranch-style duplex in a quiet, middle-class, section of Northeast Philadelphia. Tidy homes with well-tended lawns lined both sides of the street.

The middle-aged woman who answered the door introduced herself as Summer's mother. "Just a minute. I'll call her," the woman said, ushering them inside. "Why don't you have a seat in the living room?" she suggested.

Charlie Craig and Mark Keenan plopped onto one sofa; Peffall onto another. The couches were identical; both plush, both brand new. The whole room, in fact, was filled with new-looking furniture.

Summer appeared moments later looking, Peffall thought, like anything but a sexy exotic dancer. Wearing sweats, with her blonde hair up and no makeup, she could double for any of a dozen twenty-four-year-old women one saw daily in the neighborhood supermarket or the local Kmart.

"I've asked my lawyer to come over," she said in a soft, well-modulated voice. "Can we wait?"

"Sure," Peffall replied, speaking for the three. "What's his name, by the way?"

"Brian McVan."

"Oh, I know him. I've dealt with him on some other cases," Peffall explained to Craig and Keenan. "He's okay."

Peffall was about to ask her how she had met McVan when the doorbell rang.

"It's my boyfriend," Summer said, peeking through the front window.

"We're trying to conduct some business here," Peffall said when the man tried to come in. "It'd be better if you came back later."

"I believe I'm going to stay," the man insisted.

Peffall, slim but solidly built, rose to his feet. "I *said*, I think it would be better if you left. This is none of your business."

The man looked at Peffall, then at the other two officers.

"I'll catch you later," he told Summer, stomping angrily to his car.

Trying to make small talk while waiting for McVan, Charlie Craig pointed to the new sofas. "This is nice furniture."

"Yeah," Summer replied, hesitantly, Charlie Craig thought.

"New?" he asked.

"Yeah," she said, staring at the floor.

"All the furniture in here looks new," he said, glancing around the room. "Must have set you back a bit."

Summer looked at the detectives nervously. "Actually, it was a gift."

"Oh, a *gift*," Charlie Craig said, feigning surprise. "Some gift. Boyfriend? That guy that just left?"

"Oh, no," Summer smiled. "Not *him*."

"Well," the detective said lightly. "Some other boyfriend, huh?" He looked at her shrewdly.

"It was a gift from a *friend*," Summer replied, emphasizing the word.

"Uh-huh," Charlie Craig nodded. "Did Rabinowitz buy this for you?"

She looked surprised. "Yeah," she admitted.

"What did he buy?"

She shrugged. "The sofa."

The investigators looked at each other. There were *two* sofas. "Which one did Rabinowitz buy?" he pressed.

"Oh, you know,." Summer said, making a sweeping gesture to encompass the room. "Listen, I don't want to talk about this anymore until my lawyer gets here. Okay?"

"Sure," Charlie Craig said easily. "Let's wait until your lawyer gets here."

It was almost two hours before McVan showed up.

"Let's go out here for a minute," Peffall suggested, motioning for the lawyer to follow him onto the back porch.

"We're just here to *talk* to Summer," the detective explained. "We aren't looking to charge her with anything. All we want is some information about her relationship with a guy named Craig Rabinowitz. His wife was murdered in Merion last week."

"I know the case," McVan said. "Read about it in the papers. Summer was involved with him?"

Peffall nodded. "We don't know how deeply. We just know he spent a lot of time with her at Delilah's."

McVan bit his lip. "Okay. You've always been straight with me before. Let me talk to Summer."

Peffall joined Charlie Craig and Keenan in the living room while McVan and Summer disappeared into a back room. When they came out ten minutes later McVan was smiling. "She'll cooperate."

Peffall began asking Summer about Rabinowitz.

"When was the last time you saw him?"

Summer replied without hesitation: "Friday."

Peffall looked surprised. "Last Friday? May second?"

"Yeah." She nodded. "I was supposed to be at the club at one o'clock but I was running a little late. When I pulled into the parking lot it was about one-oh-five. Craig was there. He was sitting in his car, waiting for me."

"Just sitting there?" Charlie Craig asked.

"Yeah. He wouldn't get out. He said, 'I got to talk to you.' "

"And what did you say?"

"I asked him what it was about because I was running late. I needed to get inside. He said, sort of desperate, 'No, I *got* to talk to you. My wife died. I just buried my wife.' "

Peffall glanced at the other two investigators. "How did you feel when you heard that?"

"I felt real bad for him. I asked him about the baby. Who was taking care of the baby. He said she was at home with a babysitter. Then I asked him how his wife died, and he said that she slipped in the bathtub. By then I was shaking and crying. It was a shock, let me tell you. I was *really* upset."

"That's all he said?" Detective Craig asked.

She frowned. "Let me think. No. He said an autopsy was being performed and he had paid five thousand for it."

"That was it?"

She nodded. "I leaned in and hugged him but he didn't hug me back. He just sat there, real impassive."

"Then what happened?" asked Peffall.

"He drove off, and I just sort of lost it. I went screaming into the club, ran upstairs and told SherylAnn what had happened. I just couldn't believe it."

"Okay," Peffall said softly. "Before that. When did you see him before last Friday?"

"I *called* him on Tuesday. Does that count?"

Peffall raised an eyebrow. "Tuesday," he said carefully. "That's when we think she was murdered."

Summer looked puzzled. "I thought she was murdered on Wednesday. That's what the papers said."

"No, she was *declared dead* early Wednesday. We think

she was killed Tuesday night. Tell us about the conversation."

"I didn't actually talk to him," Summer explained. "I had called him on his cell phone, the number we always used, but his machine picked up. I left a message."

"What did you say? In the message?"

"I told him that I had just heard a song that he liked. I was sitting there listening to the radio, having a little tattoo removed, and the dj was playing a song I knew Craig liked. I just told him that I heard the song and I thought of him. I also wanted to know if he was still coming into the city the next day. I told him to beep me if he was. But I didn't hear from him until he showed up at the club on Friday."

"So you don't know if he got the message or not?"

"No," Summer said, shaking her head.

"Okay. Outside the phone message, when was the last time you actually saw him? Before Friday?"

She paused, staring thoughtfully into space. "I guess it was Monday. A week ago yesterday. Yeah. It was Monday. At the club."

"On April twenty-eighth? The day before the murder?" Charlie Craig asked.

Summer nodded.

"He came to the club, right? Went inside? How long was he there for?"

"He came in about lunchtime, when he usually showed up. I guess it was about one or one-thirty. He stayed until about five, like he usually did."

"And you didn't actually *see* him between Monday and Friday?"

"Nope."

Peffall asked what had transpired during the Monday visit to the club.

"He gave me some money," Summer said quietly. "About six hundred dollars, I think. I'm not sure if it was cash or credit card. I think it was cash."

Peffall raised an eyebrow. "And what did you do for that?"

Summer flashed a tight smile. "We talked."

Keenan looked at her closely. "You *talked*! Just talked?"

"That's right," Summer replied defensively. "We just talked. I've never had any kind of sex with Craig. We were just good friends. The only time I've ever seen Craig outside of the club was once last January. That's when he bought me this furniture. He said it was a housewarming gift."

"Ahhh," Charlie Craig said softly. "The whole living room?"

Summer nodded. "The dining room, too. And some furniture for my son's room. I have a five-year-old son I'm raising as a single mother. He said he wanted to help me."

"Did he ever buy you any other gifts?" Peffall asked.

"Yeah," she said, looking quickly at McVan, who shrugged. "He bought me flowers, bracelets, earrings—ones with tiny diamonds—and a necklace. I thought he had lots of money. When we first met he told me he was a lawyer, but later he said that his family owned a latex plant."

"Did he tell you that he had a wife?"

"Oh, yeah," Summer replied. "He said he loved her, but he was not *in love* with her. He said there was a difference. He said they didn't have sex much after the baby was born."

"Did he tell you about any problems he might be having?"

Summer paused. "Only that he had recently had trouble sleeping; that he had been to a doctor and was going to get something to help him sleep."

"Did he ever ask you to marry him?" Charlie Craig asked.

"Noooo," Summer replied hesitantly, "not exactly. There were several times when he said that he would marry me, that I'd make a good wife. A *perfect* wife, is what he said. But he never really asked me.''

Peffall leaned forward, locking eyes with Summer. "Did he tell you he killed his wife?" he asked pointedly.

"Oh, *no!*" Summer said emphatically. "He never said that!"

As they were leaving, Peffall turned to face Summer. "We appreciate your cooperation," he said. "We realize it probably hasn't been easy on you, either, losing your best customer and all."

Summer's eyes widened in surprise. "Oh, he wasn't my *best* customer," she said, closing the door.

On their way back to Montgomery County, the three investigators compared notes. They agreed that they believed most of what Summer had told them, although Peffall felt that she hadn't been completely forthcoming about what had transpired in the parking lot in front of Delilah's the previous Friday, or that she had been altogether candid about never having had sex with Rabinowitz. It was not unusual, Peffall knew, for rich customers at places like Delilah's to shower the dancers with gifts and cash in return for conversation or for providing a sympathetic ear while they rambled about troubles at the office or at home. But this was different. Few of those benefactors ended up with murdered wives. Despite the investigators' questions about some of the things Summer had told them, one thing was certain: Rabinowitz *had* spent a lot of money on her.

"Where the hell did it come from?" Charlie Craig asked. "There's nothing in that material we picked up in the house to indicate that Rabinowitz had that kind of money to throw around. There must be a source of revenue that we don't know about."

"I agree," Peffall said. "I think we need to go back into the house. The sooner the better. There *have* to be some records we haven't found yet."

"Are they still sitting shivah?" Keenan asked. "I hope

not, because the last time we did a search with all those
people there we weren't exactly welcomed."

"I think shivah lasts a week," Peffall said. "But we have
to get back in there. Tomorrow, if we can get another warrant."

"I don't think we'll have any trouble there," said
Keenan. "I'll start first thing in the morning on the paperwork."

"Ah, yes, tomorrow," Charlie Craig sighed, leaning
back in the seat, putting his hands behind his head, grinning
broadly. "What an experience this has been! We're probably the only three guys in all of Eastern Pennsylvania who
get paid for hanging out all day with exotic dancers."

While Peffall, Craig, and Keenan had been interviewing
Summer, they missed the early evening newscast on
WPVI–TV. The broadcast reporter, in the medium's best
you-learned-it-here vein, revealed to the public for the first
time that Rabinowitz had run up a monstrous credit card
debt.

The media bulldozer was getting cranked up. Combined
with Nolan's story, these first examples of aggressive reporting would set the stage for all future news coverage of
the case. Although the media was still circumspect about
flatly proclaiming that C&C did not exist as a viable entity,
all other reportorial moderation was about to be tossed
aside. The investigators' experience with Nolan at Delilah's
was only the beginning. Everywhere detectives went from
then on, they felt as if they were stumbling over reporters.
By the time Craig Rabinowitz's fate was sealed some six
months later, just about everyone directly involved would
be weary of media tactics, from Judge Salus, who sharply
took reporters to task during a brief but bitter legal struggle
over access to police documents, to family members and
friends, who felt as if all their privacy had been ruthlessly
stripped away in a journalistic stampede for rating points
and headlines. From May 6 on, the media seemed absorbed

in a frenetic race to see who would be first to uncover the next unsavory fact about Craig Rabinowitz's soon-to-be-revealed debauched past.

But long before all those details would be known, those who thought they knew Craig, particularly his family and close friends, discovered to their immense consternation that they did not know him at all.

NINE

On Tuesday, while Rich Peffall and Charlie Craig had been delving into Rabinowitz's ties to Delilah's Den and his relationship to one of the dancers, Bruce Castor had been on the phone with an ADA he knew in Philadelphia, listening as he explained how Rabinowitz had been linked four and a half years earlier to an escort-service–cum–call-girl-operation run by a police lieutenant named Joseph Kelly and his wife, Jayne.

The then twenty-nine-year-old Rabinowitz, married for only two years at the time, was arrested as a "john," that is, a user, of the service known as J.P. Tiffany's, a hooker-on-the-hoof operation that provided sex on demand at its Pine Street location in Center City or at the customer's home. Rabinowitz's name was not made public because he was never charged. To avoid a police department arrest record that would follow him for the rest of his life, he agreed to testify against Jayne Kelly in return for immunity from prosecution.

Rabinowitz may have thought that the immunity grant meant he was home free; that no one would ever be able to trace his connection to Tiffany's. He was wrong. While he had managed to keep his participation out of the newspapers—Stefanie, his family, and his close friends never knew about his trysts with the hookers, just as they had not

Craig Rabinowitz, a self-proclaimed entrepreneur with a house on Philadelphia's storied Main Line, with his infant daughter, Haley, not long after Haley's birth. *(Private collection)*

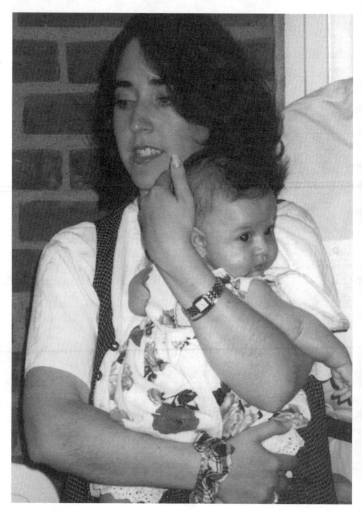

Stefanie Rabinowitz, a promising young lawyer at a prominent Philadelphia firm, with daughter Haley. Stefanie, not yet 30, was found dead in the bathtub of the Rabinowitzes' home in Lower Merion. Her husband, Craig, claimed her death was accidental, although an autopsy showed she was strangled. *(Private collection)*

Craig Rabinowitz in earlier, happier times, long before he was charged with killing his wife, Stefanie, and trying to pass her death off as an accidental drowning. (*Private collection*)

Dr. Hal Fillinger, the Montgomery County coroner whose suspicions led to the discovery that Stefanie Rabinowitz had been murdered. Wondering why a 29-year-old woman allegedly would have died in her bath, Fillinger ordered an autopsy which revealed that she had been strangled. (*Keith R. Watkinson*)

Judge Samuel Salus, the outspoken and often controversial Montgomery County jurist who presided over the murder and theft proceedings against Craig Rabinowitz.
(*Keith R. Watkinson*)

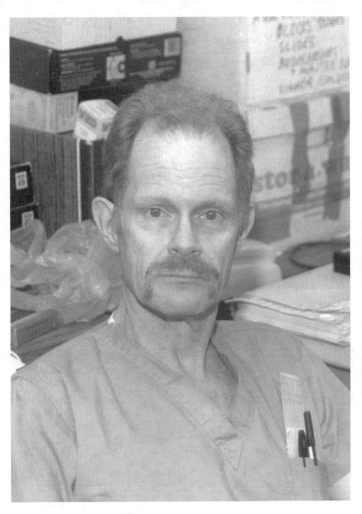

Dr. Ian Hood, the New Zealand-born pathologist who performed the crucial autopsy on Stefanie Rabinowitz, a procedure that definitively proved that the young lawyer had been strangled and had not died an accidental death, as had been originally believed.
(*Keith R. Watkinson*)

A front view of Craig and Stefanie Rabinowitz's rather modest home in Lower Merion, a tiny community along Philadelphia's fabled Main Line. Note the sheets covering the front windows, which were placed there by family members in an attempt to ensure privacy from the media during the Jewish mourning period known as shivah.
(*John Fallon*)

Charles Craig of the Lower Merion Police Department, the first detective on the scene following the discovery of Stefanie Rabinowitz's body. When Craig first examined the house soon after Stefanie's body had been removed, the investigator found no indication that her death had been anything but accidental.
(*Keith R. Watkinson*)

Mark Keenan, the sergeant in charge of the Lower Merion Police Department's detectives. It was Keenan who made the decision, based on long experience and a gut feeling that something was not right, to send Charles Craig to the Rabinowitz home in the early morning hours after the detective bureau had closed down for the night. (*Keith R. Watkinson*)

Richard Peffall, a veteran member of the elite Montgomery County Homicide Unit, who joined Charles Craig as a lead investigator in the Rabinowitz case. Over the days and weeks following the determination that Stefanie had been murdered, Peffall and Craig built a remarkably solid case against Stefanie's husband, Craig, spotlighting him as the killer as well as the clever perpetrator of a series of frauds, who was secretly in love with a blonde exotic dancer in nearby Philadelphia. (*Keith R. Watkinson*)

The prosecutorial team responsible for building the case against Craig Rabinowitz. At left is Tim Woodward, holder of dual titles as chief of the Montgomery County Homicide Unit *and* Assistant District Attorney. At center is Bruce Castor, Jr., the First Assistant District Attorney who directed the preparation of the prosecution's case and was scheduled to be the lead prosecutor at the trial. At right is Risa Ferman, a Montgomery County ADA carefully chosen by Castor to be the second chair at the trial and the one to present the fraud evidence against Rabinowitz. *(Keith R. Watkinson)*

known about his connection to Delilah's—that was about
to change. Since he did not have an *arrest* record as such
because of his agreement with the Philadelphia District Attorney's Office, his name did not pop up when Castor made
a routine computer search. However, there was a *court* record—which would not have shown up in the computer—
that clearly delineated his role. Since the Kellys pleaded
guilty before the case went to trial, Rabinowitz never had
to testify before a jury. Nevertheless, there was the transcript from the preliminary hearing, which was just as good
for the purpose it would be put to in Montgomery County.

"You want me to fax the transcript to you?" the Philadelphia ADA asked.

Castor broke into a huge grin. "You bet!"

At the 1993 hearing, according to the record, Rabinowitz
confessed that he had known Jayne Kelly since 1989 or
1990 when he had his first dealings with her service. He
admitted "seeing" her "four or five times" when she came
to his house, apparently the apartment he shared with his
new bride. Exactly what transpired on those visits was un-
clear because his testimony was interrupted by objections.
The question was not pursued because the Kellys' lawyer
successfully argued that whatever had occurred between
Rabinowitz and Jayne Kelly during that time frame was
immaterial since it was beyond the limits set forth in the
statute of limitations for the crimes with which the Kellys
were charged. However, what happened later was a different story. There was no objection to Rabinowitz's testimony about his contacts with two employees of the service,
women he knew as "Taylor" and "Courtney." In March
of 1992 and again the following August, Rabinowitz testified, he had gone to the Tiffany's location and plunked
down $150 for a shower, massage, and oral sex from each
of the women. The transcript was explicit about what Rabinowitz had done, with whom, and how much he had paid.
While this was immaterial to the murder charges, it nevertheless represented a black mark against his character,

which was Judge Salus's main consideration in determining whether Rabinowitz would be freed pending trial.

Despite the fact that the late-arriving material was going to cause them to work into the night redrafting the document, Castor and Ferman were delighted. While the prosecutors already had a considerable amount of material showing that Rabinowitz's character was deeply flawed, the Tiffany's transcript was a gift from the gods, another solid arguing point that Rabinowitz was not as spotless as his lawyers had made him out to be.

Come Wednesday morning, the prosecutors could hardly wait for court to open. Inwardly, they had been pleased about the defense's determination to seek Rabinowitz's release since that would give them the opportunity to explain in some detail why they had felt so strongly about charging him in the first place. Castor weighed the twenty-nine-page document in his hand, immensely contented with the amount of anti-Rabinowitz material that investigators had been able to put together in such a short time. "This will give Miller and DeSimone something to think about," he told Ferman confidently as they walked to the elevator.

Although couched in bland legalese, it was clear from Castor and Ferman's document that the prosecutors enjoyed ripping into defense assertions about Rabinowitz's sterling character:

- "...the Commonwealth believes and therefore avers that the defendant's employment status and history contains evidence of fraud and deceit...." *Translation: Rabinowitz has no business: C&C Supplies is a sham.*
- "...the Commonwealth believes and avers that the defendant has no appreciable assets and is heavily indebted on credit cards..." *Translation: Initial analysis of financial records recovered in the April 30 search show Rabinowitz had eleven credit cards*

and owed more than $70,000, including $33,000 to American Express alone.

- "... the Commonwealth believes and avers that the property located at 526 Winding Way is encumbered in excess of its purchase price and that the defendant has no equity therein ..." *Translation: So he put up his house as collateral? It was already over-mortgaged and would be of no value as recoverable property.*

- "... the Commonwealth believes and therefore avers that the defendant has engaged in multiple infidelities during his marriage and, in fact, was ensnared in a wiretap investigation conducted by the Philadelphia District Attorney's Office into a call-girl service being operated by a member of the Philadelphia Police Department. ..." *Translation: Rabinowitz got snagged while playing around with hookers.*

- "... the Commonwealth believes and therefore avers that the defendant has maintained, for a period of at least six (6) months prior to the murder, a relationship with an exotic dancer ..." *Translation: He left his good character at the door of Delilah's.*

- "... the Commonwealth avers that the defendant frequented that establishment at least two (2) to three (3) times per week to continue his relationship with the exotic dancer and during that time spent approximately $1,000 to $3,000 per week on her including buying her jewelry and furniture ..." *Translation: That should put the* coup de grâce *to Rabinowitz's claims to a utopian marriage.*

The Zinger: If Judge Salus still thought that Craig Rabinowitz should be freed on bail pending trial for the murder of his wife, then the amount, "in light of all the circumstances" should be no less than $5 million. That was the only way, the prosecutors contended, to make sure he showed up at trial.

"Five million dollars!" Jeffrey Miller gasped when he heard the figure proposed by the prosecution. "That isn't bail; that's ransom."

Judge Salus scheduled a hearing on the issue for May 15, only a week away.

Elaine Miller poured another cup of coffee and bent to the morning *Inquirer*. On the front page were two stories asserting that Rabinowitz continued to have the unqualified support of his family and friends.

One quoted people who had known Rabinowitz in the distant past or those who knew him peripherally, such as the owner of a popular, trendy restaurant where Rabinowitz was planning a $3,000 surprise bash to celebrate Stefanie's thirtieth birthday on June 3.

The other, headlined "Victim's parents join bail bid," was heavy with quotes from Jeffrey Miller proclaiming the family's faith in Craig Rabinowitz. "The whole family, all of them, are unanimously, 100 percent behind him," the lawyer declared.

The defense would soon have to eat its words. At the same time prosecutors were presenting their response for bail to Judge Salus, the *Daily News* was hitting the streets with Nolan's story about Craig's connection to Delilah's. It was a twin blast that no one connected to Craig Rabinowitz, least of all his lawyers, had been expecting.

In the week since Stefanie had died, none of the members of Rabinowitz's family had spoken directly to reporters and none of his close circle of friends had been contacted, which was fine with Elaine and, she was sure, with the others as well. They weren't publicity seekers; only a small group of loyal comrades who had known Craig and Stefanie for years and were determined to support him through this, the greatest crisis of his life. Despite the doubts that Jennifer and Betty were beginning to have about the degree of Craig's possible involvement, Elaine intended to remain true. Then she opened the *Daily News*. When she read about Craig's escapades at Delilah's, her resolve evaporated, totally and completely.

At first, Elaine was unable to believe her eyes. Craig involved with an exotic dancer? And none of the group knew about it?

"This isn't a case of once in a while on a Friday night with the guys," the *Daily News* quoted an unidentified source as saying. "This is a couple of times a week at one or two o'clock in the afternoon with one woman."

The story also quoted another dancer at the club, one who made it clear that Rabinowitz was deeply involved with one of the performers. "She [the dancer's so-far unidentified colleague] was the only one he wanted."

Elaine's mind was reeling. What about Stefanie? Did she know about this? No, she decided. Absolutely not. If she had, she would never have stayed with him. She would have packed up, taken Haley, and been gone in a flash. But how could she *not* know? Elaine asked herself. She answered her own question almost immediately: The same way none of *us* knew.

She stared at the newspaper, her coffee forgotten. Maybe, she thought, maybe we *did* know something. Maybe deep inside. So deep we didn't want to admit it. In a way, she told herself calmly, these revelations helped explain a lot about her friend's behavior. While she didn't want to admit it even to herself—whenever such thoughts came into her mind she pushed them away—she had long suspected that Craig's "business" had not been what he claimed it to be. No one in the circle could confirm it existed. No one had ever seen his products. Although he had promised Betty several times to bring her some talcumed latex gloves that would prevent the rash she always got when she used unpowdered ones in her clinical work, he never delivered. None of the friends had ever been to Craig's "office" or visited his "warehouse." Staring at the picture of the exterior of Delilah's Den on the newspaper's front page, she realized that the building did, indeed, have a "warehouse" look about it. And it wasn't far from the port where Craig had said his shipments of gloves arrived from Asia. Was it Craig's secret joke to talk about spending time at his "warehouse" when he really meant Delilah's?

Elaine berated herself for not saying something sooner about her misgivings. Despite her hunch about the non-viability of C&C Supplies, she had deluded herself into believing that it was just a harmless excuse Craig had dreamed up as a way for him to continue to indulge his indolence. Her attitude had always been that if Craig wanted to make up a "business" because it assuaged his guilt over being a layabout—and if it was all right with Stefanie, which it seemed to be, because surely she must have wondered about it, too—it was not up to her to question it. But that was different; Craig fibbing a little about C&C Supplies to hide the fact that he was bone lazy was one thing, while lying to his wife and his friends to protect a stripper girlfriend, maybe even murdering Stefanie to protect his secrets, was something else entirely.

As if the sun had broken through the clouds, Elaine could see the pattern clearly now. Craig had not only exaggerated his business success, he had fabricated a "colleague" from New York, the one who supposedly had an affinity for Delilah's Den. Craig had invented the New Yorker to camouflage his own activities. While he had acknowledged, amidst his friends' gentle ribbing, that he had made occasional visits to the club, he had maintained consistently that the only reason he ever went there was because his colleague insisted upon it. In actuality, from what the newspaper said, his trips had been entirely more frequent. And it was not his colleague who wanted to go there, but him.

Elaine was not sure of the connection between Craig's visits to Delilah's and Stefanie's murder, but suddenly the idea that he *could* have strangled her did not seem so far-fetched. His claims that the district attorney was trying to frame him had to be nonsense. The Delilah's incident proved that the Craig Rabinowitz currently in Eagleville Prison absolutely was not the same Craig Rabinowitz she thought she had known as well as she knew any man except Todd. This realization struck her like a lightning bolt. Craig had been living a lie the whole time she had known him. He had been leading a double life. And he had fooled everyone who cared about him. Not just fooled them; made fools *of* them.

Elaine realized that she was furious with Craig; enraged at what he had done to Stefanie, the Newmans, and his friends. Throwing the newspaper aside, she grabbed the phone. "Todd!" she cried shrilly when her husband answered. "About that check we wrote for Craig's legal expenses! Cancel it! Get that money back!"

Still infuriated, she called Betty and Jennifer to see if they were aware of developments. They were; they, too, were fuming.

However, despite entreaties from Jennifer and Betty to face reality about Craig's possible involvement in his wife's murder, Mark Hirtz and Brian Schwartz continued to believe in him . . . and to keep to themselves the fact that Craig had hinted that he might flee given half the chance. It would be several days before they—the last of Craig's once-loyal circle of friends—were ready to concede that the evidence seemed irrefutable.

While the *Daily News* had jumped into the lead in the media war with its bombshell story on Rabinowitz's connection to Delilah's, the *Inquirer* brought up several less sensational, but nevertheless important, points. The venerable old morning newspaper—the community's equivalent of the *New York Times*, which was known throughout the industry as the Gray Lady because of its plodding, sometimes prosaic approach to news reporting—had opted for volume coverage over catchy headlines. In addition to the two stories citing continued support for Rabinowitz by family and friends, the *Inquirer* also pointed out, publicly for the first time, thanks to Jeffrey Miller, that a family living next door to the Rabinowitzes may have seen a prowler in the neighborhood on the night of the killing. The newspaper did not know that investigators had already tracked this down and discounted a connection.

In contrast to the *Daily News*, the *Inquirer* barely mentioned Delilah's Den and, when it did, the reference was buried deep in the main story.

In one important way, however, the *Inquirer* got an edge on the competition. In one of its four stories that day it leaped straight to a compelling component that no one in the print media had yet addressed directly: Craig Rabinowitz may have been in jail with all the available evidence indicating that he was the killer, but investigators did not yet have a crucial element necessary for any case the prosecution might present—a motive.

Inquirer reporter Larry King astutely pointed out that although motive was not necessary, juries often were reluctant to convict without one. The implication was that motive would be extra-important in the Rabinowitz case because the couple seemed to have led such a picture-perfect life. What could possibly have generated such strong emotion in Craig Rabinowitz that he would strangle his wife to death?

The same question was troubling investigators and prosecutors as well. The only clue to motive that investigators had so far was insurance. Policies on Stefanie's life totaled $1.8 million. But even DA Michael Marino was reluctant to claim that that was why Stefanie was killed without being able to provide convincing details on why Rabinowitz would be so desperate for cash. Many Main Liners were covered by big life insurance policies; few of them were murdered.

*   *   *

After reviewing Summer's statement and facts that investigators had learned about Rabinowitz's spending habits at Delilah's, everyone involved in the case realized that Craig had been spending money no one knew he had. Lots of money. Recognizing that the source of this money could be the critical missing piece to the puzzle of Stefanie's murder, investigators and prosecutors were determined to find it.

Figuring there *had* to be some sort of financial records they had not yet been able to find, Detectives Craig and Peffall were implementing the first phase of a plan for a second search at 526 Winding Way. Since they now knew that Rabinowitz did not have an office outside the home, or a warehouse, the most logical place for him to keep the data was somewhere in his house. They agreed they would find it even if they had to tear the place apart.

While Ferman was filing their document opposing Rabinowitz's release on bail in the clerk of court's office, Castor and the two detectives were meeting with Judge Salus, asking him for another search warrant that would allow them back into Rabinowitz's house.

"One more thing, Judge," Castor asked after Salus quickly concurred with the necessity for a second search, "can you seal the warrant? The press has been hot on our heels since yesterday," he added, explaining how the *Daily News* reporter had shown up at Delilah's even before they had finished interviewing the principals. "No sense tipping our hand too much."

"You're right," Salus replied. "Consider it sealed."

Warrant in hand, Charlie Craig and Rich Peffall agreed to meet after lunch at LMPD, where the troops would gather for the new assault.

Merion
Afternoon

Thanks to the *Daily News*'s eye-opening story, the Schwartzes, Hirtzes, and Millers—and thousands of others in Greater Philadelphia—were all aware of Rabinowitz's connection to Delilah's. Those who had been listening to the radio late that morning or had tuned into the tv news at noon also knew about his involvement with the Kelly call-girl ring. But the Newmans and other religiously observant family members who had gathered at 526 Winding Way were unaware of these developments since they continued to follow shivah in the traditional way by declining to read the daily newspapers, listen to the radio, or watch tv. Although the family had bluntly refused an ever-increasing number of telephoned requests for interviews, the media continued to pursue them more aggressively than ever. Once the news about the document Castor and Ferman had filed in Norristown became public, a small army of newspeople swarmed into Merion, where they set up camp in front of the Rabinowitzes' house. In an effort to ensure some measure of privacy, the family tacked a bed sheet over the picture window that looked out onto the front yard, hoping that would deter the growing crowd of feisty reporters. It did not. As the day wore on, their number grew rather than diminished. By mid-afternoon, it seemed as if there were a reporter, a photographer, or a camera person behind every bush.

When the convoy of investigators—Detectives Craig and Peffall, accompanied by Keenan, Woodward, LMPD's Tom Hunsicker and several others—arrived at the house, they couldn't believe it.

"Look at 'em," Peffall said, encompassing the crowd of media people in a sweeping gesture. "What the hell's the matter with 'em? Why don't they go away?"

After fighting their way through the crowd of newspeople, the investigators were met with an unmistakably chilly reception from the Newmans.

"Leave us in peace," Lou Newman pleaded. "We're still in mourning."

"We can't," Charlie Craig said softly. "As much as we'd like to, we have to go through the upstairs one more time." Leaving Peffall to explain their presence, the search crew pounded up the stairs.

A few minutes later, Castor and Ferman drove up in their own vehicle. Ignoring the predictable shouted questions from reporters, the two prosecutors crossed the porch and rapped on the door. "Look at that, would you?" Ferman said, gesturing at the sheet that covered the picture window. "These people must be going through hell."

The door opened a crack and Peffall peeked out. Seeing who it was, he beckoned them inside.

Nothing in Castor's Presbyterian upbringing had prepared him for shivah. Glancing around, noting the draped mirrors and the unshaven faces of the men who glared at him coolly, the prosecutor's eyes settled on the long table covered with food that friends and neighbors had brought so the family would not have to divert their attention from their grief to spend time cooking. "Good God," he gasped. "They're having a party!"

Ferman, an observant Jew, stared at him in amazement. "Hush!" she commanded, elbowing him sharply in the ribs. "It's *not* a party. Don't say anything else. I'll explain it to you later."

Hurrying up the stairs, the prosecutors ducked into the master bedroom where Charlie Craig and Tom Hunsicker, LMPD's senior detective, already were at work, Hunsicker looking through the dresser while Charlie Craig went through the drawers in the night stands.

"We'll go back here," Castor said, striding toward the back of the house to the room that Rabinowitz called his "office."

"Hey-hey," Hunsicker called out a few minutes later. "Take a look at this."

Stepping back so Charlie Craig could see, he pointed to two items that had not been there on the first search: Rabinowitz's wallet, which probably had been in his pocket earlier, and a large wad of bills.

"What've you got?" asked Woodward, who had just entered the room, apparently alerted by Hunsicker's excited comment.

"How's this?" Hunsicker said, lifting the thick packet of currency.

"How 'bout that!" Woodward whistled. "How much?"

Hunsicker was already counting. "One thousand . . . two . . . three . . . four . . . five . . . six . . . seven. Seven thousand and . . . one . . . two . . . three . . . four . . . five . . . six . . . seven . . . eight. Seven thousand, eight hundred dollars even. Mostly big bills. Now I wonder what he was going to do with that." He grinned.

"Why would he have that much money sitting in a dresser drawer, of all places?" Woodward mused. "Bruce and Risa will be happy to see it, though," he said, taking the money and disappearing back into the other room.

Encouraged by the find, Charlie Craig and Tom Hunsicker went back to searching, methodically opening every drawer and examining every piece of paper they could lay their hands on. Two hours later, however, they had not added anything else to their store of new evidence.

"Why do women have so many clothes?" Charlie Craig mumbled half to himself as he replaced a stack of Stefanie's sweaters which he had removed from a shelf in the closet.

"How's it going in here?" Risa Ferman asked cheerily, joining them from the other room.

"Nothing more yet," Charlie Craig said, "but there's something in the closet I want to check out."

"What's that?" Ferman asked, peering inside.

"Up there," Charlie Craig said, pointing at a rectangular-shaped indentation in the ceiling. "That's the outline of a panel. In houses like this there's usually a space between the ceiling and the roof where a lot of people store things. I want to check it out. I'm going to try to find something to stand on."

Five minutes later he was back, lugging an old stepladder and a flashlight. "Give me a hand?" he asked Ferman.

With Ferman steadying the wobbly ladder, Detective Craig started upward. With one knee resting on a stack of out-of-season clothing and the opposite foot braced against a small shelf that had been inexpertly nailed onto the wall, the investigator struggled to remove the panel so he could get to the musty empty area behind it.

"If you fall on me, I'm dead," the diminutive Ferman joked, watching intently as Charlie Craig struggled to maintain his balance. "There," he grunted, sliding the panel aside and shining his light into the opening.

"See anything?" asked Ferman.

"Nope," Charlie Craig replied, his voice muffled. "Nothing . . . Wait a minute!" he said excitedly. "Here's something."

"What is it? What do you have?"

"It looks like a shopping bag. Like one of those paper things you get at a department store."

"Well, bring it down," Ferman urged. "Let's see what's in it."

Carefully, Detective Craig lowered the bag through the opening, heedful not to spill the contents as he twisted and pulled. Handing it to Ferman, he jumped down and followed her across the room.

"You guys better come in here," she called, summoning Castor, Woodward, and Hunsicker.

As they gathered around her, Ferman began removing the items one at a time, placing them on the Rabinowitzes' bed. There were several soft-core porn magazines—not the kind a man would would want his mother, wife, or daughter to see, but not anything that would get him thrown in jail either . . . some Delilah's Dollars . . . a half-dozen slips of paper printed with the name of Carver W. Reed & Co., an upscale Center City pawn shop . . . and a handful of what appeared to be receipts. One was for a $300 golf club; others were for flowers, diamond earrings, bracelets, and a pearl necklace. To Charlie Craig the receipts corroborated Summer's story about gifts she had received from Rabinowitz. There also were receipts for living room, dining room and children's furniture, which further corroborated what the dancer had said. At the bottom of the bag, looking at first glance like trash, was a note-sized piece of inexpensive paper covered with figures and lettering.

"Let me see that," Castor said eagerly, extending his hand.

Written by hand, complete with scribbles, circles, and some cross-outs, the document looked like this:

	OUT		IN	
Feldman—	52	7.5	F.C.	1,000,000
Schwartz—	25	12.5	P.M.	500,000
Kaplan—	51.5	40	ABA	360,000
Smolen—	88	8.5	F&B	10,000
RAB—	85	—	STOCK	7,500
Newman—	34	7.5	Car	6,000
Hirtz—	13	1.5		1,883,500
	348.5	77.5		1,212,500
	426	+10	HOUSE	270,000
		J.S.		
Mort	200			1,482,500
CC	35.3			
	235.3	671K	$1,000,000	6600/MO/
				6875/MO/

"Those are some of Rabinowitz's friends," Detective Craig exclaimed, reading over the prosecutor's shoulder and pointing to the names on the left side of the paper. "Feldman . . . Schwartz . . . Kaplan . . . Hirtz. 'Newman' must mean his in-laws," he added.

"Who's Smolen?" Castor asked.

The detective shook his head; it meant nothing to him.

"RAB?"

"I'd guess 'Rabinowitz.' "

"Down here," Castor pointed. " 'J.S.' What's that?"

The investigator shrugged and shook his head a second time.

Castor tapped the piece of paper, his excitement boiling to the surface. "I think this is a ledger of sorts," he cried, his boyish face breaking into a huge grin. "This is great! Hot damn, I can't believe it! This piece of paper," he said, waving it in the air, "is going to show us where Rabinowitz was getting his money. Oh, God! This is *precisely* what we've been looking for. Good going, guys! This is the most important thing we've found so far."

The detectives were passing it around, studying it.

"It's going to take some work to get it all sorted out," Peffall said.

"That doesn't matter," Castor said, his face flushed. "No problem. Once we get it deciphered, it's going to tell us *why* Craig Rabinowitz killed his wife and prove that he had been planning to do it. This clearly demonstrates pre-meditation. There's no way Miller and DeSimone are going to be able to claim heat of passion when we hit 'em with this. This piece of paper right here is going to make our first-degree murder case! It's going to put Rabinowitz away for the rest of his life!" Staring at the paper, he slowly shook his head. "This is absolutely staggering."

Reaching for his cell phone, he began punching in a number. "I'm going to call Mike. He'll definitely want to know about this." Covering the mouthpiece, he looked at the investigators. "You guys start working on it right away. But," he cautioned, "not a word to anybody. I mean *any-body*. I don't want this to get to his lawyers before we have it all sewed up."

It would take the detectives weeks to confirm the paper's usefulness, but Castor's instincts proved correct. What looked at first glance like idle doodling on a piece of scrap paper would turn out to be the Rosetta Stone to understand-ing Craig Rabinowitz and to establishing the motive for Stefanie's murder.

Stuffing the material back in the bag, the detectives gathered what they had found and hurried back to Ardmore. Gathering in the LMPD's conference room, they emptied the shopping bag onto the table and began going through the items more carefully, sorting them, speculating about them, assigning priorities, and deciding who would track down what.

The second search had taken almost four hours, so it was already late in the day; too late to hope to accomplish much in the way of interviews before Wednesday. "Let's call it quits," Woodward suggested. "We can start again in the morning. In the meantime, not a word to the media about what we found, especially about the piece of paper. That's going to be our ace in the hole."

Bala-Cynwyd
Evening

Despite Woodward's instructions to call it a day, Detectives Peffall and Craig elected to make one more stop before going home. Climbing into Peffall's car, they drove to a nearby community where they knew that one of the people whose name had been on the paper lived.

Mark Hirtz was polite but firm. When investigators asked him why his name would be on a piece of paper found in a storage area above Craig and Stefanie's bedroom, and what the figures beside his name meant, Hirtz shook his head. Perhaps recalling the warning relayed by Anne Newman about how Rabinowitz's friends might be held accountable for possibly destroying evidence when cleaning up the house the night of Stefanie's death, Hirtz was cautious.

"You know I'm an attorney?" he asked.

"Sure," said Charlie Craig. "You were with Rabinowitz the night he gave his statement. I remember."

"Well," Hirtz smiled. "you know how attorneys are. I'll

be happy to talk to you, but I'll have to talk to *my* attorney first.''

Thanking him for his time, the detectives climbed back into the county sedan.

"Jeez," said Peffall, "seems like everyone involved in this case is either an attorney or has an attorney."

Within days, however, Hirtz would meet with the detectives again to give them information that would plug one more gap in their investigation. Details that Hirtz and Brian Schwartz would provide would kill any last hope Rabinowitz and his lawyers may have had that he would be released on bail.

TEN

Norristown
Thursday, May 8
Morning

If prosecutors had seemed frustrated in their efforts to nail down a motive for Stefanie Rabinowitz's murder, the defense team of Frank DeSimone and Jeffrey Miller must have felt even more thwarted in their attempts to win his speedy release from jail. If they thought his freedom was imminent, based on their claims to his good character, they undoubtedly were left aghast by more than the prosecutors' suggested $5 million bail fee.

In a sense, DeSimone's and Miller's own reputations were on the line. They had vouched for Rabinowitz's good standing, only to see the very points about his character which they had stressed as being unsullied being trashed, in spades, by Castor and Ferman:

- Miller and DeSimone had cited Rabinowitz's image as a doting father, but, according to those friends who had seen him daily during the period before he went to jail, Rabinowitz had, in his last hours of freedom, stayed as far away from Haley as he could get;
- They had crowed about his standing in the local business community, but the district attorney's office had preliminary evidence that C&C Supplies was non-existent;

- Miller had been very vocal with the media about how much support Rabinowitz had from his family and friends. But by Thursday morning the only ones still in his corner were Brian Schwartz and Mark Hirtz. And soon they would be gone, too. Even the Newmans—after Lou finally heard on his car radio, en route to a doctor's appointment, what investigators had uncovered about his son-in-law—would, within days, withdraw their backing and align themselves with a lawyer of their own choosing, abandoning DeSimone and Miller as ''family'' spokesmen;

- But what may have wounded the defense lawyers the most was getting ambushed on their claim that Rabinowitz had a clean police record. As it turned out, this was not exactly so, witness his bust for repeatedly patronizing the tarts from Tiffany's. True, Rabinowitz had never been charged in connection with his involvement in the call-girl operation, but he had been grabbed up as a semi-regular customer. And he had confessed. If he had not cut a deal with the Philadelphia District Attorney's Office to testify, Stefanie would have known about it years before and may have left him then.

Being good defense lawyers, Miller and DeSimone took the only action they could under the circumstances. In an effort to cut their losses they attacked the prosecution's right to bring up the Tiffany's incident. Within hours after Ferman and Castor filed their document, Miller and DeSimone asked Judge Salus to expunge the transcript of Rabinowitz's testimony in the Kelly case on grounds that its presence violated his immunity agreement. Additionally, they said, the prosecutors had prejudiced the case against their client by making it public.

In reply, Ferman and Castor pointed out that they were not attempting to use Rabinowitz's testimony against him in the murder case. Instead, they brought it up simply to show that his *character* was not as spotless as Miller and DeSimone had portrayed it to be. Since the decision on whether to release Rabinowitz pending trial for Stefanie's killing depended almost entirely upon Judge Salus's conclusion about Rabinowitz's reputation, evidence of his involvement in the call-girl scandal was both pertinent and permissible. "It is inconceivable," the prosecutors contended, "that the defendant could allege that he is of good character in a written bail motion and then endeavor to hide behind a previous shield of immunity granted under circumstances directly tending to prove his good character— an issue injected by the defendant in an effort to fool this court into believing he is of good character."

DeSimone and Miller, in the meantime, apparently could not stop from digging themselves deeper into a hole of their own making. In an effort to minimize the damage done by the prosecution's revelations against their client, the defense lawyers only made themselves look worse. Miller was quoted in the *Daily News* as saying that the information about Rabinowitz's connections to the Kellys and his fling with Summer had little to do with the murder charges, and, by the same token, were unrelated to whether he might try to flee if he were freed. Soon, they would have to eat those words, too.

Despite the bitterness that was evident to anyone who knew the history of the Miller/DeSimone–Castor pairing, the legal slug-fest was barely getting started. In weeks to come the defense vs. prosecution competition would come to resemble a no-holds-barred tag team event on late-night tv. The entry of a battery of attorneys representing various broadcast and print concerns would just add spice to the show.

After all but ignoring the Delilah's Den angle in its Wednesday story on the Rabinowitz case, the *Inquirer* splashed it on Page One on Thursday. Under the headline, "The double life of Main Line murder suspect," the story covered the points outlined by Ferman and Castor, livening them up with some fresh quotes from a Den waitress and the club's night manager. The *Inquirer* also mentioned the afternoon search, pointing out that investigators left the house "carrying three boxes containing such items as a black binder, a shopping bag, and numerous brown evidence bags," but did not attach any special significance to the items. A picture of a frowning Craig Rabinowitz illustrated the piece.

The *Daily News*, on the other hand, went straight to the issue they knew would get their readers' attention: sex. Wednesday's photo of an exterior of Delilah's Den was filed away. In its place was a pic of Summer embracing the brass pole used as a prop by Delilah's dancers. The headline on the adjacent story—the *News*'s headlines are always snappy and bright—read, "Steamy Summer raised sweat." The *News*'s story, like the headline, was colorful and catchy, describing Summer, for example, as being clothed "in a skin-tight evening gown with spaghetti straps, a slit from her toes to her crotch" with parted lips and a hair style that looks "like a woman who just got out of bed." But there was one problem. While the picture was indeed Shannon Reinert, aka Summer, the newspaper made a mistake in identification. Instead of *Shannon* Reinert, the *Daily News* used the similar first name of another young woman in Northeast Philadelphia. Ten days later, the *News* published a fifteen-paragraph story on the woman who was incorrectly identified as Summer. In effect, it was an apology, although the newspaper blamed the mixup on television news crews, not their own reporting.

On May 8, the toxicology report came back from the National Medical Services lab in Willow Grove, Pennsylvania. Tests on Stefanie's blood and gastric fluid certified that shortly before her death she had taken a common hypnotic sedative known to the scientific community as zolpidem. Sold under the name Ambien, it is an effective sleeping potion that begins acting within twenty minutes after it is ingested. NMS's analysis showed that when Stefanie died she had about three times what would be considered a normal dose in her system.

Ambien, Detectives Peffall and Craig recalled, was what Rabinowitz had said he had obtained a prescription for because he and his wife had been suffering from mild insomnia. The bottle the drug had come in was still missing; it had not been found in either of the two searches at the Rabinowitzes' house.

When he saw the toxicology results, Dr. Ian Hood became more convinced than ever that his original theory about how Stefanie had died was correct. In his opinion, Rabinowitz had drugged Stefanie with Ambien and, once she was unconscious, carried her upstairs and put her in the bathtub, intending to drown her. However, the water probably revived her and she woke up, at least enough to struggle and bruise her outer arms by banging them against the sides of the tub. When it became apparent that he was not going to be able to drown her, Rabinowitz strangled her, hoping that an autopsy would not be done and the death would be ruled accidental.

Bruce Castor was almost as elated over the toxicology report as he had been about the discovery of Rabinowitz's ledger. If the hand-written note showing how he planned to dispose of the money that he would collect if Stefanie were dead did not absolutely prove premeditation—since it was undated, Rabinowitz might try to claim that he wrote it after Stefanie's death, not before—the presence of Ambien would seal the issue. Castor would be able to argue that, under Pennsylvania law, the zolpidem was, in this case, a poison, and a poison, per se, augured premeditation. While the defense might try to counter by saying that Stefanie took the drug voluntarily, prosecutors could respond by pointing out that it was Rabinowitz, by his own admission, who sought the prescription; that Stefanie *never* took drugs unless it was absolutely necessary, and that if she had ingested the Ambien voluntarily she would not have taken three times the recommended dose.

Even though it had been less than twenty-four hours since they found the shopping bag, investigators already were starting to mine its riches. From receipts and other documents in the bag, detectives learned that Rabinowitz:

* spent $8,500 for furniture for Summer's house;
* splurged for *two* memberships at the upscale Sporting Club, one for himself and one for Summer, at $375 apiece, plus an additional $136 a month each in fees, *plus* extras for laundry service, shoe shines, and a locker in the VIP section on the same row as those of Mayor Ed Rendell and Dr. J, the 76ers star;
* repeatedly pawned Stefanie's jewelry—his favorite item was a diamond-studded band that had belonged to her grandmother, getting $1,250 for it each of the five times he borrowed against it—at Carver & Reed, a 127-year-old Center City dealer popular with Philadelphia's more affluent residents; an avuncular type of place where most of the items left are eventually reclaimed;
* charged hundreds of dollars' worth of items, apparently gifts, from major stores like Bloomingdale's and Saks between the time that he first met Summer and the end of April;
* had, on Valentine's Day, 1997, only ten weeks before Stefanie's murder, plunked down $1,980 in cash for a pearl necklace from Tiffany's in Center City (whoever it went to, it was *not* Stefanie).

Investigators were delighted with the largesse of information they got from documents in the shopping bag, since each lead led to another, and every one tightened the noose about Rabinowitz's neck. "It was like Christmas," Montgomery County's John Fallon cracked later, explaining the investigators' good fortune in the rapid accumulation of evidence against Rabinowitz, an avalanche of material that dazzled even the veteran detectives. "It was like unwrapping presents under the tree. Every day, everywhere we went, we kept finding something that was even more incriminating than what we had before."

Friday, May 9

While detectives were scrambling to build on the leads from the documents found in Rabinowitz's shopping bag, the *Daily News* turned briefly from its pursuit of Summer to a rather bizarre attack on the investigators.

In a curious article that appeared to be half-editorial, half-news, under the headline, "Cops slow to catch on?" reporter Nicole Weisensee took Montgomery County authorities to task, implying that from the beginning they had bungled the investigation, perhaps irretrievably.

Without quoting the sources directly, or identifying them, other than saying that they were "forensic pathologists," Weisensee wrote that the characteristic signs of manual strangulation should have been apparent by the time Rabinowitz found his wife in the bathtub twenty minutes after hearing the "thud" he professed to believe was the shampoo bottle falling off its perch.

". . . By then, marks on her strangled neck should have begun to appear and the skin around her eyes would have already been blackened by the force of the assailant who strangled her . . ." she wrote. "And then, there was the unusual hour—after midnight—that [Stefanie] went to take a bath."

Reverting again to an unidentified source, Weisensee proclaimed: "All of this should have alerted cops that her death wasn't an accidental drowning."

At that point, the article reiterated the defense claims that Stefanie may have been killed by a mysterious stranger and evidence of his presence was destroyed because police failed to secure the house as a crime scene. "In the meantime," Weisensee wrote, using earlier statements from Miller and DeSimone as apparent source material, "Rabinowitz and his friends traipsed in and out of the house and cleaned it, destroying any possible evidence that could have linked either him or someone else to her murder, including muddy footprints his friends said they saw in the bathroom where she was killed."

Weisensee also quoted a man named Joel Moldovsky, "a veteran criminal defense attorney and former homicide prosecutor," as saying that he thought Castor and Ferman had a "weak case." "Where's the confession?" the *Daily News* had him asking. "Where's the evidence linking his hands to that neck? Where's the witness?" He concluded by predicting that the district attorney's office would not be able to convict Rabinowitz.

Noting that DeSimone and Miller declined to comment, Weisensee added: "But they have begun to weave their defense, creating the specter of a mysterious intruder who first knocked on a neighbor's door about two hours before she died. They point out that it was Craig's habit not to lock his back door and that previous owners had been liberal in giving out keys to people. They say the muddy footprints could have been put there by the real killer."

Although the story lacked direct quotes from Miller and DeSimone, it precisely mirrored the spin the defense attorneys had been trying to impart on the case from the time that Miller first talked to Castor.

The prosecutor also declined to speak for the record, but privately he was furious.

"You guys did a terrific job," he told Tim Woodward. "What the hell does the *Daily News* expect? Most of the time when somebody dies at home it's not a homicide. When there's no evidence of a murder, why make the family go through the inconvenience of having the house sealed up, having fingerprint dust all over the place, all that crap?

Especially in this case with all the ceremony attached to mourning in the Jewish religion and the use of the house. What would you guys have found anyway? Rabinowitz's fingerprints? His hair? He *lived* there, for Christ's sake! Of course you'd find it! A forensic examination wouldn't have turned up a damn thing that you wouldn't expect to be there in the first place. The first officer on the scene . . . what's his name? He didn't see any indication that Stefanie had been strangled. Her eyes weren't black and there weren't any bruises on her throat. The paramedics didn't see anything, either. And neither did the emergency room doctor. Does the *Daily News* think these people are all blind? The signs didn't start showing up until Hood looked at her twelve hours later, after the blood had a chance to drain from the surface. And when they did, they were not nearly as pronounced as the paper makes 'em out to be; there was almost nothing visible to the naked eye.

"And look at this," he said, slamming the newspaper with the back of his hand: " 'there was the unusual hour . . . that she went to take a bath,' " he read aloud with heavy sarcasm. "Jeez. There're a lot of people who wouldn't think it unusual at all for someone to take a warm bath at midnight if they were having trouble getting to sleep. And this, dammit," he added, his face reddening, "this guy saying we won't be able to get a conviction! Just watch. Wait and see."

To Elaine Miller and Jennifer Hirtz, the implication that potentially valuable evidence had been destroyed because they helped clean the house for shivah was an uncomfortable echo of what Anne Newman had told them four days earlier, on the morning that Craig surrendered: that the friends might one day be called accountable for their action. In actuality, there was no compelling reason, neither then nor later, why this should not have been done.

*   *   *

While the defense attorneys apparently declined to talk to Weisensee, Miller was voluble with the *Daily News*'s print competitor. The page one story in that morning's *Inquirer* emphasized defense comments debunking prosecution contentions that Rabinowitz's infatuation with Summer may have been connected to the murder of his wife.

Under the headline "Lawyer: Kin knew of suspect's club visits," Miller was quoted as saying that Rabinowitz's family knew about his visits to Delilah's Den. "They were not upset about it. They joked about it."

He conceded, however, that they may not have known about the *frequency* of Rabinowitz's appearances at the club.

Despite the family's knowledge about Rabinowitz's obsession with Summer and his admitted experiences with Jayne Kelly's call-girls, they were, according to Miller, continuing to stand by him. "They wanted me to know they were more eager than ever to help him."

Deeper in the story, reporters Monica Yant, Ralph Vigoda and Anne Barnard clarified reports about Rabinowitz's $88,000 loan from Allied Mortgage, an angle their tv competitors also were fighting fiercely to exploit.

The day before, after investigators had identified the name "Smolen" from Rabinowitz's ledger as that of a partner in Allied Mortgage, Detectives Craig and Peffall set out to find him to see what he could tell them about Rabinowitz's finances. The only "Allied Mortgage" listed in the local directory was in nearby Bala-Cynwyd. But before going there they swung by the district justice's office to pick up a warrant they felt they would need to secure the information they were looking for. To their surprise, KYW–TV reporter Walt Hunter and a camera crew were waiting for them in Narberth.

Grabbing the warrant, the detectives, with the tv crew in pursuit, raced to the Bala-Cynwyd office building where they believed the mortgage company was headquartered.

After negotiating with Hunter to keep the cameras in the hallway while they talked to company officials, the investigators disappeared inside, only to reappear in less than five minutes.

"Sorry to disappoint you," Peffall told Hunter, grinning broadly. "Wrong Allied Mortgage. These guys have never heard of Craig Rabinowitz, much less made him a loan."

Having learned that the Allied Mortgage they were seeking was, in fact, in the community of Villanova, a dozen miles to the northeast, the two detectives jumped back into Peffall's car and hurried there, again with the tv newspeople right behind them. However, since the company was run from an office in the rear of a private residence, the reporters had to wait on the street.

While Detectives Craig and Peffall were playing tag with reporters, Castor and Ferman were drawing up an amended affidavit of probable cause for District Justice Henry Schireson in Narberth. Since the murder had occurred in Lower Merion Township, documents relating directly to the homicide itself would have to be filed with him. The bail issue, on the other hand, would be handled by Judge Samuel Salus of the common pleas court in Norristown, the seat of Montgomery County, since that decision was beyond the authority of a district justice. The preliminary hearing—a procedure to determine if there was enough evidence to bring Rabinowitz to trial for the murder of his wife—would also be held before Schireson. If he ascertained that Rabinowitz *should* be called to account, the trial itself would be in the common pleas court, where all felonies were adjudicated. It was a somewhat confusing procedure necessitated by the state law that set forth which courts had jurisdiction in which matters. If a trial were ordered, the presiding judge would be picked at that time.

Incorporating a smattering of the information they had found in the shopping bag, the prosecutors' amended affidavit would provide fresh fodder for the media and kick off a new round of titillating coverage that featured headlines ranging from lurid ("From porn to pawn . . . Did sex-obsessed Craig Rabinowitz trade wife's jewelry for cash just a day after her death?"—the *Daily News*) to dull ("More contacts of husband, dancer found"—the *Inquirer*).

Detective Craig filed the papers on Friday, even as readers of the *Daily News* were being told how police had botched the investigation. The fourteen-page document revisited the scene at the Rabinowitz house on the morning that Craig had called 911; repeated the high points of Craig's statement—including his assertion that he had locked his doors and windows before going upstairs to bed—described Craig's surrender; and went into what was then old news about Craig's relationship with Summer. Halfway through, it segued into material that was not yet publicly known: how Rabinowitz had showered Summer with gifts of flowers and jewelry; how he furnished her house; how he had seen her the day before Stefanie was murdered and given her $600 in cash; how Summer had telephoned Rabinowitz at eleven o'clock on the night of the murder and left a message on his machine; and how they had met in the Delilah's parking lot on May 2, when Rabinowitz told the dancer about his wife's death.

Although the document did not mention Rabinowitz's pawning of his wife's jewelry, reporters had dug up that information on their own. "A day after he cradled the body of his strangled wife in the lukewarm water of her bathtub," Jim Nolan wrote in the *Daily News*'s story about the filing of the document, "Craig Rabinowitz expressed his grief in a rather peculiar fashion." Printed pause. "He pawned her engagement ring." Printed pause. "And the rest of her jewelry, too."

No one was more shocked at these revelations than the tight group of Craig and Stefanie's friends, who thought they had already learned as much as they wanted to know about Rabinowitz's duplicity. "I can't believe it!" a dazed Mark Hirtz said, switching off the evening news. "I can

understand about him pawning Steffi's jewelry," he told
his wife, Jennifer, "because he was desperate and desperate
people do strange things. But I *can't* tolerate the fact that
he gave that woman six hundred dollars."

It was the blow that irrevocably severed a friendship
which he had nurtured and held onto despite the travails of
the previous week. Picking up the phone, Hirtz dialed Brian
Schwartz, who also had been watching the newscast. They
decided they would go to investigators and tell them about
Rabinowitz's hints that he would run given half the chance.

Another thing that purposely was not disclosed in the
amended affidavit was information about the scrap of paper
found lying loose in the shopping bag, the item that detectives and prosecutors had come to refer to as "the hand-
written ledger." Bruce Castor remained convinced that it
was the key to Rabinowitz's motive. Because of the importance of the piece of paper to the prosecution's case, he
insisted on extreme secrecy about its existence. If the media
found out about it, so would Miller and DeSimone. And
the last thing Castor wanted at that stage was the defense
tumbling to what the district attorney's office had on Rabinowitz before Castor was ready to make it public.

Saturday, May 10–Sunday, May 11

It was characteristic of the Rabinowitz case, as it is in many
developing stories, that information ebbed and flowed; developments tended to come in spurts with lulls in between.
This was especially true over weekends and holidays, when
public offices were closed and sources sought by reporters
and investigators alike had a habit of disappearing.

The media filled the gap that weekend by reprising what
was already known, bolstered by details revealed on Friday
in the amended affidavit. In an unusually long piece, the
Daily News, in its Saturday edition, summarized the revelations about Rabinowitz's secret life, stressing his relationship with Summer and the lengths to which he had gone

to keep the liaison a secret. There was no mention at all about C&C Supplies, or family support for Rabinowitz. There was no more speculation about alleged police incompetence. Absent, too, was any further mention of defense claims about an unknown killer who might still be on the loose. Rabinowitz's lawyers, in fact, were uncommonly mute about the situation facing their client. While the story noted that they had visited Rabinowitz for the first time since he surrendered, neither lawyer appeared eager to speak at length on what they had discussed. DeSimone relayed the hardly startling news that Rabinowitz planned to plead not guilty when the time came. Miller added that their client "relentlessly" continued to affirm his innocence.

Other than demonstrating that it, too, could have a problem getting Summer's real name straight—calling her Reinhart rather than Reinert—and that it had more of an inside line to Miller and DeSimone, the *Inquirer* added little to the body of public knowledge about Stefanie's murder.

In reality, statements from defense lawyers were beginning to look rather strange. Insisting that Rabinowitz's family continued to support him—although by this time he almost certainly knew otherwise—Miller asserted that the information that had surfaced about Rabinowitz's double life tended to "crystallize" rather than "fragment" his supporters. "They simply do not believe he killed this woman, or is capable of it," he said.

On one point, though, Miller was precisely on target: Rabinowitz had absolutely no history of violence or abuse, no record of anything to indicate an uneasy marriage, and there were no reports from neighbors about loud arguments emanating from the house on Winding Way. "It just doesn't make sense," Miller said candidly, evidencing more so than anything he had said so far, the true state of confusion that must have reigned in the defense camp.

On Sunday—in a questionable bow to Mother's Day—the *Inquirer* weighed in with its own thumb sucker, a lengthy piece by reporter Anne Barnard imparting no new information about Rabinowitz or Stefanie's murder, but emphasizing instead the reactions of a half-dozen or so people who either lived near the Rabinowitzes, attended Bryn Mawr—Stefanie's alma mater—or were themselves mothers.

More pertinent to the issue was a sidebar story headlined "Suspect talked in brothel case," since it cleared up some of the perplexity resulting from the snippets of testimony attached to the prosecution's May 7 document that exposed Rabinowitz's contacts with the call-girl operation. The testimony filed with Judge Salus was from a preliminary hearing in which Rabinowitz had testified and, because of objections from the Kellys' lawyer, the exact connection between Rabinowitz and Jayne Kelly was ambiguous.

The *Inquirer* dug deeper, going back to what Rabinowitz told prosecutors in the district attorney's office months before his testimony was interrupted at the hearing. In the DA's interview, Rabinowitz admitted having sexual intercourse or engaging in oral sex "about ten times" over a two-year period beginning in "March or April of 1989" with a woman he knew as "Jeannie," whom he later identified as Jayne Kelly. In return for the service, Rabinowitz paid $150–$175 per event. The story showed that Rabinowitz was meeting the prostitute both before and after he married Stefanie in June 1990, not only cheating on his fiancée/wife, but bringing "Jeannie" into the apartment that he shared with his new bride. Kelly herself never elaborated upon Rabinowitz's claims because she and her husband pleaded guilty to charges of running a house of prostitution before the case came to trial.

ELEVEN

Although it was Mother's Day weekend and Castor and Ferman would have preferred to be at home with their spouses and children, they were feeling the pressure of the bail hearing that was scheduled for Thursday, only three days away. While Castor still had confidence in the strength of the material he had filed on May 7 listing the prosecution's reasons why Rabinowitz should not be freed, he wanted to make sure every angle was covered. To get ready for what they were anticipating would be the first in a series of showdowns with DeSimone and Miller, he and Ferman had driven to the courthouse to prepare still another document for the judge's attention. As soon as the clerk's office opened on Monday, Ferman took the elevator downstairs and had it stamped into the growing file.

Mainly, it was a recapitulation of what was already on the record, at least in general terms. Where it went further was in adding tiny nuggets of information, interesting little details that further elaborated on the prosecution's attack on the defense's claims about Rabinowitz's good character and his reputation in the local business community. Specifically, the document said that Rabinowitz had spent a minimum of $28,913.55 during thirty-nine visits to Delilah's Den in the three-month period beginning on January 7, 1997, an average of $2,224.12 per week. The operative word was "minimum." That was the amount that could be documented from analyzing Rabinowitz's credit card statements. In actuality, not Castor, not Ferman, not anyone but Rabinowitz himself knew how much he really spent. Prosecutors figured it was considerably more than the minimum because he often walked around with large wads of cash in his pocket. In April alone, Rabinowitz withdrew $27,100 in hard currency from his C&C Supplies account. Where all of that money went was a mystery.

Implying that it showed an additional lack of "character," the prosecutors also pointed out to Judge Salus that Rabinowitz had bought the exotic dancer her own membership at a well-known Center City health club, spent $8,501.80 to furnish her house, and pawned his wife's jewelry, even her engagement ring, to help finance his affair. Furthermore, the document concluded, Rabinowitz was not only *not* a highly regarded member of the business community, he didn't even *have* a business.

It was not mentioned in the document, but the assertion that C&C Supplies was a phantom operation raised an extremely important question: If there was no latex glove business, where was Rabinowitz getting the money that he was spending on Summer? It wasn't coming from Stefanie, since she was making only $33,000 a year as a part-time litigator. Rabinowitz spent almost that much at Delilah's just in the first three months of 1997. He had no day-job; no independent source of income that investigators had so far been able to determine. So where was he getting the money he was throwing around like confetti?

Realizing that the defense must be wondering the same thing, Castor ordered investigators to increase their efforts to nail down Rabinowitz's mysterious money source. Obviously, judging from Miller's and DeSimone's public statements and the absence of legal pleadings, Rabinowitz was not being candid with his own lawyers. Therefore, Castor reckoned, he had not told them about his income source either. It *had* to be illegal; Castor was sure of that. But that much money couldn't be garnered through penny-ante schemes; he must have found a steady, seemingly bottomless, source of cash. And the prosecutor was bent on finding it, preferably before the defense could seal off possible sources of information.

Under pressure to start making progress on deciphering the ledger, Tim Woodward summoned Detectives Craig and Peffall to his office. "We need to get cracking on this," he said, slapping a copy of the ledger onto his bare desktop.

Earlier, after studying the paper and batting around the possibilities of what the names and figures represented, they had tentatively concluded that the "Out" side represented Rabinowitz's indebtedness, assuming that he had been able to tap his friends and associates for considerable amounts of cash. The names and figures on the right, or "In" side of the document, they reckoned, showed what Rabinowitz stood to gain by the death of his wife. Risa Ferman had volunteered to track down the insurance companies, leaving the investigators the chore of talking to Rabinowitz's friends.

However, if the first column of figures on the left of the "Out" side represented the amount of money that Rabinowitz had borrowed, they were unsure what the second column of figures stood for.

"I think that's the interest he had to pay," Charlie Craig said. "Look here," he added, jabbing at the copy on Woodward's desk. " 'Smolen . . . 88 . . . 8.5.' The people at Allied told us that Rabinowitz had borrowed eighty-eight thousand dollars last February 13. So that matches. And he agreed to pay back the original loan plus eighty-five hundred in interest. So that fits, too. Eighty-eight and eight-point-five."

"I don't know," Peffall said doubtfully, studying the paper. "Look at this. 'Kaplan . . . 51.5 . . . 40.' He can't be paying anyone forty percent interest."

"Uummmm," Charlie Craig agreed. "You have a point."

"Listen," Woodward said impatiently. "We don't have time to sit around all day speculating about this. Let's go talk to some people. Hear what they have to say and go from there. You," he said, pointing at Peffall, "go talk to Mark Hirtz and Brian Schwartz. Find out why their names are on this list and what the figures mean. And you," he said, looking at Charlie Craig, "talk to Brian's father, Alex, who's also on the list. I'll take Robert Feldman. We'll meet back here this afternoon."

Peffall jumped in his car and pointed it toward Philadelphia, where both Hirtz and Schwartz worked. As he turned onto I-276 he flipped on the radio, punching buttons until he found a local talk station. The mid-morning dj's—not wanting to be left behind by the newspapers and tv—were milking the Rabinowitz case for all it was worth. Although they seldom had anything important to say, Peffall enjoyed listening to the give-and-take with the listeners who called in. As far as the Rabinowitz case was concerned, most of the callers, Peffall felt, seemed particularly outraged by the cold-bloodedness that Stefanie's killer had exhibited.

The one on the air currently was no exception. Identifying herself as a homemaker from Bridgeport, she was telling dj Phil Valentine about the Scott Flander story in that day's *Daily News*, a gripping piece that went into considerable detail describing what Stefanie's last moments must have been like.

Peffall picked up the paper that was on the seat beside him and quickly re-read the first two sentences. "It took four minutes for Stefanie to die. And if what prosecutors say is true—that her husband was the one who killed her—what was he thinking as he tightened his hands around her throat, squeezing the life out of her?"

Valentine's raucous laugh broke Peffall's concentration on the newspaper. The talk-show host was replying to a caller, who was requesting something called "Down at Delilah's."

"Okay, okay," Valentine chuckled. "My own little creation. Back by popular demand."

There was a half-second of dead air, then the singer began:

> He paid a fortune to watch her dance 'round
>   in the nude.
> His gold MasterCard and his Visa kept her in
>   the mood . . .

Peffall burst out laughing. Am I hearing what I think I'm hearing? he asked himself. An eighteen-wheeler roared up behind him, drowning out the radio as it inched by on his left. Peffall cursed quietly, spinning the volume knob and urging the semi forward. It cleared in time for him to hear the rest of the song.

Fumbling for his notebook, the detective scribbled a brief reminder to himself: "Call WWDB."

"I've got to get a copy of that," he laughed aloud. "The guys'll love it."

Norristown
Late afternoon

"I don't know how he did it," Peffall said when the group re-gathered in Woodward's office late that afternoon. "He must be one smooth-talking son of a gun."

"How's that?" Woodward asked, lifting an eyebrow.

"He got a bunch of money out of Hirtz and Schwartz," Peffall explained, "and then left them holding the bag."

Reading from his notes, Peffall briefed the other two investigators on what he had learned. "Okay," he said, "this is Hirtz. He loaned Rabinowitz $10,000 in October 1995. Seven months later, in May 1996, Rabinowitz repaid $1,000, leaving a principal balance of $9,000. On that same day—you believe that? The same day!—Rabinowitz borrowed another $5,000. That brought his total outstanding indebtedness to Hirtz to $14,000. Five months later, in October 1996—a year after the original loan—Rabinowitz gave Hirtz $3,500, chopping his debt to $10,500. Last February, Rabinowitz paid Hirtz another $4,500, lowering the debt to $6,000, which is where it stood when Rabinowitz was arrested.''

"And Schwartz?'' asked Woodward.

"Same, identical pattern.'' He glanced at his notes. "In November 1995, three weeks after going to Hirtz, Rabinowitz borrowed $10,000. In December 1996—more than a year later without repaying a damn penny—he borrowed another $30,000 . . .''

"Phew,'' Charlie Craig whistled.

"That's not all,'' Peffall smiled. "A month later—we're talking this past January now—he borrowed yet another $10,000. This brought his total debt to Brian Schwartz to $50,000.'' He paused, looking at Charlie Craig and Tim Woodward. "That's a lot of money.''

"So what happened?'' Woodward asked.

"Two months ago, in March, Schwartz was repaid in full.''

Charlie Craig chuckled. "That must have been a shock.''

"If it was, it was short-lived. 'Cause a few weeks later, in April, only a little more than two weeks before Stefanie was murdered, Rabinowitz borrowed another $10,000. It's still outstanding,'' he said, flipping his notebook shut.

"I got more or less the same story from Feldman,'' said Woodward. "He loaned Rabinowitz $10,000 in January 1996, *but* it was promptly repaid in full. Then Rabinowitz came back in October and asked for $52,000. In January, he repaid $7,500, and on April 15, another $20,000. That left the principal debt at $24,500. But Feldman said Rabinowitz promised him fourteen-five in interest so he figures Rabinowitz still owes him $39,000.''

"My turn'' Detective Craig said, clearing his throat. "Mine's simple. My man, Alex Schwartz, loaned Rabinowitz $15,000 on April 1. None of it has been repaid.''

"Jesus! This is getting confusing,'' Woodward exclaimed. "Give me those figures again,'' he said, grabbing a sheet of paper. As Detectives Peffall and Craig repeated the numbers, Woodward scribbled them down on a makeshift chart.

"My God!'' Woodward gulped, doing some quick arithmetic. "Rabinowitz owes just the five people we've talked to $158,000!''

"According to this ledger,'' Peffall interjected, "the total is actually $348,500.''

"Holy shit,'' mumbled Charlie Craig. "No wonder he needed the insurance.''

"If that's not a motive for murder, I'll kiss your ass in Wanamaker's window.''

"Wait a minute, Peff,'' cautioned Woodward. "This doesn't tally with what we found out. You said Hirtz told you that Rabinowitz owes him $6,000?''

"Right.''

"But according to this ledger, it's thirteen, plus one-point-five in interest, if that second figure *is* interest. Charlie, you said Alex Schwartz told you fifteen, but this says ten. Feldman told me thirty-nine, including interest. This ledger says fifty-two plus seven-point-five something-or-other. Damn! I know we're on the right track, but we're not there yet. We still have a lot of work to do.''

"Hang on,'' Peffall interjected. "We don't know when this ledger was written. There's no date on it. Maybe he paid back some of the money after he wrote it. Or borrowed some more.''

"That's a good possibility,'' Woodward agreed.

"And we still don't know who this 'RAB' is,'' Charlie Craig pointed out.

"We'll find out,'' Woodward said grimly. "Don't worry about that. We'll find out. But it's not going to be tonight,'' he added, glancing at his watch. "Let's call it a day.''

"Wait a minute!'' Peffall said, holding up his hand.

	95	96	97	BORROWED	REPAID	BAL	OUTSTNG 4/29/97
Hirtz	Oct.			10		10	
		May			1	9	
		May		5		14	
		Oct			3.5	10.5	
			Feb		4.5	6	6
B. Schwartz	Nov			10		10	
		Dec		30		40	
			Jan	10		50	
			Mar		50	0	
			Apr	10		10	10
Feldman		Jan		10		10	
		Jan		10		10	
		Jan		10		10	
			Jan		10	0	
		Oct		52		52	
			Apr		7.5	44.5	24.5
					20	24.5	+14.5
							int=39
A. Schwartz			Apr	15		15	15
Allied/Smoler			Feb	88		88	88

"Don't you want to hear what else Schwartz and Hirtz told me?" he asked, grinning broadly.

While the three investigators had been working on the listings under the "Out" side, Ferman had been calling the insurance companies to see if she could make sense out of the initials and figures on the "In" side. She had much better luck.

The previous January 30, Ferman learned, Rabinowitz had arranged for two new insurance policies on his wife, supplementing two others that already were in effect: one from New York Life for $360,000, which Stefanie held through the bar association, and a relatively small one for $10,000 through her employers, Fineman & Bach. One of the new policies, from a company called First Colony, was for $1 million; the other, from Provident Mutual, was for $500,000.

The Provident Mutual policy had gone into effect immediately; by April 18 he had paid $2,100 in premiums to make sure it stayed in force. However, there was a delay in the activation—the industry term was "binding"—of the larger policy from First Colony. Apparently anxious to get it in place as soon as possible, Rabinowitz asked the agent why it was being held up. She explained that because of the large payout amount there were more bureaucratic hurdles that had to be vaulted; if Rabinowitz wanted a million dollars in insurance that would go into effect immediately he could substitute the single large policy with two for $500,000 each. Or he could wait for the paperwork to clear. Rabinowitz apparently decided to wait. In late March, First Colony asked Rabinowitz to make out another check, since the original had been returned to him by the agent pending the "binding" process. On April 3, he mailed the agent another check. A week later, on April 10, an impatient Rabinowitz again called the agent.

"I have one question for you," he said. "Is Stefanie fully insured by First Colony?"

"Yes," the agent replied.

In less than three weeks Stefanie would be dead.

While conceding that the timing of the new policies could have been strictly coincidence, Ferman nevertheless was struck by the implications of Rabinowitz having suddenly quintupled the amount of insurance on his wife. Furthermore, the figures on the "In" side of the ledger agreed precisely with what she had learned from the insurance companies. The ledger said "F.C., 1,000,000," which to the prosecutor clearly meant First Colony, $1 million. The ledger said "P.M., 500,000." That matched with the Provident Mutual policy for $500,000. The other figures also agreed: "ABA 360,000" undoubtedly meant American Bar Association, $360,000, and "F&B 10,000" was Fineman & Bach, $10,000.

Ferman asked herself why Rabinowitz would be keeping track of exactly how much he could collect if Stefanie were dead if his reason was not sinister? The answer: The reason *was* sinister; as far as Ferman was concerned Rabinowitz had been planning for some time to kill his wife for the $1.8 million in insurance money. What was still unclear, however, was why he needed the money desperately enough to murder the mother of his daughter, a woman he had been with for almost fourteen years. He couldn't spend *that* freely at Delilah's, or be *that* generous with Summer. What possessed him?

The detectives had the answer: He needed it to repay his debts. Castor had been right; the ledger did provide the elusive motive for Stefanie Rabinowitz's murder. But the details were still unrefined. It would be weeks yet before investigators and prosecutors would be able to make sense of the scribbling, and more weeks after that before they could fit the facts together into a comprehensive form that a jury could understand and accept. To accomplish that, they eventually would have to spend $20,000 for an outside expert, a forensic accountant, because only a specialist would be able to untangle Rabinowitz's ultra-complicated financial affairs.

Tuesday, May 13
Morning

Both newspapers made official what investigators had known for days: Craig Rabinowitz's support among family and friends had all but evaporated. Under the headline, "Accused wife killer may be standing alone," the *Daily News* quoted lawyer Neil Epstein as saying that Anne and Lou Newman were "re-considering" both their offer to put up their house to help Craig meet bail and an earlier promise to testify on his behalf as character witnesses at the hearing, now only two days away. The Newmans, Epstein told reporters, had found the details about Rabinowitz's past "unsettling."

The *Inquirer* more conservatively reported that the Newmans "have moved to distance themselves from their son-in-law," but also quoted Epstein as saying that they had not made a final decision on whether to withdraw their offers of support. The *Inquirer* also quoted Jeffrey Miller, who tried to pass the latest developments off as nothing particularly unusual. "If anybody is jumping ship," Miller told the newspaper, "it's not because they think he killed her." If there was a shift in loyalty, he added, it would only be because the family was upset by the revelations in the prosecution's document that exposed Rabinowitz's spending.

Significantly, for the first time the *Daily News* also raised the issue of whether Stefanie may have been drugged on the night she died. Although details of the statement Rabinowitz made to Detectives Craig and Peffall had not yet been made public, the *Daily News* seemed to know that he had mentioned sleeping pills. Investigators, who were still searching for the bottle of Ambien, declined to comment other than to repeat the coroner's finding: that Stefanie had died of manual strangulation.

Norristown
4:24 p.m.

Bruce Castor was on a roll. Investigators were bombarding him with new information, and he, in turn, was bombarding the court. Feeling that he had DeSimone and Miller staggering, if not exactly on the ropes, he followed Monday's filing of additional material opposing Rabinowitz's bail with a four-page document attacking the defense's contention that the testimony Rabinowitz gave in the Kelly hearing could not be used in the murder case because it violated the promise of immunity that Rabinowitz had been granted four years previously.

The prosecution was not seeking to use the information *against* Rabinowitz, Castor explained, but raised it only as an indicator of Rabinowitz's character, which was important to Judge Salus in determining if Rabinowitz would be freed. "Additionally," Castor wrote, "the notes of the defendant's immunized testimony do not tend to incriminate him in any way because they do not tend to show he is guilty of the crime for which he is charged," which was murdering his wife. "Since the defendant was immunized by Philadelphia because he asserted his Fifth Amendment privilege against self-incrimination," Castor continued, "and since the evidence at issue here does not bear on whether he committed this homicide, it does not 'incriminate' him and therefore the use of the evidence is not protected by the previous immunity order."

He could have left it there, but he couldn't resist a final jab at Miller and DeSimone. "It is inconceivable," he added, "that the defendant could allege that he is of good character in a written bail motion and then endeavor to hide behind a previous shield of immunity granted under circumstances directly tending to prove his good character—an issue injected by the defendant in an effort to fool this court into believing he is of good character.''

It didn't take Judge Salus long to rule in Castor's favor on the issue. The testimony would remain.

But even as Castor was filing that document, he already was making plans for yet another that he hoped to file the next day, literally on the eve of the scheduled bail bond hearing. Entitled ''Additional Supplementary New Matter,'' it would offer still more reasons why prosecutors felt that Rabinowitz should remain in Eagleville Prison until he went on trial, reasons which would not fully play out until investigators could follow through on information Mark Hirtz and Brian Schwartz had given to Peffall on Monday.

Merion
5:05 p.m.

''Oh, no,'' Anne Newman sighed. ''Not again.''

Rich Peffall looked somewhat abashed. ''I'm afraid so, Mrs. Newman. We need to examine Craig's car.''

''His *car*?'' she asked, surprised. ''Whatever for?''

Peffall paused, wondering how much he should reveal. ''It has to do with a tip we got,'' he said, deciding to be forthright. ''We understand that Craig was ready to flee. We think he might have a packed bag in the trunk. It won't take long for us to look and we won't disturb you. We have a warrant,'' he added, reaching into his jacket.

Mrs. Newman waved the document away. Turning to a woman behind her, she said resignedly, ''I guess we're going to have to let them, Joyce. Maybe this will be the end of it.''

Jews have a word for the relationship that existed between Anne Newman and Joyce Rabinowitz as a result of their children's marriage. A Yiddish word, *machetayneste*, it refers to a son's or daughter's mother-in-law. Joyce and

Anne were each other's machetayneste. The word, however, is neutral in the sense that it does not reflect any
feeling the mothers-in-law might have for each other.
Sometimes, there is no feeling; the women simply tolerate
each other. In this case, however, Joyce Rabinowitz and
Anne Newman were fairly close, and the tragedy which was
profoundly affecting them had not driven a wedge into the
relationship. However, it did put it in a new light, since
there was the baby girl, Haley, who was now without either
a mother or a father. Haley would live with Anne, but Joyce
would not be excluded.

"If you have to, I guess you have to," Anne Newman
said, turning back to Peffall. "You don't mind if we wait
inside?"

"Certainly not," the detective replied quickly. "Would
you mind giving us the keys to the Honda? We'll be gone
as soon as we can."

"Damn!" Charlie Craig said fifteen minutes later, after
a cursory search of the black Honda turned up nothing.
"Maybe the information was bad. Or maybe someone already removed what we were looking for."

"Let's tow it in anyway," Sergeant Mark Keenan suggested, reaching for his mobile phone. "Maybe the lab
guys'll find something of interest."

While they waited for the tow truck to arrive, Peffall
returned to the house to tell the two women that nothing
had been found.

"You know, don't you," Joyce Rabinowitz said, "that
Craig sometimes drives the Volvo? Technically, the Honda
is *his* car, but he likes the way the Volvo handles."

Peffall's eyes widened. "No kidding!" he said, smiling.
"You wouldn't happen to have the keys for the Volvo, too,
would you?"

"We have to get a new search warrant," Keenan pointed
out. "The other was only for the Honda. I'll go get it."

While Keenan was in Narberth seeking fresh authoriza-
tion from District Justice Schireson, Charlie Craig, Rich

Peffall, and John Fallon waited near the Volvo, which was parked in the driveway at the rear of the house almost directly beneath a kitchen window that the two women had opened because of the balmy spring night.

"What do you think we might find?" asked Fallon.

"If we're lucky, a packed suitcase and maybe some more money," said Detective Craig.

"Oh, just like O.J.," Fallon quipped. "Maybe a mask and a passport, too."

"That's uncalled for!" a female voice said angrily from inside, carrying easily through the open window. "Who said that? That's not right. You have no right to make a comment like that."

Fallon blushed. "Sorry, ma'am," he apologized. "I just got a little carried away."

An hour later, Keenan returned.

"Let's see what we've got!" Charlie Craig said, inserting the key that Joyce Rabinowitz had given them into the lock on the trunk.

"Ah *hah*!" Fallon exhaled when the lid swung open. "Now whatcha think we have here?"

Sitting in the otherwise empty trunk was a beige nylon suitcase, the type one could throw over a shoulder and carry on a plane.

"Do you believe this?" Peffall laughed, pointing at the label on the bag. " 'RUNAWAY!' By God, I think I've seen everything now."

Fifteen minutes later they were back at LMPD headquarters in Ardmore.

"Okay," Charlie Craig said, rubbing his hands together, "let's see what Rabinowitz had packed for his trip."

Unzipping the bag, they began removing the clothing that was jammed inside.

"Polo shirts . . . shorts . . . swim trunks . . . nothing but summer clothing here," Detective Craig said, "no pun intended."

"Doesn't look like he was heading for Canada or Alaska," Fallon added.

"You notice anything strange?" Peffall asked, sifting through the pile.

"What do you mean?"

"No baby clothes! Wherever he was going, it doesn't look like he planned to take Haley along."

"By God, you're right," Charlie Craig exclaimed. "So much for the defense's claim that Rabinowitz isn't a flight risk. Bruce and Risa are just going to *love* hearing about this."

When reporters told Jeffrey Miller about the investigators' find, the defense lawyer waved it off as inconsequential. Rabinowitz was going to visit his mother at her home on the New Jersey shore, Miller said, but his plans were interrupted by his arrest. Miller ignored the fact that Joyce Rabinowitz had been in Merion since the day Stefanie died, plus the fact that not even the tradition-breaking Craig would have dared leave the state until shivah was over on May 8, three days after he surrendered.

As Charlie Craig was driving home that night he had his radio tuned to his favorite soft-rock station, a low-key outlet that prided itself on a minimum of chatter but lots of music. "Stay tuned," the dj said, "I have another set of seven songs coming up. I'd like to dedicate them to the only seven people in Philadelphia who think Craig Rabinowitz is going to make bail on Thursday."

The detective laughed aloud. After the media gets hold of what we found tonight, there won't even be seven, he said to himself.

TWELVE

Bruce Castor was primed. A sturdy cardboard box bulging with twenty-three files supporting his argument that Craig Rabinowitz should not be released on bail sat on the floor by his desk. And offstage, just waiting to be summoned, were fifteen witnesses waiting to testify about the Mr. Hyde side of Craig Rabinowitz, an aspect that only two weeks before would have seemed ludicrous. At that time, the thirty-three-year-old self-professed entrepreneur was being lauded as a Main Line Dr. Jekyll, a hard-working, self-effacing independent businessman; a harmless, jolly, hockey-crazy sports fanatic; a dream husband who was super-solicitous of his lawyer wife's merest whim; an adoring father who worshiped baby Haley with an ardor bordering on preoccupation. But Castor was waiting almost gleefully to shred that reputation.

For seven days, Castor and his co-prosecutor, Risa Ferman, had been besieging the defense with a series of paper attacks that turned the once-accepted image of Craig Rabinowitz inside out. But for Castor, paper wasn't enough; the first assistant DA wanted a direct nose-to-nose confrontation, not a paperwad fight. He wanted to drag Rabinowitz into Judge Samuel Salus's courtroom and publicly demolish what Miller and DeSimone continued to insist, much to Castor's indignation, was a spotless reputation.

But there was a problem. Not with the prosecution, but with the defense. Two days before, the odds of Castor getting his wish for a face-off seemed high. But all the revelations about Rabinowitz's fixation on strippers and whores, plus his apparent abandon with credit cards, had perhaps been too much; the prosecution's zeal may have been overkill. In the previous twenty-four hours, judging by DeSimone's and Miller's comments to the media, the defense seemed to be back-pedaling as fast as they could away from the prosecution-sought fracas.

That morning's *Inquirer* had featured a Page One story quoting DeSimone as saying an unidentified lawyer friend of Craig and Stefanie's, while in their house during shivah, had found what appeared to be a suicide note signed by Rabinowitz. DeSimone's co-counsel, Jeffrey Miller, mentioned the possibility of having Rabinowitz examined by a psychiatrist or psychologist. But it was all rather vague. The defense attorneys declined to reveal the contents of the note, although they hinted that its existence might be a reason to postpone the bail hearing.

Curiously, in comments to the rival *Daily News*, Miller seemed to retreat from the suicidal aspect of the missive. The note did not directly say that Rabinowitz was considering killing himself, Miller told Nicole Weisensee and Jim Nolan, but it did indicate that he was experiencing "deep sorrow" over Stefanie's death.

Investigators and prosecutors were highly skeptical. If such a note existed, why hadn't it been found during the April 30 or May 7 searches? Why had no one else, like Anne Newman, mentioned it? Why were DeSimone and Miller keeping its contents secret? In the end, it turned out to be a smokescreen. Like the second autopsy, the note was never mentioned again.

Also without going into detail, Miller floated another theory about Stefanie's death, posing the possibility that, in the wake of the toxicology report that confirmed she had a sedative in her system, she may have died as a result of a drug overdose.

When Castor heard that claim he exploded, uttering an expression he frequently relied upon in such circumstances. "Fucking nonsense!" he told Mike Marino angrily. "First it was an accidental death, not a homicide, and the matter would be cleared up by a second autopsy. Then it was a mysterious stranger who left muddy footprints on the bathroom floor. Now it's a drug overdose. I can't wait to see what's next."

Pacing his office like an expectant father, Castor reflected on the prosecution's progress so far. Actually, it had been going much better than he could have hoped. Rabinowitz had sealed himself in by making it so plain at the beginning that he, Stefanie, and Haley had been alone in the house, so there was really no one else to consider. On the surface, given the way events had developed, that had seemed an incredibly stupid thing to do—provided he had, indeed, killed his wife, about which Castor had not the slightest doubt. But why had Rabinowitz put himself in that position?

He and Ferman discussed it at length. Finally they agreed that it had not been stupid at all, but remarkably clever. Very chancy, but very canny: Rabinowitz had been taking a calculated risk. His whole plan had hinged on his ability to convince police and emergency room personnel that Stefanie's death had been accidental. He had no choice. What Rabinowitz absolutely could *not* have done on April 30 was tell officers that he had not been at home at the time his wife died, or that someone had broken in and killed her. Then her death would have been investigated as a murder from the get-go. Once investigators started looking for someone with a motive, they would have settled on him very quickly. Not known among his friends as a gambler— in fact his reluctance to tempt fate was a mild in-joke among his friends—he had staked his life on the chance that no one would suspect a murder. If the accident story had been convincing enough, there would have been no autopsy and Stefanie would have been quickly buried. If at some later date suspicions were aroused, it would be a horrific fight to have her body exhumed. And even if it was, what would show up? Only the drug zolpidem, and certainly not enough of that to have killed her, despite the suggestions by the defense. Even for that, though, Rabinowitz had already proffered an alibi. On April 30 he had told Detectives Craig and Peffall that both he and his wife had been having trouble sleeping and he had gotten a prescription for a mild sedative. He could not be blamed, could he, if Stefanie took too much?

But the autopsy had been his undoing. Looking back, Castor silently thanked Dr. Fillinger. Based on the first reports he received about Stefanie's death—if he had been the one making the decision rather than the pathologist— he probably would not have requested an autopsy, simply because police and emergency room personnel said they had no reason to suspect a homicide. If it had not been for Fillinger's inflexible rule about doing an autopsy in *every* unusual death, her murder might have gone undetected.

Castor was content to accept things as they were; the murder *had* been detected. Concerned only with Rabinowitz's prosecution, he did not give another thought as to *why* Rabinowitz thought he might have gotten away with the crime.

Charlie Craig, however, was different. Time and again, the detective asked himself what Rabinowitz must have been thinking to believe that everyone would be fooled. After turning the idea over in his mind for weeks, the investigator suddenly recalled something about a book at the Rabinowitz house that had seemed very odd. Unable to recall the title, he dug in the file until he found the photographs that had been made of the interior of the Rabinowitz house during the April 30 search. Flipping through the black and whites, he stopped when he reached one that depicted the house's only bookcase. There, among the

Reader's Digest Condensed, the Tom Clancys, and the Danielle Steels, he saw a title that was curiously out of place: *How We Die*.

Why, the investigator wondered, would a healthy man Rabinowitz's age have a book like that in his library? Was it because his father had died of cancer and his father-in-law had been diagnosed as well? Or was it something else? Finally, his curiosity got the best of him. Charlie Craig went to his local library and checked out a copy of Dr. Sherwin B. Nuland's best-seller. What the detective found was surprising. The author devoted almost two pages to death by drowning, going into extensive detail about the process and ending with the statistic that almost 5,000 people drown in the U.S. every year. There was another statistic that hit him as well: According to Nuland, autopsies are performed on only about 13 percent of the people who die of indefinite causes.

Maybe, Charlie Craig thought, Rabinowitz really *did* believe he could get away with it. Perhaps he figured that, because he was a Main Liner, with a good reputation and a well-respected lawyer wife, no one would seriously question his word. Perhaps he figured being Jewish might work in his favor, too. An autopsy might be averted altogether on religious grounds, or, if one was ordered, family pressure to have the body released quickly might result in an incomplete examination, in which case the true cause of death might not be discovered.

But the autopsy only proved that Stefanie had been strangled; it did not prove that her husband was the killer. Castor still hoped that tests done on her fingernail scrapings might reveal traces of DNA. Weeks later, however, that prospect was shattered when the lab results showed nothing in the samples to point to Rabinowitz. In any case, the prosecutor was banking on his real jewel—the hand-written ledger. Now *that* was stupid on Rabinowitz's part, Castor reckoned. Gambling on getting by without an autopsy was one thing, but chancing that investigators were not going to find the attic hiding place was another. Did Rabinowitz think the shopping bag was safe because it was well-hidden? Because police were incompetent? Because they never would have been looking if it had not been for the autopsy? Or did he simply think they wouldn't be able to figure it out?

Castor smiled to himself. Thank God for the ledger. It had been a fantastic find; absolutely astonishing in its implication. Even better, despite an oblique reference to some kind of money scam in Wednesday's *Daily News*, Rabinowitz and his lawyers almost certainly did not yet know that the material had been discovered. If they suspected something, there was no way they could grasp its importance unless Rabinowitz told them. And that was highly unlikely, given that Rabinowitz evidently did not tell them about Summer or the Tiffany women. Castor's heart had skipped a beat when he had read the *News* story that hinted at financial improprieties; he still wanted to keep the information quiet until investigators could get it all sorted out. Although it had not been confirmed, it appeared that Rabinowitz had been running a pyramid ploy, a type of fraud more commonly known as a "Ponzi scheme."

Named after its most famous perpetrator, Charles Ponzi, a diminutive Italian immigrant who got fabulously rich with the gambit in 1920s Boston, it basically centered around widespread borrowing, using funds from one source to pay another. In Ponzi's case, he claimed to be buying International Postal Union Coupons at a tremendous discount in war-torn Europe, then selling them for their full value in the United States. Contending that he needed more money with which to buy more coupons, Ponzi advertised for investors, promising huge returns. In actuality, he was using one investor's money to pay another, robbing Peter to pay Paul, as it were. Later, when the scheme came crashing down, it was learned that there were no postal coupons; Ponzi had been taking money in one door and shoveling it out another, holding onto enough to line his own pockets. Ponzi had to declare bankruptcy, was sentenced to five years in a federal prison in Massachusetts for fraud, and eventually was deported to Italy. Not long afterwards, he died penniless in the charity ward of a Brazilian hospital.

Castor figured that Rabinowitz, intentionally or not, was following Ponzi's blueprint, substituting shares in C&C Supplies for postal coupons. Not physical shares, such as those issued by IBM or General Motors, but a stake in his alleged latex glove business.

From what investigators had discovered so far, Rabinowitz used the same pitch every time. After first planting the belief among his friends that C&C's business was booming, he then went to them and said he needed ready cash to buy containers of latex gloves. Once he sold the gloves at a handsome profit, he would pay back the money along with substantial interest. Besides the money, he asked only one thing of his friends: Don't mention the arrangement to Stefanie. He was anxious to prove his skill as a businessman, he said, and he wanted to get firmly established before he told her.

What he was actually doing was using money from later "investors" to pay back earlier ones. While it worked for a while, the debt began to snowball, especially after he met Summer and began spending so extravagantly at Delilah's Den. Eventually, it was bound to catch up with him, since he had no business, therefore no hope of future income. As the months slipped by, his investors, just as Ponzi's had some three-fourths of a century earlier, began pressing him for their money. He put them off with token repayments, using money he got from fresh sources of revenue outside the group of friends who were willing to lend him money, such as Allied Mortgage. Finally, with no more revenue wells to dip into, Rabinowitz found himself in a hole he could not climb out of. What he needed was a huge infusion of cash, somewhat in excess of a quarter of a million dollars. Without such a windfall, he was in a predicament. He would either have to confess what he had been doing and throw himself upon his friends' mercy—probably losing his wife and daughter in the process—or he could find an untapped source of money large enough to allow him to pay off his considerable debt. Castor was certain that Rabinowitz had believed that source would be Stefanie's life insurance.

Although there were still a lot of holes to be filled, the prosecutors' plan was to zero in on Rabinowitz's financial juggling, developing it as the motive for the murder. But there was still a long way to go; investigators were making steady progress but there was not yet enough evidence for Castor to bring it all out in the open by charging Rabinowitz with fraud. Once he did that, the defense would know everything.

In the meantime, while investigators chased down Rabinowitz's investors, Ferman and Castor had enough to keep them busy. Foremost on their slate was the bail situation. Their strategy had been to thoroughly trash Rabinowitz's character, mainly through the filings with Judge Salus. By doing that, DeSimone and Miller would not be able to come back with any type of credible claim that Rabinowitz was the upstanding person they had originally portrayed him to be. Prosecutors reckoned that if the defense tried to argue in court that their client was an honorable, trustworthy individual, they'd look foolish.

On May 15, the media gathered in Salus's courtroom, sitting restlessly on the hard wooden benches with nothing to stare at but each other and the fading murals on the back wall that depicted scenes from Pennsylvania's past. According to local legend, when the legislature cut off funding for the paintings a number of years ago, the artist who had been living on the subsidy was so enraged that the focus of his last subsidized courtroom painting was that of a horse's butt.

As the room filled up, the lawyers filed in: Castor and Ferman, looking pleased with themselves; Miller and DeSimone, looking resolute.

As soon as everyone was present, Salus stood and beckoned them to follow. "Let's go out here for a minute," he commanded, leading the way into a nearby room normally used for jury deliberations. Taking the spot at the head of the long table, the judge motioned for the lawyers to sit. Lining up on one side, they lowered themselves stiffly into the wooden chairs—Castor on the judge's immediate right, Ferman beside him, Miller on her right, and next to him, DeSimone.

"What are you planning to do in there?" Salus asked Miller.

The defense attorney answered promptly: "Withdraw the request for bail."

Castor exhaled slowly, smothering a grin. The defense's capitulation signaled a major victory for the prosecutors. For Miller and DeSimone to have to withdraw their motion was much more humiliating than it would have been if there had been a big fight and the DA's office had won. A withdrawal represented a full-fledged retreat by the defense. There was no way Miller and DeSimone could sugarcoat it; they were being forced to surrender their once fiercely held position on Rabinowitz's good character without a shot having been fired.

On the other hand, Castor was inwardly disappointed. He had desperately wanted the media to see the prosecution's evidence so that they would inform the world about what a louse Rabinowitz was. Then maybe the Newmans and Rabinowitz's friends would understand why he had seemed so aggressive. The prosecutor still remembered the reception he had been given by Anne and Lou Newman when he and Ferman had shown up at Winding Way for the second search on May 7. Although Anne had been cool toward the detectives, she was absolutely frigid toward him. Castor reckoned it was because she blamed him personally for all the misfortune that had fallen upon her family. Later that afternoon, as soon as he had the opportunity, he pulled Lou Newman aside and suggested that he and his wife might want to hire their own lawyer rather than letting DeSimone and Miller continue to be their spokesmen. Two days later, after he learned from a reporter that the Newmans had engaged a Center City attorney named Neil Epstein, he called Epstein and made him a rare offer. If you want, Castor said, you can see what evidence we have, and what the investigators have as well, against Craig Rabinowitz. That way, Castor figured, the word would get back to the family and friends.

"Does the defendant agree with that decision?" Salus asked.

"Yes, Your Honor," Miller said, with DeSimone nodding in accord.

"Just to make sure, let's bring him in and ask him," Salus added, signaling to a bailiff to fetch Rabinowitz from the basement holding cell where he was being temporarily housed.

As soon as the bailiff was gone, Castor used the opportunity to address the judge. "Would it be convenient, Your Honor, for this court to retain jurisdiction in this case?" In other words, would Salus consent to remain as judge throughout the proceedings relating to the Rabinowitz case?

Miller and DeSimone, apparently caught by surprise, quickly concurred. "Yes, yes," Miller said hurriedly. "That would be a great idea."

Nodding slowly, the sixty-three-year-old Salus confirmed that he would.

Castor beamed, reckoning that he had racked up another huge win. "Tell you later," he whispered to Ferman when she glanced at him inquisitively.

After explaining the situation to Rabinowitz, Judge Salus asked him if he understood.

"Yes, sir."

"And you agree with it?"

"Yes, sir," Rabinowitz replied in a strong voice.

On his way out of the jury room, he ignored shouted questions from reporters, deliberately keeping his head down and his eyes on the floor so photographers would not be able to get a clear full-frontal shot. When the elevator arrived that would take him back downstairs, where he would board a van that was standing by to return him to Eagleville Prison, Rabinowitz walked quickly to the back of the cage and stood facing the rear wall so only his back would be on film.

The hearing, which had been anxiously awaited by reporters from all of Eastern Pennsylvania, was over in less than three minutes. After asking for a postponement to give them more time to collect material, and being rejected by Judge Salus, Jeffrey Miller repeated what he had already said in the jury room: that the defense was withdrawing its request for bail. But, he added, they were reserving the right to re-introduce it later. It never was.

The media filed out of the room, unhappy because there had been no tantalizing new revelations; nothing that reporters could sink their teeth into.

For the defense, it had been a demeaning experience, a time for Miller and DeSimone to eat crow after bragging about their client's sterling reputation. It was not their fault, actually, that they had been so far off course. They had been acting in good faith on what they had been told. If anyone was to blame for them being in the situation they were in, it was their client, Craig Rabinowitz.

For Rabinowitz himself, nothing was changed; he would remain locked up at least until his trial. His only ray of hope lay in the belief that his hiding place had not been discovered and that his deepest secrets remained protected.

For Castor and Ferman, the hearing had been a series of triumphs. Not only had they forced the defense into a de-grading flight, they had two unexpected bonuses as well. Before going into the jury room, Jeffrey Miller, without comment, handed Ferman a small item that investigators had been looking for for two weeks: a bottle, now empty, that once had contained thirty tablets of Ambien. It was another fortuitous find for the prosecution, not exactly on the level of the shopping bag, but nevertheless a vital piece of physical evidence, since it joined the loop they had suspected existed but had been unable to complete. They knew that Rabinowitz had obtained a prescription for the drug, and that a significant amount of the sedative had been found in Stefanie's system. But until Ferman actually clasped the bottle in her fist, it had been only a theory that Rabinowitz had actually brought the drug home to Winding Way. Now they could prove it. They had no idea where the bottle had been hidden and the defense was not obligated to tell them. It had not turned up on two searches of the Rabinowitz house, but that was immaterial. What mattered was that they had it.

While waiting for the elevator that would take them to their upstairs office, Ferman leaned close and whispered to Castor: "What was that about with Judge Salus? You looked like the cat that swallowed the canary."

Castor looked around to see who might be in earshot. "It's great for us," he said. "We couldn't have been luckier."

"How do you figure that?" Ferman asked. "Everybody in Montgomery County knows his reputation."

A balding, bespectacled, third-generation lawyer, a graduate of Cornell and the University of Pennsylvania law school, Samuel W. Salus II was known throughout Pennsylvania for his crustiness. He was, to hear the tales, an abrupt, free-speaking jurist with no patience for inefficiency and little toleration for blatant criminality.

Before taking a seat on the Common Pleas bench in 1980, Salus had been a public defender for fourteen years, a vocal spokesman for the poor. On the bench, however, he showed a different side. One of the first trials he presided over was that of well-known anti-war protestors Daniel and Philip Berrigan, two Roman Catholic priests who first leaped into the headlines during the Vietnam War. When they appeared before Salus in 1981, some dozen years after their first brush with prosecutors and judges, it was because they apparently had lost none of their fervor for spectacular demonstrations. Charged with damaging nuclear missile cones and pouring blood on documents at the General Electric plant in King of Prussia, another Montgomery County community, the brothers were among a group known collectively as the Plowshares Eight, the name coming from the Biblical admonition to beat swords into plowshares to insure peace.

It didn't take Salus long to express his contempt for their actions, commenting that he wished he could send them to "a leper colony, where they could really do some good." The Pennsylvania Supreme Court later found that Salus had been too emotionally involved in the trial to pronounce fair sentences and ordered another judge to review the case. In 1990, York County Senior Judge James Buckingham resentenced the members of the group to time already served—periods ranging from five days to 17½ months.

Salus's comments at the Berrigan trial marked the first public recognition of his predilection for brusqueness. As time went on, he built a reputation unmatched in Montgomery County. Any lawyer who appeared in his court acknowledged that he was a judge who said what he felt, not what he thought was politically correct. In 1993, while presiding at the trial of a Haitian man accused of rape and assault, the judge angrily declaimed against illegal aliens who defrauded the U.S. government. In 1995, when Salus thought a black public defender named Raymond Roberts was dawdling unnecessarily during a theft trial, he called him a Stepin Fetchit, a racially inflammatory term referring to a 1940s entertainer whose roles exemplified unfavorable stereotypes of blacks; Salus later apologized. And in 1996, apparently disturbed by the dissolution of the career of a once-promising local black athlete named Michael Simpkins, who was charged with providing cocaine to an undercover officer, Salus took it upon himself to deliver a lecture at his sentencing hearing. Too many athletes, Salus

told Simpkins, begin thinking of themselves as sports stars
rather than humans.

"You become Muhammad Alis and O.J. Simpsons and
you get cut down to your size very quickly," he said before
ordering Simpkins to serve five to ten years in prison and
pay a $30,000 fine. Salus's lecture set off a furor among
black church leaders and community activists who staged
a rally on the courthouse steps. Afterwards, Salus arranged
a meeting with the leader of the black group, apparently
hoping to hammer out an understanding. "I admit that I
am blunt, very blunt. But being blunt does not mean you
are a racist," he told the *Inquirer* after the incident.

"How do you think he's going to help us?" Ferman
persisted.

Castor put his finger to his lips, nodding toward two
approaching lawyers. "I'll tell you when we get upstairs."

"Okay," Ferman said, once they were in Castor's office.
"What's with Salus?"

"It's a *major* step forward for us," Castor grinned, peel-
ing off his jacket. "We couldn't have a better judge. Salus
and I go back a long way. I don't know how many cases
I've tried before him. We have great rapport."

"But how's that going to *help* us?"

"He *knows* me," Castor replied. "He knows he can trust
me when I say something regarding the law. He'll understand our legal points, and believe me, we're going to need
somone like that in the next few months. We won't have
to spell everything out for him."

Ferman looked slightly dubious. "I'm not sure I understand."

"Look," Castor added, plopping into his chair, "if we
had a really conservative judge, he'd be worrying all the
time about being reversed. Salus won't give it a second
thought. Some other judge, every time he would be required
to make a ruling, would feel the appeals court was looking
over his shoulder. More likely than not he'd rule in the
defense's favor if he had to make a close call because he

wouldn't want to be overturned. Salus doesn't worry about being second-guessed.''

"If having Salus for a judge is so advantageous to us, why didn't Miller and DeSimone object?"

Castor laughed. ''What the hell were they going to do? Tell the judge to his face that they didn't want him? What kind of position would that put them in if they ever had to come before him on another case? Trust me,'' he said, leaning back, ''when Salus agreed to stick with the case, it was *big*.''

THIRTEEN

Narberth
Thursday, May 22

This time Bruce Castor and Risa Ferman looked calmer, less anxious. At the bail hearing they had been tense, unsure if the paper case they had constructed to demolish Craig Rabinowitz's hyped-up reputation was sufficient to keep him in jail until he could go to trial. To Castor's disappointment, the defense had collapsed without a public fight. He had wanted a confrontation; been ready for one. But he harbored no such illusions about a possible face-off during the preliminary hearing.

Designed to make sure that a defendant is not being unjustly persecuted by an over-zealous prosecutor, a preliminary hearing is a proceeding in which the prosecutor has to prove, in open court, that there is a good reason for the charges that have been filed; that the evidence is sufficient to warrant a trial. They are virtually always all-prosecution shows. Smart defense lawyers—and Miller and DeSimone definitely fit into that category—ordinarily did not do much at preliminary hearings except ask a few questions on cross-examination and take notes about the prosecution's evidence, hoarding their ammunition and energy for the trial itself. By the same token, prosecutors tried to keep as much of their evidence as they could to themselves, exposing only what is absolutely necessary. In Pennsylvania, an indicator of the preliminary hearing's standing in the judicial scheme of things can be seen by the fact that it is conducted by a district justice—essentially was downright abrupt. Although Rabinowitz himself was there, along with his full four-man legal team—DeSimone and Miller, plus the local lawyer, Bill Honig, and Rabinowitz's long-time lawyer friend, Jeffrey Solomon, who had been sitting next to him when he made his statement to Detectives Craig and Peffall—the defense did not present any witnesses of its own. Miller's cross-examination of the prosecution witnesses also was brief, limited almost exclusively to a few questions of Officer Driscoll.

Had Rabinowitz been distraught when the policeman had arrived at Winding Way? Miller asked.

Yes, answered Driscoll.

If Rabinowitz had been visibly upset, Miller added, Stefanie's murder—*if* Rabinowitz did it, he said, emphasizing the "if"—may have been committed "in the heat of passion," therefore it was not a premeditated killing. If that was the case, the first-degree murder charge would not apply.

Rabinowitz, wearing the same dark suit and blue polka-dotted tie that he had on when he surrendered two and a half weeks earlier, sat impassively throughout the short proceeding, exhibiting only a flicker of emotion when Castor introduced a small black-and-white headshot of Stefanie taken after her death.

Outside of an effort to convince Schireson that the prosecution's evidence did not substantiate the first-degree murder charge against Rabinowitz, the defense offered little in the way of argument.

To no one's surprise, Schireson ignored the defense's suggestion and ruled that there was enough evidence that Rabinowitz strangled his wife to bring him to trial as charged, meaning the first-degree accusation would remain. An actual trial date would be set by Salus, the presiding Common Pleas judge.

Hearing Schireson's ruling, reporters began hurriedly filing out of the room, anxious to phone in their reports or prepare for stand-up tv commentaries. In their haste, they missed a development that later would lead to considerable friction between the media and the court.

As was his usual custom, Castor bundled the documents he had brought into the courtroom into a file that he planned to take back to his office for safekeeping until the trial. Never did he release documents used at a preliminary hearing to the media. In this case, though, the documents represented material that the reporters were particularly keen to get; material that Castor was just as anxious they not have, particularly the text of the autopsy report, the small collection of autopsy photos, and the text of Rabinowitz's April 30 statement.

As far as the prosecutor was concerned, the media had no business knowing the details. If all the information contained in the files were disseminated, it could threaten the forthcoming trial. Also, Castor could envision every item, including personal medical information about Stefanie that had no relation to the strangling, being hashed out in excruciating detail on the front pages of the papers, on the evening news, and in news talk shows. That possibility made Castor worry that the pool of potential jurors would be so saturated with information about the case there would be difficulty picking a panel when Rabinowitz eventually came to trial.

The defense, as well, had much to gain from keeping the documents out of reporters' hands, specifically Rabinowitz's statement. Already DeSimone and Miller were planning to ask Salus to rule that the statement not be admissible at trial on grounds that Detectives Peffall and Craig should have told their client that they knew Stefanie was murdered *before* asking him to commit himself. By not telling him about the autopsy report in advance of asking him to make a statement, the defense lawyers would argue, the investigators had violated Rabinowitz's rights, deliberately keeping from him the fact that he already was being considered a suspect.

Castor, who had no intention of turning this material over

unless he was forced, asked Schireson to formally declare the documents sealed. After the defense team concurred, Schireson agreed. Later, the district justice secured the papers in an envelope, which he turned over to Salus.

Merion
Tuesday, June 3

While all the attention was focused on Craig, Stefanie's family and friends continued to grieve quietly, out of the spotlight. On what would have been her thirtieth birthday, instead of the $3,000 party Craig had planned, Elaine Miller wrote a poem she dedicated to her friend:

> *The world forever mourn*
> *Hell unleashed its scorn*
> *A life so hallowed, pure*
> *Upon this earth no more.*
>
> *A vile wind and thus*
> *Eternal loss for us.*
> *It choked her life away*
> *Foul evil free to prey.*
>
> *Her face remains unchanged.*
> *I see it through my pain.*
> *Body live and strong,*
> *Her laugh plays like a song.*
>
> *Reality sets in*
> *In knowledge death is grim.*
> *To know I cannot see*
> *My lovely Stefanie.*
>
> *Gone the life of a friend,*
> *All reason has to end.*

To never understand
Darkness's looming hand.

Norristown
Late June

For six weeks, ever since the shopping bag was found in
the ceiling above Stefanie's closet, investigators and prosecutors had been working frantically to make sense out of
Craig Rabinowitz's finances. Risa Ferman had been on the
telephone with insurance company executives, bank officials, financiers, and lawyers. Detectives Peffall, Craig, and
Hunsicker, along with Deputy Chief Tim Woodward, had
put thousands of miles on their vehicles, racing around
Montgomery and Philadelphia Counties, talking to people
who had loaned money to Rabinowitz. Stacked in a pile in
the LMPD squad room were scores of slips of paper: credit
card statements, telephone bills, pawn tickets, promissory
notes, canceled checks, old contracts, checkbooks, receipts,
and dozens of faxes that had flown between Ardmore, Norristown, Philadelphia, and points in between. Uncounted
hours were spent checking phone calls, bank deposits and
withdrawals, credit card receipts, and sales slips.

Buried in this small mountain of paperwork were a series
of fewer than a dozen receipts that frustrated Detectives
Craig and Peffall as much as any other single factor in the
case, charges they were never fully able to explain.

When investigators first began working their way
through the documentation on Rabinowitz's ten credit
cards, they noticed a number of charges for lodging in Philadelphia, Montgomery County, and across the Delaware
River in Cherry Hill, New Jersey. Charlie Craig made a list
of the hotels and motels, putting it aside for later.

"What are these?" Woodward asked weeks afterward,
scanning the list. "What was Rabinowitz doing there? Who
was he with?"

"Don't know," replied Peffall.

"Well, find out," Woodward said, handing the list back.

Starting on May 24, 1996—some three weeks after his daughter, Haley, was born—Rabinowitz began a series of periodic visits to easily reachable hotels and motels, roughly one every three to four weeks, that continued through April 4, 1997, only twenty-five days before Stefanie was killed. In all, Rabinowitz's statements showed ten unexplained visits over the eleven-month period at a total cost of $4,100.

The first establishment to show up on his statements was a Marriott in West Conshohocken, between Merion and Norristown, only four and a half miles from Rabinowitz's house.

The next—and by far the most expensive—was the Four Seasons Hotel on Logan Square in Center City. When Rabinowitz checked in on June 6, 1996, less than two weeks after his visit to the Marriott, he didn't ask for just a room, he demanded the Presidential Suite. The most expensive room in the tony hotel—its features include a Jacuzzi, skylights, and mirrors everywhere—it rented at the time for $1,900 a night, or, in Rabinowitz's case, a day, since he checked in that morning and checked out that afternoon. His bill, including tax but excluding room service, was $1,959. In the next nine months he made two more trips to the Four Seasons: one on November 13, 1996, when he paid $499, and another on March 20, 1997, which cost only $493.

Two more of the hotels, like the Four Seasons, were repeat visits. On December 11, 1996, and again on April 4, 1997, he checked into the Adams Mark, which was only two and a half miles from his house.

Two more of the check-ins were to different hotels in the same chain: The Inn of the Dove, whose properties are specifically designed as romantic hideaways. Each features cottages—as opposed to a central building—which are tucked away behind locked gates, like an upscale condominium complex. Amenities in the cottages include a Jacuzzi, a fireplace, and a large bed surrounded by mirrors. Each also comes stocked with wine and champagne. One of the Inns Rabinowitz visited was in Northeast Philadelphia, the other in Cherry Hill.

On September 10, 1996, and again almost exactly a month later, Rabinowitz visited the Sheraton in Philadelphia's Society Hill section.

While Detectives Peffall and Craig learned from room service receipts and from talking to hotel personnel that there had been *two* people in the room on each of Rabinowitz's visits, they were never able to determine who Rabinowitz may have been entertaining. The most obvious answer, of course, was Summer, but she had denied ever meeting Rabinowitz outside the club, except for once when he took her furniture shopping. All the same, the Sheraton was within walking distance of Delilah's Den.

During their frequent trips to Philadelphia to take care of one piece of business or another relating to the Rabinowitz investigation, Detectives Craig and Peffall had fallen into a loose routine. If their duties required them to be in the city over the lunch hour, they had agreed on a dining custom. Since neither was especially fond of fast food, they focused on another type of cuisine.

Heading for the South Street section on the edge of Little Italy, Peffall would stop at a non-descript, wooden-fronted building and disappear inside, returning five minutes later with a paper bag full of hot, soft pretzels and two sodas. From there, it was only a five-minute drive to Penn's Landing, where he would pull into a parking space facing the broad Delaware River. There was a distinct advantage to the spot: It was quiet and peaceful along the riverfront; there was none of the noise and bustle of a crowded restaurant. More importantly, it was private. The detectives could talk about the case freely, discuss their morning interviews and plan the afternoon without worrying about who might be listening.

"You know, Peff," Charlie Craig said thoughtfully one afternoon, taking a bite of pretzel, "I can't quite understand these people who don't believe that Rabinowitz killed her. It's been all over the news; how Rabinowitz himself admitted—with his lawyer sitting right next to him—that there were only three people in the house that night and it was locked up tight. All this bullshit about muddy footprints and mysterious strangers—what a crock. Maybe if he had a chimney someone could have gotten in that way. But I saw those doors and windows. I *know* they had not been tampered with. Nobody else came in that house."

"It gets me, too," Peffall replied. "But I'll say this: He's cool."

"Someone asked me the other day if I thought he'd done it in a fit of passion, like the point DeSimone was trying to make when he grilled Driscoll. You know, maybe he and Stefanie had an argument and he just lost his head. I don't think that's the case at all. I think he's a cold fish. He had his mind made up to kill her, and he did."

"I agree with you all the way," Peffall replied, staring across the river. Being so close to the ocean, the Delaware rose and fell perceptibly with the tide. At that point, the tide was out and a forty-yard-wide plot of black muck stretched outward from the seawall, exposing a bottom littered with empty cans and broken bottles. A half block away, the Moshulu, a graceful sailing ship–turned–restaurant, safely moored in its scooped-out slip, bobbed on the wake of a passing vessel. An avid saltwater fisherman, Peffall felt especially comfortable along the waterfront; it was one reason he had chosen this luncheon spot. "In a way, it's ironic," he said so softly that Charlie Craig had to lean forward to hear him. "I've been thinking about this a lot. I believe he loved Stefanie. I think he really did. She was his best friend; they'd been together a long time." He paused again, listening to the squawking sea birds, debating how to continue. "But at the same time, I can see him choking her to death. I can hear him saying, 'There's nothing personal in this, Steffi. It's just business. In the end, it's going to be better for me and Haley.'"

For several minutes, neither man spoke.

"Well," Peffall sighed, draining his Coke, "that's what I think, for what it's worth. Now I guess we'd better get back to work."

"Look at that," Charlie Craig commented as Peffall pulled onto I-95. "I never noticed that before."

Peffall looked to where he was pointing. It was a huge billboard overlooking the freeway; a gigantic multi-colored advertisement for Delilah's Den.

By the third week of June, investigators had talked to everyone whose name appeared on Rabinowitz's list. All of them except two had been willing to cooperate. Rabinowitz's mother, Joyce, believed to be the "RAB" who was marked down for $85,000, and Jeffrey Solomon, whom investigators thought was the "J.S +10," both refused to talk. See our lawyers, they told Detectives Craig and Peffall.

At first it had looked like a simple task, decoding the single scrap of paper investigators and prosecutors now referred to only as "the ledger." But the more they got into it, the more complicated it became.

One of the problems was that Rabinowitz was inconsistent with the figures he had written in the second column on the "Out" side; sometimes they referred to a percentage and sometimes to a flat amount. After hours of juggling what Rabinowitz's friends had said in interviews, Ferman began to understand that when Rabinowitz, for example, had written "Kaplan . . . 51.5 . . . 40," he had not meant that he owed his friend 40 percent interest on a loan of $51,500. Rather, Rabinowitz had been reminding himself that he had promised Russ Kaplan a fee of $40,000 in addition to the $51,500 principal. In essence, Rabinowitz was planning to pay Kaplan $91,500 by September 4, 1997, a date Kaplan told Charlie Craig that they had agreed upon earlier.

Detective Craig also learned, after talking to Kaplan at length, that he had a special arrangement with Rabinowitz that went beyond the deals that Rabinowitz had made with the others. Kaplan was a sort of silent partner in C&C Supplies, a business that he believed not only existed but was highly profitable. That's why he negotiated a special fee.

By mid-April, only days before Stefanie was strangled, several of Rabinowitz's creditors were pressing him for payment. However, Stefanie's death gave him a perfect excuse to put them off still further, saying that he couldn't concentrate on business when his wife had just died. During shivah, Kaplan—who knew nothing about Craig's financial mess—pulled Rabinowitz aside and volunteered to collect C&C's accounts for him so he would not have to worry about that during the mourning period. Rabinowitz declined the offer.

Another problem was that investigators and prosecutors did not know *when* the ledger had been written. When Charlie Craig interviewed Kaplan on May 28, Kaplan told him that, on April 18, Rabinowitz had given him a check for $10,000. Since this was not reflected on the ledger, Ferman assumed it had been written before April 18. By the same token, Ira Newman, Stefanie's younger brother, said that he had given Rabinowitz an additional $4,000 on April 14. Neither was this reflected on the ledger, so that pushed back still farther the date when Rabinowitz scribbled the figures.

As they moved toward the end of June, Bruce Castor was getting nervous. So far, the defense seemed totally unaware that investigators had uncovered such a wealth of detail about Rabinowitz's alleged business; as far as he could tell they were ignorant of the massive fraud their client was involved in. Write this off, as well, to Rabinowitz not being candid with his lawyers. But the media had been sniffing around and were getting close to exposing the situation. For weeks, reporters had been hinting that there was something major brewing on the financial front, referring in almost every story to the large insurance policies and the iffy status of C&C Supplies.

Finally, Castor decided to cut it off. "We've got to quit investigating and get down to prosecuting," he told Woodward and Ferman. "Let's go with what we've got and hire an expert to try to get it all straightened out."

"We're about three-fourths of the way there," Woodward protested mildly.

"I don't care," Castor replied. "We can't drag this on forever. It's not cost-effective for us or time-effective for our case to keep going. Risa," he said, turning to his assistant, "we need to get started on a probable cause affidavit slamming Rabinowitz for theft. Use what's there. It's plenty."

On Thursday, June 26, Charlie Craig, as the lead investigator, filed an eight-page affidavit which he and Risa Ferman had labored over for a week with District Justice Schireson in Narberth, charging Rabinowitz with eight counts each of theft by deception, performing deceptive business practices, and three other fraud-related charges: theft by unlawful taking, receiving stolen property, and theft by failure to make the required disposition of funds received.

"An exhaustive search of the Rabinowitz home disclosed no evidence of any business being operated [by him]," the affidavit said. "The search failed to disclose any of the following items that I believe are normally associated with the operation of a business: names or addresses of customers, names or addresses of suppliers, accounts receivable, accounts payable, invoices, contracts, receipts, bills of lading, warehouse contracts or receipts, marketing materials, order forms, or any item that would provide evidence that Rabinowitz was buying or selling latex gloves.

"At the time of the murder of Stefanie Rabinowitz," Charlie Craig continued, "I was unable to locate any evidence that the business, C&C Supplies, was actually operating anytime between 1995 until the time of Stefanie Rabinowitz's murder."

The document went into some detail, explaining how much Rabinowitz had borrowed from whom and how much had been repaid. It listed Robert Feldman, Mark Hirtz, Alex and Brian Schwartz, Russ Kaplan, Alan Abrams of Allied Mortgage, Philip Moyer, Andrew Pauson, and his partner, Robert Malmud, as the victims of Rabinowitz's fraud—eight in all if the Pauson/Malmud partnership was counted as one.

Four of them—Feldman, Hirtz, Brian Schwartz, and Kaplan—were friends of Rabinowitz's. Mark and Brian were his last two supporters among the once-loyal group of buddies. Feldman often played cards with Rabinowitz and the others. Kaplan was a cousin of Stefanie's who had known Rabinowitz for more than a decade. As a result of trusting Craig Rabinowitz, Hirtz lost $6,000; Schwartz, $10,000, and Feldman, $39,000. The biggest loser of all was Kaplan. Over the fourteen months that he did business with Rabinowitz, he lent him a total of $119,500, of which $74,500 was repaid. That left Kaplan on the hook for $45,000, which did not include the promised fee.

Alex Schwartz, Brian's father, had simply been looking for an investment and ended up losing $15,000. Moyer and the partners, Pauson and Malmud, did not know Rabinowitz directly but C&C Supplies had been recommended to them as a good place to invest. Pauson/Malmud lost $10,000. So did Moyer. Allied Mortgage was out $88,000.

All told, as best as anyone could figure, Rabinowitz owed the group a total of $223,000.

Still, there was more. Rabinowitz also had debt other than what he owed his investors. According to the affidavit, he still owed Accubank $181,000 on his house; American Express, $33,000; the credit line at Corestates Bank,

$19,600; the Corestates credit card, $14,800; the company that financed his Volvo, $10,500; the Jefferson Bank credit card, $8,111; American Express Optima (another AE credit card), $4,538; Citibank Visa, $3,524; PECO (a utility company), $329, and Comcast Metrophone, $159—a total of $275,561.

Add the amount he owed investors to his other debt, and Rabinowitz allegedly was in the hole for $498,561.

That was according to the affidavit. *Not* listed in the document were loans from the Newmans ($42,500), Joyce Rabinowitz ($85,000 if the ledger was correct), and Jeffrey Solomon (who, according to the scrap of paper, had put up $10,000). Rabinowitz's total debt, as best could be figured at that time, probably exceeded more than two-thirds of a million dollars.

"Is that or is that not," Castor asked Woodward, "sufficient motive for murdering his wife?"

It was not as though Rabinowitz was totally without funds, however. The C&C account at PNC Bank, as of the day before Stefanie was murdered, showed a balance of $70. And Craig and Stefanie's joint account had a balance of almost $7,300, thanks to the check for $7,710 that Stefanie had received for her stock portfolio and turned over to her husband as a loan on April 28, the day before she was killed.

The affidavit was filed in the morning. By afternoon, Rabinowitz, through his lawyers, had agreed to waive a preliminary hearing and was taken immediately to Narberth, where he appeared before Schireson and pleaded not guilty to the new accusations. That meant they would be forwarded, as had the murder charges, to the Common Pleas court in Norristown.

The media, whose interest in the Rabinowitz case had not slackened in the least, jumped on the affidavit with renewed glee.

The *Daily News*'s Jim Nolan was in Narberth when Rabinowitz, after waiving a preliminary hearing on the theft accusations, was shuttled there from Eagleville Prison to make his not guilty plea. "He stumbled out of a Lower Merion police van into the sun and stifling heat, unshaven, pale and perspiring in the same gray-suit he wore to his wife's funeral," the reporter wrote. In response to a shouted question about whether he missed his daughter, Haley, Rabinowitz replied: "It breaks my heart about how much I miss her . . . I miss everybody." The headline in the next day's *News* read: " 'It breaks my heart . . .' Rabinowitz misses baby; DA says pals missing 223G."

Also according to the *News*, Rabinowitz, at Miller and DeSimone's request, had taken three polygraph tests since he was first jailed on May 5. Not surprisingly, the defense refused to confirm the report or reveal the results. Instead, Miller's comment was limited to three sentences in which Rabinowitz was said to have claimed his abiding love for Lou and Anne Newman. "He speaks very affectionately about them," Miller concluded.

Ironically, at about the same time that Rabinowitz was being transported to Narberth, his other lawyer, Frank DeSimone, was speaking at a Philadelphia Bar Association seminar entitled "TV News: Reporter, Judge and Jury."

As expected, DeSimone was heavily critical of the media, attacking reporters particularly for their lack of sensitivity when they swarmed to Winding Way while the family was still sitting shivah. "We had a dead lady, a baby and a grieving family and all we were hearing about was Summer," he was quoted in the *Inquirer* as saying. "The media made the story every night. It was important because they said it was important."

The significance of the intense media coverage, he said, in addition to being distasteful, was that it could drastically affect his client's future. What if he wanted to try to plea-bargain the case? he asked, stressing that the question was hypothetical. What effect would unrelenting coverage on *any* case have on the desire of the district attorney to prosecute to the full extent of the law?

DeSimone made one statement before the group that came as a surprise to everyone. "I asked for a gag order," he announced. "TV coverage cannot help us. I couldn't put a positive spin on the case no matter what I do."

Earlier, before the avalanche of evidence that tore apart Rabinowitz's untarnished image, Castor had been opposed to a decree that would have prohibited him from speaking publicly about the case. "Things are looking bad for us," he explained to Ferman when the issue first came up very early in the investigation. "We don't want to seal ourselves off from the opportunity to give our side of the story."

Later, after the tide turned in the prosecution's favor, Castor became a proponent of formal restraint. "Things can't get any better for us," he said to his assistant. "A gag order now will help us because it will allow us to concentrate on our case. We won't have to worry about what's being said in the media." Five days later, on July 1, Judge Salus signed an edict prohibiting investigators, potential witnesses, and lawyers from both sides from making "extrajudicial statements which might interfere with the rights of the accused to a fair trial by an impartial jury." The directive would remain in effect until the case was finished.

By the time he signed the paper forbidding just about anyone connected with the case from talking to reporters, however, Salus was involved in a bitter fight of his own with the media. On June 6, lawyers for the major news organizations in the Philadelphia area had asked the state supreme court to force the Common Pleas judge to release two of the three files that had been sealed after the preliminary hearing on May 22: the text of the autopsy report and Rabinowitz's statement.

Contending that the documents were part of the public record, since they had been entered into evidence at the preliminary hearing, the media demanded that either Salus hold a hearing on his refusal to release them, or that the supreme court go over his head and order them turned over without Salus's approval.

However, the judge stubbornly refused to bow. The documents had been entered into the record en masse, he asserted, and not with specificity. Therefore he couldn't release them individually. Besides, he averred, the autopsy *conclusion* was available, if not the entire report. As for Rabinowitz's statement, the highlights had already been published, which was sufficient since the document, seen as a whole, was an exercise in ''self-serving braggadocio'' and had no relevance to the case. Salus was referring to the part in which Rabinowitz talked about trying to seduce his wife on the night she was killed, something the judge felt didn't need to be exploited by the media. The dispute would not be settled for another three months.

FOURTEEN

Time was flying. One day and three months before, Stefanie Rabinowitz had been strangled to death in her bathtub, allegedly by her free-spending, stripper-obsessed husband. And only eight days earlier, on July 22, to the surprise of absolutely no one, a seemingly self-assured Craig Rabinowitz had appeared before Judge Salus to formally plead not guilty to all the charges against him.

For the media, the arraignment was a non-event, important only in that it gave reporters and photographers an opportunity for a rare glimpse at the jail-pale, chunky defendant. But the court appearance was significant for Castor and Ferman because it was a vivid reminder that the days were galloping by. Although a trial was still weeks or months away it was not too soon for the prosecutors to begin mapping their strategy.

There are two distinct phases in a criminal case. The first is the investigatory one, which is handled largely by the police and consists primarily of the gathering of evidence. The second is the prosecutorial one. That's where the district attorney's office assembles the material collected by investigators and begins organizing it, getting it ready to present to a jury, provided the accused does not plead guilty and the case goes to trial.

By pleading not guilty, Craig Rabinowitz was assured of the opportunity of a trial. So Castor and Ferman, who until then had played mainly passive roles, leaving the investigation to the LMPD and Tim Woodward's crew, moved to the forefront. At the same time, the investigation, which was largely complete anyway, slipped more into the background. Although Detectives Craig and Peffall would continue working on the case, largely in trying to pin down the hotel mystery, the bulk of their work was finished. On the other hand, Castor and Ferman were shifting into high gear.

An important part of pre-trial preparation, for both the prosecution and the defense, involves deciding who will be called as witnesses. To a layman, it may seem like a routine chore. But to prosecutors and defense attorneys it is an art. The right witness can make a case; the wrong one can wreck it.

Highly conscious of the necessity of carefully selecting who he would call to the stand, the perfectionist Castor had already been giving the subject considerable thought. Some people involved in the case were obvious choices. Castor was certain that he would call investigators like Tim Woodward, Mark Keenan, Charlie Craig, and Rich Peffall. Also the pathologists, Drs. Fillinger and Hood. The Newmans were on his "definite" list, along with the friends and associates whom Rabinowitz had duped out of tens of thousands of dollars. Inevitable, too, was the appearance of the forensic accountant, Ricardo Zayas. But in prosecuting, as in life, nothing was problem-free; there was one potential witness whose possible presence on the stand was causing Castor extraordinary anguish. That was Shannon Reinert, aka Summer.

Increasingly, Summer had become more of a thorn in the prosecutor's side and less of a potentially helpful witness who would willingly testify about her fling with Rabinowitz. Except for that first interview with Keenan, Peffall, and Charlie Craig on May 6, Summer had not talked again to the detectives or to the prosecutors. She had changed lawyers, replacing Brian McVan, and, with the change in legal representation, she seemed to grow more difficult. First she waffled about being a willing witness, informing Castor that she would appear only if subpoenaed. Then, much to Castor's surprise, she demanded immunity. When she said that, the prosecutor's antennae started to vibrate. What does she need immunity *from*? Castor asked himself. If she had been truthful with detectives, there was nothing to immunize. But what if she had not been entirely forthcoming? What if she had held back? If so, what was she hiding? The fact that she wanted immunity made Castor wary.

Immediately, he discarded the idea of giving her a walk. But that didn't solve the problem of what to do about her. His instincts told him she was a landmine waiting to explode.

Castor had been mulling the situation for weeks, trying to make a decision. Then one morning, halfway through his shower, it struck him. Drying and dressing quickly, he hurried to the courthouse. Grabbing his phone, he summoned Tim Woodward, his dual-purpose confidant, who was both an assistant district attorney and the deputy chief of the county detectives. Castor and Woodward had been working closely together for nine years, ever since Woodward was transferred to homicide from narcotics. Some eighteen months earlier, they had prosecuted and convicted Thomas DeBlase, the last of the participants in the murder of David Swinehart. Castor respected Woodward's opinion and legal savvy, knowing Woodward would tell him if he saw a flaw in his strategy.

"You know what I'm thinking?" Castor asked excitedly before Woodward could get comfortable.

Woodward smiled indulgently. "No idea."

"I'm thinking about Summer," he said.

Woodward raised an eyebrow. "Summer? The season or the person?"

"The person," Castor replied. "Shannon Reinert. I'm thinking we don't need her at all. As a witness, I mean."

Woodward blinked. All along it had been assumed that

Castor would use Summer as a prosecution witness at Rabinowitz's trial. After all, she had played a major role in his life; was, in fact, probably *the* major influence over him for the nine months or more before he killed his wife. She could provide details about Rabinowitz—his feelings toward his wife, for example—that would be available from no other source.

Woodward frowned. "How do you figure?"

For the next thirty minutes, Castor used Woodward as a sounding board, throwing out the pros and cons of dragging the capricious performer into the box. At best, she could be unpredictable; at worst, actively hostile.

"I've been thinking about what I would do if I were Frank DeSimone," Castor said. "And you know what I think?"

Woodward shook his head. "Haven't the faintest."

"Remember Patricia Swinehart? Terry Lee Maute? The sleazebag who DeSimone spent five hours tearing apart in his closing arguments? More importantly, remember Tom DeBlase? Remember how we agonized about calling that dirtball prison mate of his? At the last minute we decided we didn't need him because he might harm us more than he could help us. We decided that calling him was just too much of a risk. Well, I feel this way about Reinert. She makes me nervous as hell. She could ruin everything."

"What about DeSimone?" Woodward asked.

"I *know* him," Castor said with a tight smile. "I know how he thinks. He's going to see Reinert as the vehicle he can use to sabotage our case. If I were DeSimone, I'd blame Stefanie's murder on Reinert. I'd say that she drove Rabinowitz to strangle his wife."

"How would he do that? What's the connection?"

"The phone call!"

"The one on the night Stefanie was murdered?"

"Absolutely!"

"But we don't know if Rabinowitz ever got that message."

"That's the point!" Castor shot back. "Reinert will say she called and left a message. The defense doesn't have to prove that Rabinowitz got it. What if DeSimone argues that Stefanie, not her husband, picked it up? If I were Frank DeSimone, I'd say the message was the key to Stefanie's death; it was the trigger that sent her into a rage. I'd try to convince the jury that she and Rabinowitz had a huge argument, that she threatened to leave and take the baby. So Rabinowitz says, 'You're never going to take *my* baby!' and he grabs her by the throat and chokes her. Then he tries to cover it up by passing it off as a drowning." The prosecutor paused, studying Woodward. "Does that make sense?"

"Yeahhhh," Woodward replied slowly. "But . . ."

"If DeSimone can get that to fly with the jury, it knocks the hell out of our premeditation argument."

"He still *strangles* her . . ."

"That's true. Strangulation is a damn good argument for premeditation because it's such a lengthy process. But by then the situation has changed. Suddenly, we've gone from first-degree to voluntary manslaughter. Rabinowitz isn't such a cold-blooded s.o.b. anymore; he's an angry man trying to keep an irrational, jealous woman from taking the thing he loves most in the world—his child, his baby daughter. DeSimone could fucking wring that for sympathy like you wouldn't believe."

"Okay," Woodward said, rising. "I see what you're saying," he continued, pacing in a tight circle in front of Castor's desk, the bright sunshine streaming in from the windows on the left side of the room throwing alternating halves of his face into deep shadow. "I think you're probably right about DeSimone. But *Summer* . . ."

"No! No!" Castor interrupted. "You don't see my point. We don't *need* her! There's no benefit to us to have Reinert testify. She could be devastating to our case."

Woodward stopped pacing and stared at his boss.

"Listen," Castor said excitedly. "What's she gonna say?

Rabinowitz had a thing for her? We've got other dancers who'll say that. He spent a lot of money on her? We have the credit card statements. He bought her furniture? We have the receipts. He spent a lot of time with her? Half the people at Delilah's will testify that's true. What she has *never* said is that Rabinowitz was going to leave his wife for her; that he was interested in marrying her. So we're not going to get that out of her. The way I see it, we aren't going to get *anything* from her that we can't get from somebody else.''

"By God, you're right," Woodward grinned. "I just never looked at it that way before."

"Hang on," Castor said, raising his hand. "I'm not through."

Woodward returned to his chair. Crossing his legs, he looked expectantly at the prosecutor.

"This is where I want to get cagey," Castor said with a hollow laugh. "Like I said, I *know* DeSimone. If he thinks we're going to call Reinert he'll spend *days* preparing to cross-examine her."

"Yeah," Woodward nodded. "You're right about that."

"So," Castor grinned, "what if we can fool Miller and DeSimone into thinking we're going to call her and then we don't? All that time that DeSimone put in on his prep not only will have been wasted, but it benefitted us because it was time he could have been spending on something else. If we're lucky, he and Miller will tie their defense to her. If they make a connection in their opening statement, then we can go back and say they promised but didn't deliver. It'll make them look like fools."

Woodward grinned. "I love it."

"Great!" Castor said, slapping his hand on the desk. "Let's go ahead and subpoena Reinert. That way, we can always use her if we decide we want to. Only we figure we're not going to call her unless it's an emergency. That puts the burden on Miller and DeSimone. If they want to call her as one of their witnesses, that's great. Then *we* get to cross. We'll tear her ass apart. Since we're the only ones who can grant immunity, she might be scared shitless about testifying about something that's going to result in charges against *her*. Let her be a timebomb for the defense instead of us. If we ask her something she doesn't want to answer, her only option will be to take the Fifth. If she has information the defense feels it needs, their only choice will be to put Rabinowitz on the stand. And you *know* they don't want to do that; there's no way they want us to cross-examine him. Plus, by not calling her we'll throw 'em off-balance. They'll be scrambling.''

"I think it'd work," Woodward said, laughing, getting into the spirit of the plan. "What does Risa think?"

"I don't know," Castor said, reaching for his phone. "Let's ask her."

Ferman was as excited about the idea as Woodward. "It's been bothering me, too; how we'd handle her," Ferman confessed. "This sounds like a perfect solution. I'd say let's do it."

To Castor's surprise, the main opposition came from Mike Marino.

"Have you gone crazy?" the DA asked, horror-struck. "You *have* to call Summer."

"What do you mean?"

"The press is expecting her," Marino said. "The jury is going to be expecting her. *Everybody*'s going to be expecting her."

"That's exactly my point," Castor argued.

"I still think you ought to call her," Marino said solemnly.

"Oh, fuck, Mike," Castor sighed. "Are you *telling* me to call her?"

"No," Marino said, shaking his head. "I'm not going to tell you how to do your job. It's your case. You handle it. And," he added, after a pause, "that's all I'm going to say about it."

What Marino did not say—what he did not need to say—was, "you have to live with the consequences."

While it had been apparent from the beginning that motive was going to be particularly important at Craig Rabinowitz's trial, it was becoming more so as the date got closer and no physical evidence surfaced to tie him directly to Stefanie's murder.

Presenting an entirely circumstantial case was always a dicey undertaking for any prosecutor. It was not unlike building a house of matchsticks; one unexpected bump and everything could come tumbling down. In the Rabinowitz situation, prosecutors would have to make sure that all the parts fit together into a solid whole; they would need an argument constructed of Lincoln Logs instead of Diamond brand matches.

Complicating their quest for a first-degree murder conviction was the fact that they had nothing tangible—no gun, smoking or otherwise—to present to a jury. To win a conviction, Castor and Ferman would have to convince jurors of their hypothesis that it was Rabinowitz's precarious financial position that led directly to Stefanie's murder; that the only way he could see to free himself of debt was to collect on her life insurance, which, in turn, meant throttling her to death. Under that scenario, her murder would have been premeditated. If it was not premeditated, it was not first-degree. And if it was not first-degree, Rabinowitz conceivably could one day be back on the street.

But this was where it got tricky for the prosecution. Ferman and Castor were convinced that their theory was highly viable; it was the only explanation for Stefanie's murder that made sense. However, for the prosecutors to get their thesis before the jury they would have to present evidence dealing simultaneously with Rabinowitz's finances and his wife's death. Technically, under Pennsylvania law, the prosecution could simply declare that all the charges were connected and announce to Judge Salus that they planned only one trial. This would position them to ask the jury to convict Rabinowitz of first-degree murder.

But it was not so easy as that. Pennsylvania law also allowed the defense to object to a one-trial plan. DeSimone and Miller could file a formal request asking Salus to sever the two cases, make the prosecution hold not one trial, but two—one on the fraud charges, the other for the murder. If the defense made such a request, Salus would have to decide.

Castor and Ferman never doubted that the defense would challenge their attempt to force a single trial. They would claim, Castor was sure, that the fraud and the murder were unrelated issues, neither of which had anything to do with the other. Their argument would be this: Allegedly, Rabinowitz was a thief. Allegedly, he was a murderer. But being a thief did not mean, *ipso facto*, that he was also a killer, although that would be the implication if he were tried on both charges at the same time.

DeSimone and Miller, Castor knew, would do whatever they could to prevent prosecutors from having the opportunity to explain to a jury the connection between Rabinowitz's debt and his wife's strangulation. If they could convince Judge Salus to order separate trials, it would be a major victory for them and Rabinowitz. On the other hand, if the prosecution prevailed and there was only one trial, Castor and Ferman would have a huge advantage.

Conversely, if the defense lost the one-trial/two-trials campaign, the situation would look bad for Rabinowitz. And if the prosecution lost, Ferman and Castor could wave good-bye to any chance for a conviction on first-degree murder.

Viewed in that light, the almost certain battle between the prosecution and the defense over whether Rabinowitz would face two juries or one would be the most significant legal fight to date, second in importance only to the actual trial or trials.

Castor had set the wheels in motion for the showdown

on July 3, a week after filing the fraud charges, when he
formally notified Judge Salus of his aim to try Rabinowitz
for fraud and murder before the same jury. On August 1,
DeSimone and Miller filed a brief opposing the prosecution's plan for consolidation, asking Judge Salus instead to
decree that there be separate trials. Salus told both sides to
appear in his court to argue their positions.

Norristown
Wednesday, August 20

The prosecutors were tense going into Judge Salus's courtroom to present their case for a single trial for Rabinowitz.
At the bail hearing, the defense team had no chance and
both sides knew it. By the same token, at the preliminary
hearing the odds were stacked overwhelmingly in the prosecution's favor. But the hearing on the Motion to Sever
was another story. Castor and Ferman knew that DeSimone
and Miller were too good at their business not to have thoroughly researched the matter; their arguments would be
strong and persuasive. It didn't matter that DeSimone was
on vacation. Miller was a skilled orator and an astute lawyer; his legal arguments would be on the money.

Going in, Castor knew that if he and Ferman were going
to be able to convince Salus, they would have to be sharp
on several somewhat ambiguous points of law. For days,
they had been researching and discussing their strategy,
boning up on past cases that might apply so they would be
ready to counter Miller's contentions. Ferman had handled
another case with similar issues not long before, so she felt
she was on top of the matter. She and Castor had heatedly
discussed putting their points in the form of a brief they
could present to the judge. Ferman had argued in favor of
a written document, but Castor had decided it wasn't necessary. For one thing, the prosecutor felt that his history
with the judge gave him and Ferman a slight edge. It was

not that Salus did not trust or respect Miller, it was just that he had not dealt with him as much as he had with Castor.

The prosecutors had no sooner settled into their chairs than Miller rose and cleared his throat. Because opposing lawyers rarely address each other directly in the courtroom, Miller directed his remarks to Judge Salus.

"Your Honor, I would inquire of the prosecution, if they have an extra copy of their brief. If they do, I'd be obliged to see it. For some reason, we never received it."

Castor's jaw dropped. "What the hell's he talking about?" he whispered to Ferman.

"I don't know."

"I asked both sides to submit briefs," Salus interjected. "Didn't you get my order?"

Castor looked at Ferman, who shook her head. We should have done the damn brief, she thought.

"The order must have gotten lost or misdirected," Castor said, reddening.

"Well," Salus said, "let's just go ahead and see what we can do with what we've got. It's your motion," he said to Miller. "You start off."

The defense attorney wasted little time getting to the heart of the dispute. If the jury were to be allowed to see a prosecution-painted picture of Craig Rabinowitz as both a thief and a killer, it would be highly prejudicial to his client, he argued. Since the jury was to be required to view both issues, they undoubtedly would form an opinion of Rabinowitz as an "evil" person, especially after the prosecution finished describing him as someone who would steal even from his wife's parents. "If," Miller said, warming to the subject, "you say to a jury, 'Hey, folks, guess what? This same man also defrauded a bunch of people out of a bunch of money,' then the prosecution calls the murdered woman's parents as witnesses, and they get up and testify with tears in their eyes," that was prejudice, Miller averred. "By that time, the jury is thinking of the defendant as a reprehensible person. They would be unable to separate the accusations in their minds. As a result, they would be, in my opinion, ten times more likely to convict him of both crimes simply because they would think of him as 'bad.' ''

Salus made a few notes on the pad in front of him, then nodded at the prosecution.

Castor nudged Ferman. ''You're up.''

She stood and squared her shoulders. Even though she was standing, her head was barely above Castor's.

For jurors to get a true picture of *why* the murder occurred, she began carefully, it is necessary to understand how one crime, the theft, led to the other, the murder. ''The defense,'' she continued, glancing quickly at Miller, ''doesn't want us to be able to explain the 'why.' They want the jury to see a rosy picture of a perfect marriage and an unexplained killing.''

Rabinowitz's downfall, she went on to say, began when he started borrowing from his friends under the guise of investing in a company that did not exist. This indebtedness, she explained, was what led Rabinowitz to murder his wife.

Salus shook his head. ''I don't see that I want every debt or credit pounded out in a homicide trial,'' he said, eliciting groans from the prosecutors.

''These are not two crimes that should be tried separately,'' Ferman argued with as much passion as she could muster. ''One is the continuation of the other. These were a series of events that culminated in a capstone of murder.''

Looking at Salus, Castor knew he and Ferman were in trouble. The judge's lips were compressed and his jaw was clenched.

Castor waited until the judge finished scribbling on his pad. ''Your Honor,'' he said, rising, intent on trying to rescue what was left of the prosecution's chances, ''may I respectfully ask that you take the matter under advisement and give us a chance to write a brief?''

Salus did not reply immediately. He was under no obligation to grant the prosecutor's request; he had ordered that written arguments be prepared in advance of the hearing and if the prosecution had somehow misplaced his directive, it was not his problem. On the other hand, to agree to the request would be the courteous thing to do. While he could easily refuse, it would be rude. "Have it in to me by Monday," he said curtly, signaling that the session was over.

"Fuck!" Castor said with feeling once he and Ferman were back in his office. "That did not go well *at all*. We're in deep trouble. Salus was telegraphing to us that he's going to rule in the defense's favor. He couldn't have made it much clearer."

"You think it's that bad?" Ferman asked with a worried frown.

"Oh, yeah," Castor nodded. "Absolutely. It's that bad. We're lucky he didn't turn us down flat today and rule immediately for the defense. I'm *sure* that's the way he's leaning."

"But he *did* give us a chance to file a brief," Ferman pointed out.

"He's humoring us," Castor said, sounding despondent. "He did everything but tell us he's going with Miller and DeSimone. But," he added briskly, struggling to look on the bright side, "that doesn't mean we're going to give up. We have five days to get the brief together. And it has to be damn good. If we don't turn the judge around, we're dead. We could lose everything before we can even present our case to a jury."

Ferman sighed. "There goes the weekend."

"Tell me about it," Castor replied sourly. "Sunday's my wife's birthday. She's not going to be very happy about it, either."

Judge Salus was walking across the courthouse parking garage, his footsteps echoing off the concrete, when a man called to him.

"Hey, Skip," a fellow judge said in greeting. "How's it going?"

Salus looked up. "Hey," he replied. "Not bad."

"You look distracted. Another hard day?"

Salus managed a tight smile. "You know how it is. Some decisions are really tough."

The other judge nodded sympathetically. "That's why we make the big bucks. What is it? That Rabinowitz thing?"

"Yeah," Salus said. "The motion to sever."

"Oh. No wonder you look worried. I'm glad it's you and not me. It's a touchy one."

" 'Touchy' doesn't come close to describing it."

"That bad, huh? I gather you haven't made a decision."

"Not yet," said Salus, "but I'm definitely leaning toward severing it. Bruce is drawing up a brief, but he and Risa are going to have a hard sell. I think he's over-exaggerating its importance. I'm trying to keep an open mind, but the defense has a damn good argument."

"I don't envy you the decision," the second judge clucked. "Here's my car. Good luck."

"Thanks," Salus replied absently. "I'll need it."

FIFTEEN

By late in the day, Castor and Ferman were feeling considerably better about their chances of swinging Judge Salus over to their one-trial scenario. Working right up to the deadline—with Ferman drafting the basic document and Castor serving as editor—they completed a 24-page brief that they felt cogently summed up their position.

"Let's go through it one more time. This may be the last shot we have," Castor said, placing the document squarely in the center of his large mahogany desk. Leaning over, bracing himself with his elbows, he began reading: " '...*From November 1995 until April 29, 1997, Craig Rabinowitz deceived friends and family into thinking he operated a latex glove business. In fact, Rabinowitz converted money invested by these people to finance a lavish lifestyle, showering gifts on a stripper while maintaining a covert identity to fool those closest to him...,*' blah, blah, blah. Here we go. Here's something to catch their attention. The media'll eat it up. " '...*His debt had become so staggering that only two options were open to him: he could tell his wife, friends, and family that his whole life—as of that time—was a fraud, or he could murder his wife to collect approximately two million dollars in life insurance. The second of these options carried with it the added benefit that he would then be free to live out a fantasy come true, a life with a beautiful exotic dancer nicknamed "Summer." ' "*

"Great!" Ferman grinned, quickly turning pages. "Here's another good point:

' *. . . Because the progression of events leading up to the defendant's decision to commit murder provides a clearly understandable motive for the killing, the defense wants the theft charges severed from the murder charges. The defense reasons—correctly—that a jury will more easily be able to understand that this was a wilful, premeditated killing with malice if they are told of the events leading up to the killing . . .* ' That 'correctly' ought to get 'em." She paused, taking a breath, then continued: " ' *. . . The defense, admittedly, does not state its position so succinctly . . .* ' "

Castor smiled. "That'll piss 'em off, won't it?"

They read quietly for several minutes. "How's this sound?" Castor asked. " ' *. . . The Commonwealth believes that the defendant's illegally acquired debt is a significant portion of his motive for killing his wife. In order to fully establish the defendant's motive for murder, the Commonwealth needs to introduce all of the evidence of the fraudulent business transactions which put the defendant into debt and ultimately led up to the killing . . .* ' "

"Sounds good to me," Ferman replied.

"We can't simply show that Rabinowitz was in debt when he strangled his wife," Castor said. "We have to demonstrate to Salus that the nature of his debt—who he owed money to and why—formed the basis for motive to murder. Everyone who's in debt doesn't go out and strangle his wife, which is what Salus was saying the other day. He hasn't grasped our point: Rabinowitz killed Stefanie because it was the only way he could see to get money to pay off his loans and continue his lifestyle, therefore his debt led directly to the murder."

Ferman nodded. "Here you go. This is where we emphasize that we couldn't find any other instance of a judge refusing to join cases in which the prosecution wanted to use one crime to prove motive for a second crime: '... *Similarly, the Commonwealth has found no case* ...' We have to make sure the judge understands *no case*, '... *where a conviction was overturned on the basis of an improper consolidation when one crime forms part of the motive for the principal crime. There simply is no precedent supporting what the defense here asks of the court* ...' That should make it pretty clear.''

"It sounds really good," said Castor. "But we have to be very positive about our purpose. I think this does it: '... *The Commonwealth will prove*,' " he read, verbally underlining *prove*, " '*that the murder of Stefanie Rabinowitz was partially the result of a long series of criminal acts that drove the defendant into a desperate financial situation from which he needed to escape without revealing the fraud of his business activities* ...' "

"You know what still bothers me a little bit?" asked Ferman.

"What's that?"

"This 'heat of passion' thing. You think that's going to be their defense?"

Castor shrugged. "Who knows? But we mention it ..." he flipped more pages "... right here: '... *The evidence will prove that when he strangled his wife it was an intentional, premeditated, reasoned action designed to achieve a particular purpose: to collect money. It was not an accidental killing in the heat of passion or under the slightest bit of provocation* ...' "

"Remember that 'evil' stuff?" Ferman asked. "How Miller argued that a jury made to listen to the theft accusations during a murder trial would be likely to convict Rabinowitz of murder simply because the theft allegations made him out to be an 'evil' person? Don't you think this covers it? " '... *The jury is not being asked to conclude that this defendant is an evil person, but rather, they will be asked to conclude that he possessed legal malice in his heart when he killed his wife* ...' Just in case, we've also added the definition of legal malice: ' ... *It is an intent to kill or inflict serious bodily injury, wickedness of disposition, hardness of heart, cruelty, recklessness of consequences, a mind regardless of social duty and an extreme indifference to the value of human life* ...' "

"And," Castor added, grinning, "we've tossed in a final jab at the defense. If they weren't pissed off before, they will be now: " ' ... *The Commonwealth believes that all these efforts on the part of the defense are designed to sanitize the trial and remove as much evidence of motive and intent as possible,*' " he paused. " ' ... *This is a blatant attempt to hide the truth from the jury by shielding them from relevant evidence that would explain the defendant's conduct. While the defense will try to remove the motive and intent evidence from the case, this court should not support such efforts, as the evidence is relevant, admissible, material, and necessary to the Commonwealth's case* ...' "

Ferman chuckled. "No doubt about it. This is hardball."

For several seconds, neither of them spoke. "What do you think?" Ferman asked nervously, breaking the silence. "Honestly?"

"Honestly," Castor laughed, "I think it's a slam-dunk. How can the judge not be convinced? This is a damn good brief. It not only points out the fallacies of the defense arguments, it also outlines fully and publicly for the first time how we think this crime went down." The prosecutor tapped the document. "Let's get this filed first thing in the morning. Unless I'm reading Salus all wrong, I think this is going to do it."

"The defense still has the chance to respond ..." Ferman began.

"Doesn't matter," Castor said confidently. "They can say what they want. Salus is going to *love* this. I'm sure of it."

*   *   *

Two days later, Jeffrey Miller filed the defense's reply.

Apparently stung by the prosecution's remarks, Miller contended that Ferman and Castor, by asserting that homicide evidence should be admitted in a fraud trial, "demonstrate the frustration of the District Attorney's Office in trying to force a round peg into a square hole."

He also contradicted the prosecution's claim that Rabinowitz's alleged theft was part and parcel of the murder. While conceding that some crimes, such as threatening a witness who was subsequently killed, or securing a pistol before shooting someone to death, might be linked, this logic did not follow in the Rabinowitz case, where the crimes occurred at different times and involved different people. One, the defense said, was a crime of deceit, while the other was a crime of violence.

The defense attorney also introduced a new element. Not only would Rabinowitz be deprived of a fair trial if the two charges were to be tied together, but it would have a "chilling effect" on his right to testify. If he took the stand to defend himself against theft, for example, he would be exposing himself to increased risk on the murder charge, and vice versa. It would create a Catch-22 for Rabinowitz, Miller argued. "A defendant should not have to make such a choice in the defense of a serious criminal charge such as first-degree murder."

If there was only one trial, there were other dangers involved as well, said Miller. Among them was the likelihood that the appeals process would be unduly complicated; another was that the jury might decide that Rabinowitz was guilty simply because of the weight of the combined charges, while they might not think him guilty if he were to be tried on the charges separately. But most importantly, Miller said ominously, was the fact that Rabinowitz "may be prejudiced" if the accusations were consolidated, a flag notifying Judge Salus of a possible point on appeal.

*   *   *

On August 29, nine days after the first hearing, Salus ruled in favor of the prosecution. In explaining his decision, Salus repeated the cases listed by Ferman and Castor in their brief, adding, "... All [the cases] indicate that evidence from the theft case is generally admissible in the homicide case where it tends to establish motive, intent, malice, premeditation, mistake, or accident, commission of the crime, or where it was a culmination or the end result of a chain or sequence of events which formed the history of the case ..."

Stripping away the legalese, Salus was saying that similar cases in the past had been consolidated and as far as he was concerned, this one would be as well.

When he read his decision in court, Castor and Ferman looked at each other and grinned. "I told you!" Castor whispered in exhilaration, resisting the urge to shout. "Didn't I tell you?"

Salus softened the blow slightly for the defense by promising to remind the jury during the trial not to jump to conclusions about Rabinowitz's guilt based on the fact that he did some not-so-nice things, such as running around with an exotic dancer behind his wife's back, or maybe cheating his friends and family out of tens of thousands of dollars.

"The prejudice of trying the cases together will be minimalized by these cautionary instructions indicating that the commission of one crime is no indication of the commission of another, nor is the evidence introduced to establish that defendant is of bad character or is a bad person," Salus said in his written order.

But no matter how much the judge tried to pillow the shock for the defense, he was unable to camouflage the reality: It was a major victory for Castor and Ferman; a major defeat for DeSimone and Miller. Come October 27, which was the tentative date for the start of the trial, the prosecutors would be able to line up a long string of witnesses to testify about every aspect of Rabinowitz's distasteful past, from his relentless scrounging of money to his shameless philandering. Nothing would be off limits for the prosecution, there would be no dark corners into which they would not be able to probe.

Norristown
Tuesday, September 2

Although news coverage had dropped markedly in the past weeks, the reason was Judge Salus's July 1 gag order and not media disinterest in the case. With everyone involved in the case prohibited from talking, the flow of available information was reduced to a trickle. However, as an indicator of how strongly reporters and their bosses felt about the ongoing drama, they still were trying to force the judge to release the files that had been sealed after the preliminary hearing in May: the full autopsy report and the text of Rabinowitz's April 30 statement to Detectives Peffall and Craig.

Although it had been just four days shy of three months since lawyers representing virtually every major news outlet in Philadelphia, both print and broadcast, had first filed suit in an attempt to force Salus to unlock the documents, there had not yet been a hearing on the issue. That was because the media got impatient and tried to go over Salus's head, appealing directly to the state supreme court. Seemingly trying to prove it was impervious to such pressure, the high court sat on the request for weeks, stymieing media attempts to bring the question to a head.

Finally, the suit had come back to Salus. But just because he scheduled the long-sought hearing didn't mean he was ready to rule.

Spectators in the packed courtroom, mostly reporters, were treated to a rare sight: For the first time in the Rabinowitz proceedings, DeSimone and Miller sat alongside Ferman and Castor, since both sides, along with Neil Epstein, were united in their agreement that the documents should not be unsealed. Across the aisle, at the plaintiff's table, was the media lawyer, Samuel Klein.

Speaking first, Klein demanded release of the documents, insisting that they were part of the public record and were entitled to be perused by reporters.

One-by-one the Rabinowitz-case lawyers offered their arguments in opposition. The law did not require their release, said Rabinowitz's lawyers. If the media had full access to the documents, it would damage Rabinowitz's right to a fair trial, said the prosecutors. And to turn them over to reporters would result in an invasion of the family's privacy, said Epstein, who was aware that the autopsy report contained information about a pre-existing medical condition from which Stefanie suffered, one that was totally unrelated to her death.

When all the lawyers had finished, it was Salus's turn. With his eyes flashing angrily, the outspoken judge launched into a bitter attack on the local media, accusing reporters of muckraking and practicing a brand of sensationalism not seen in the area since the mid-Eighties bombing attack on a Philadelphia compound occupied by a radical group called MOVE, which was the most publicized incident in modern local history. "We've seen over the weekend what extensive, dogging, sensational media pursuit does to the lives of people," Salus growled, referring to the car accident in Paris that killed Princess Diana and Dodi Al Fayed.

In the first place, he declared, the records were not *trial* evidence, but only documents filed by the prosecution in an attempt to prove that there was sufficient reason to justify the filing of murder charges against Rabinowitz. "I certainly don't in any way feel it is a matter of public record for scrutiny by the press until it becomes a matter of evidence at the public trial," he insisted. There was "no way" he was going to release the documents, he added.

Klein jumped to his feet. "All we're asking," he implored, "is that the public be afforded the same opportunity to see the evidence that the district attorney saw."

Salus shook his head vigorously. "The press has got to come to grips with this exploitation, when the right to a fair trial runs headlong into the rights of a free press," he replied, adding that he was seriously worried about whether Rabinowitz could receive a fair trial in Montgomery County, considering the volume of print and air time devoted to the case. "I'm very concerned," Salus said, "that we may find it difficult to pick a jury."

It was the first hint that the judge was considering moving the trial elsewhere.

While the hour-long hearing itself ended inconclusively, it triggered another event that would have a profound effect on Rabinowitz's trial. Less than a week later, on September 8, DeSimone and Miller filed two motions with Salus.

One asked the judge to prohibit the trial jury from having full access to Rabinowitz's April 30 statement on grounds that detectives did not tell him that he was a suspect, or that they knew his wife had been murdered, when they asked him to come to LMPD to give his version of events on the night she died.

The other motion, which should have been no surprise considering Salus's earlier comments during the document hearing, asked Salus either to move the trial out of Montgomery County—a change of venue—or bring in a jury from some distant county to hear the case—a change of venire.

Somewhat surprisingly, the prosecution readily agreed to a change of venire. Almost a year and a half earlier, Castor had agreed to a similar request in the trial of Caleb Fairley, again because of extensive pre-trial publicity. Court historians were unable to find a previous example. The closest they could come was a change of venue, which was granted in a case more than thirty years before.

"Why did you go along so readily?" Ferman asked.

"The judge was going to order it anyway," Castor explained. "We don't want to look like obstructionists."

Ferman looked at him closely. After weeks of working together, she was beginning to understand him better. "Are those the only reasons?"

Castor grinned. "No," he admitted. "I figure the defense just shot themselves in the foot. Wherever the trial goes, or wherever a jury is picked, the jurors are going to be more conservative and even more pro-law than any panel that could be picked here. For us, it's a win–win situation."

His prediction that a county more conservative than Montgomery would be chosen proved correct. Two weeks later, the Pennsylvania Supreme Court, which makes such decisions, selected Westmoreland County in the western part of the state, near Pittsburgh. A rural county with a population a little more than half that of Montgomery, Westmoreland—county seat, Greensburg—was a Nineteenth Century coal mining center whose current best-known industry was the company that produced Rolling Rock beer. Among those who called Westmoreland County home were golf great Arnold Palmer and the tv personality Mr. Rogers.

While he did not oppose the change of venire motion, Castor remained adamantly against the attempt by the defense to suppress Rabinowitz's statement during trial. "I want the whole world to see what an arrogant son of a bitch he really is," the prosecutor explained.

Norristown
Wednesday, September 10

With the trial only six weeks away, the pressure was beginning to build, especially on Ferman, whose task it was going to be to explain Rabinowitz's complicated financial dealings to the jury. Ricardo Zayas was still working on his analysis. When he turned in his final report it would be almost a half-inch thick and seventy pages long. But Ferman couldn't wait for the forensic accountant to finish; there was too much to be done.

Even at this late date there was still only one piece of physical evidence tying Rabinowitz to his wife's murder: the ledger. Its significance could not be overemphasized. It represented, in Rabinowitz's own handwriting, his motive for wanting to kill his wife. It was also the all-important link between the fraud and the murder, a connection that prosecutors would have to prove if they hoped to get the first-degree conviction.

But before Ferman could introduce it into evidence and ask a jury to weigh its importance, she and Castor would have to be able to account for every single notation. And this was where they had run into a stone wall. The figures on the scrap of paper were not as unambiguous as the prosecutors would have liked; the ledger, they had learned, could not be taken too literally.

While investigators were interviewing Rabinowitz's investors—that is, checking out the figures on the left side of the ledger, the "Out" column—Ferman had been working on the figures that Rabinowitz had jotted down on the right, or "In," side. The numbers, she found, were close but not bookkeeper-absolute. While she already had confirmed that the amount of insurance Rabinowitz apparently would have received was $1,870,000—and that coincided perfectly with Rabinowitz's jottings—some of the other numbers varied slightly from what he had written down.

After talking to Anne Newman, Ferman learned that the "STOCK 7,500" notation represented a check for $7,711 that Stefanie had received from the sale of her stock portfolio and turned over to Rabinowitz on April 28. Rabinowitz probably had not been able to list the exact amount because when he wrote the ledger—Zayas had tentatively set the date as April 13, based on what was and was not included—he did not know what it would be. "Car 6,000," Ferman determined, represented what Rabinowitz thought he could get for the Volvo if he decided to sell it. It was an arbitrary figure, but probably accurate. The total, then, that Rabinowitz expected to receive after Stefanie's death was $1,883,500, which Ferman reckoned was very close.

Not quite as exact was the amount that Rabinowitz figured he would have left after subtracting his estimated debts from his estimated income. That was because the debt figures—which Rabinowitz listed on the ledger at $671,000—were not precise. But assuming they were in the ballpark, Rabinowitz planned to have $1,212,500 left over after paying off everything he owed. He signified the importance of the figure by circling it.

It was clear to Ferman that Rabinowitz was using that as the base amount. To be added to it was $270,000, which he reckoned he could get if he sold the house ("House 270,000") that he had purchased for $230,000. Therefore, Rabinowitz's final estimation of what he would receive if Stefanie was dead was $1,482,500, which also was circled.

What puzzled Ferman for quite awhile were the three figures on the very bottom of the piece of paper: "*$1,000,000* [which was underlined] . . . 6600/MO/ . . . 6875/MO/."

Zayas came to her rescue. As a Certified Public Accountant, a Certified Fraud Examiner and a former special agent for both the IRS and the U.S. Department of Labor, he was a man who knew how to unravel a financial tangle. Those figures, he explained to prosecutors, represented what Rabinowitz reckoned he would earn if he invested $1 million of the $1.48 million. If the investment paid 8 percent, he would make $6,600 a month; if it paid 8.25 percent, he would clear $6,875 a month.

Still, there was a hole in Ferman's presentation. And it was not something that Zayas would be able to help her with. In order for prosecutors to be able to use the ledger as part of its case, they would have to be able to explain every single figure that Rabinowitz had written. And, as of early September, there were two notations they could not back up with testimony: "RAB 85" and the circled "+10 J.S."

Although they felt certain that the "RAB" referred to Joyce Rabinowitz, and the "J.S." alluded to Jeffrey Solomon, both Mrs. Rabinowitz and Solomon continued to refuse to talk to investigators.

Facing an approaching deadline and confronting an enduring reluctance to testify from Solomon and Mrs. Rabinowitz, Castor used his last card: He subpoenaed them to appear before a Montgomery County grand jury, hoping that would push them into agreeing to testify. It worked. Although what happens before a grand jury is secret, Castor explained to Mike Marino afterward that he had won an agreement from Solomon to take the stand and confirm that he had loaned Rabinowitz $10,000 as an investment in his latex glove business. However, since Castor was reluctant to call Joyce Rabinowitz to testify against her son, he worked out an arrangement with Rabinowitz's attorneys where both sides would agree to stipulate that the "RAB 85" notation represented a loan of $85,000 from Joyce to Craig.

While the grand jury appearance solved one problem for prosecutors, it opened the door to two others.

The most immediate was that it did not remedy another dilemma relating to Jeffrey Solomon. A long-time friend of Rabinowitz's as well as the lawyer who sat by his side when he made his statement to Detectives Peffall and Craig on April 30, Solomon also—and this concerned Castor—was the last known person except for Rabinowitz himself to have talked to Stefanie before she died.

Prosecutors knew that Solomon had called the Rabinowitz house at about 8:30 p.m. on April 29, only two hours before the time they thought that Stefanie was strangled. He talked to her for only a few minutes and what was said was not important. What was significant, however, was that Solomon would be able to swear that Stefanie was alive as of 8:30, that she sounded normal—that is, that she was not upset, as if she and Craig had been arguing—and that she did not sound as if she were drugged. The last point was particularly consequental because it allowed prosecutors to build their timetable of what happened inside 526 Winding Way later that night. Castor wanted to be able to tell the jury that Stefanie was totally coherent at 8:30, so she must have ingested the Ambien after she talked to Solomon. Dr. Hood estimated that she died no later than 10:30. Since it takes Ambien about an hour to act, Rabinowitz must have duped her into ingesting the drug shortly after she talked to Solomon. Castor's problem was that Solomon was refusing to testify about the conversation, claiming that he was part of the defense team and, as one of Rabinowitz's attorneys, he could not be forced to testify against his client.

On September 22, ten days after Solomon appeared before the grand jury, Castor asked Judge Salus to issue an order formally removing Solomon from the list of defense attorneys. The judge complied. One problem down, one to go.

Norristown
Wednesday, October 8

Castor's decision to bring Solomon and Joyce Rabinowitz before the grand jury drew a strong response from De-Simone and Miller. Shocked by the tactic—a chilling preview of what would happen much later when independent counsel Kenneth Starr called Marsha Lewis before a federal grand jury in Washington to talk about her daughter, Monica Lewinsky, and Lewinsky's alleged affair with President Clinton—the defense lawyers filed a new motion with Judge Salus asking him to reconsider his earlier order that allowed prosecutors to introduce evidence of fraud and murder in one trial. Although Salus would toss out the motion, DeSimone and Miller made a strong argument for second-thinking the decision:

"Since the determination of the severance/consolidation
issue, the District Attorney has strongly suggested that they
intend to call defendant Craig Rabinowitz's mother as well
as attorney Jeffrey Solomon, Esquire, as 'victims' in con-
nection with the fraud allegations," the defense complained. "This anticipated evidence would heighten the
inflammatory nature of the fraud charges and substantially
exacerbate the 'spillover' impaction [on] the homicide
charge. In a just and fair due process consideration by the
jurors of Craig Rabinowitz's guilt or innocence of the murder charge, it is highly improbable that the jury could fairly
analyze the homicide case knowing that the defendant allegedly defrauded his own mother and attorney."

It was bad enough, the defense lawyers were saying with
as much indignation as they could command, that jurors
already would be compelled to hear tearful testimony from
Rabinowitz's mother-in-law (his father-in-law, Lou Newman, after a long battle with cancer of the pancreas, had
died of a heart attack on September 28, just ten days earlier), but now the prosecutors wanted to add his mother and
his personal attorney to the witness list as well.

The defense lawyers waxed even more indignant in an
accompanying document entitled a "Memorandum of
Law." In the three-page paper, they contended: "It is not
so much the receipt of funds from [Solomon and Joyce
Rabinowitz] which may be probative to motive, but the
alleged deceptive, manipulative nature of the accused's
character which carries the overwhelming prejudicial, in-
cendiary potential. It is not a quantum leap for a juror to
conclude that while he may or may not have murdered his
wife, any individual who defrauded his mother and attorney
should, nonetheless, be convicted of the murder because of
his apparent reprehensible character. This methodology,
analysis, and contemplation is both unfair and unwarranted.
While it may certainly enhance the probability of conviction, it certainly constitutes an injustice."

Bruce Castor slammed down his copy of the document.

"Fucking nonsense," he barked. Don't they realize the irony here? he thought. Exactly—he paused to count—five months and two days after they asked Judge Salus to release Rabinowitz on bail, citing his unimpeachable character, they are back asking the same judge to protect their client who now "appears" to be "reprehensible." From the perfect husband and doting father, Rabinowitz had morphed into someone who had robbed his own mother.

While the prosecution and defense were maneuvering over whether Joyce Rabinowitz and Jeffrey Solomon might testify at Craig's rapidly approaching trial, other things were popping on the legal front as well:

- On September 12, Judge Salus tossed the media a bone, agreeing to partial release of the documents they were trying to shake loose: the autopsy report and Rabinowitz's April 30 statement. It was a hollow victory. Salus agreed only to let them have the autopsy *conclusion*, which did not include the information about Stefanie's pre-existing medical problem, and an *edited* version of the statement, in which Rabinowitz's assertions about trying to make love to his wife on the night she was killed were blacked out.
- On September 25, the defense asked that charges against Rabinowitz be dismissed on grounds that prosecutors had inappropriately used his testimony at the J.P. Tiffany hearing in their attempt to stop Rabinowitz from being released on bail. The testimony was immunized, Miller and DeSimone argued, and prosecutors violated the agreement which prohibited his words from being used against him "in any criminal case." By using it, Ferman and Castor had poisoned their case against Rabinowitz.
- On October 7, following a strong nudge from Judge Salus that included a threat to impose sanctions if

they did not respond, Miller and DeSimone tardily filed a certification—required of defense lawyers under Pennsylvania law—that they did not plan to use an alibi defense or an insanity plea. It was a signal to Castor and Ferman that the defense had few options left.

- On October 15, Judge Salus rejected the defense request to dismiss the charges against Rabinowitz because of the J.P. Tiffany testimony, noting that "the use-immunity granted in Philadelphia pertained to that case only and could not have predicted the subsequent events of the instant case and any relevancy to the motion before the court."

- On the same day, in a second order, Salus turned down the five-week-old defense plea to prohibit prosecutors from using Rabinowitz's April 30 statement at the trial. The defense had contended that investigators had violated Rabinowitz's rights when they failed to tell him before he made the statement that his wife had been murdered and he was being considered a suspect. Salus gave three principal reasons for his rejection: 1. Rabinowitz was not in custody, so there was no reason for him to be advised in advance of his rights; 2. The statement was voluntary and Rabinowitz's lawyer was present at the time; 3. The statement was made before Rabinowitz was arrested.

Norristown
Friday, October 24
Afternoon

"What the hell's so funny?" Bruce Castor asked irritably.

His first assistant's crabbiness only caused Mike Marino to grin wider. "You want to hear something great?" he asked, teasingly.

"I sure hope it's good," sighed Castor, plopping into the

chair in front of his boss's desk. "Risa and I are trying to get ready for jury selection and we could use a good laugh. No matter how many of these cases you try, you can't help getting uptight."

"I thought for a minute you might not have to *go* to Greensburg," the district attorney replied, dragging out his private joke.

"C'mon, Mike. Don't play games. I still have a lot to do."

"You won't believe who I just had a call from," Marino said, sobering.

Castor's mouth fell open. "No kidding! Don't tell me! Jeffrey Miller!"

Marino smiled. "Close. Frank DeSimone."

"Well, don't keep me guessing. What the hell did he want?"

"He said, and I quote: 'What kind of offer will you make me in return for a guilty plea?' "

"No shit!" Castor said, grinning even wider than Marino. "What'd you tell him?"

"What do you think I told him?"

"*Mike!*"

Marino laughed heartily. "I told him I'd agree to life."

Castor slumped into the chair, exhaling. "You scared the crap out of me, you know that? So what did *Mr.* DeSimone say to that?" he asked, emphasizing the "Mister."

Marino turned his palms up. "What the hell could he say? Nothing. He hung up."

Castor laughed. "That figures."

Marino shook his head. "Don't dismiss it. My gut feeling is, he's going to plead."

"Aw, Mike, get serious," Castor replied. "*Nobody* pleads guilty to get life in prison unless he has a death sentence hanging over his head, too."

"He's gonna plead," Marino said. "Mark my words."

"No way!" Castor said.

"He is," Marino argued. "Just remember I told you so."

"Have to go get packed," Castor said, rising.

"Okay," Marino replied, smiling. "By the way, happy birthday. How old are you?"

"Thirty-six."

Marino shook his head. "Ah, to be thirty-six again. Have a good trip. Pick a good jury, but I don't think you'll need 'em."

SIXTEEN

Greensburg, Westmoreland County, Pennsylvania
Wednesday, October 29
Morning

"What did I tell you weeks ago?" Bruce Castor asked, shoveling suitcases into the trunk of his 1991 Cadillac Sedan Seville, a tan behemoth that he had inherited from his grandmother. "Didn't I predict the defense was making a mistake by asking for a change of venire?"

"I would never have believed it could have gone this well," replied Risa Ferman, shoving a cardboard box onto the back seat. "I can't imagine how it could have been any better."

Castor laughed. "Not anywhere in Pennsylvania could we have gotten a better jury. A librarian . . . an electrical engineer . . . a pharmacist . . . an insurance agent, for crying out loud . . ."

"Don't forget the dog groomer."

"Yeah," Castor chuckled. "A dog groomer whose husband owns about twenty Midas Muffler shops."

"And the pretzel salesman. God, I love it."

"Here," Castor said, tossing the keys to Ferman. "Why don't you drive?"

"Sure, no problem. Any special reason?"

"I want to go over our lineup and start working on our opening statement."

"Can you believe it?" Ferman asked, turning the key, still high on their success. "I thought I'd die when that guy said he already figured Rabinowitz was guilty and deserved the death sentence.''

Castor laughed. ''And DeSimone's reply, once he picked his jaw off the floor: 'Your Honor,' '' he said, imitating his rival, '' 'I think we have cause for dismissal of this juror.' ''

''You didn't have to add that you thought he'd be terrific.''

''Why not?'' Castor grinned. ''I did. Still do.''

''I think we followed our game plan down to the letter,'' Ferman added. ''And it went like clockwork.''

''Yeah. We came out here looking for a group that wasn't too young or too old, some family-oriented people with a record of stable employment. And that's exactly what we got. Seven men, five women, almost all of them married with children. Good, conservative people, pro–law enforcement to the bone. Every one was better than the one before. It's a fucking dream jury.''

''I don't think the defense would agree with that,'' Ferman smiled.

''No,'' Castor agreed. ''They wanted an all-male jury if they could get it. Obviously thinking about Summer.''

''Sure. They probably figured men would be more sympathetic to Rabinowitz once they saw his young blonde girlfriend.''

''What they definitely didn't want was women with young children. They'd take one look at Haley and be ready to pull the switch on Rabinowitz themselves.''

''I'll bet they were surprised when you struck that teacher, the one with the two little kids.''

''Oh, boy, that was close,'' Castor said. ''I was ready to take her. She looked perfect. Then she happened to mention that she had directed a school presentation of *Twelve Angry Men*. As soon as she said that, I had visions of her thinking of herself as a female Henry Fonda out to convince everyone else on the panel that Rabinowitz wasn't guilty. I couldn't get rid of her fast enough after that. You know who was my favorite, though?''

"The pretzel salesman?" Ferman said tentatively.

"No," Castor laughed. "The manager of the auto parts store. The very first one we questioned."

"Oh, *really*?" Ferman said, surprised. "Why's that?"

"See, you didn't spot it, either."

"Spot what?"

"His ring," Castor said, lifting his right hand. "Just like mine."

Ferman shook her head. "I don't understand."

"Neither did the good Catholic DeSimone. This is a thirty-second-degree Mason's ring. We're like fraternity brothers. I knew as soon as he noticed mine there'd be an automatic bond. He'd be in our camp all the way."

Ferman swung up the entrance ramp and pointed the DeVille east on I-76.

"Drop it in cruise," Castor suggested. "We'll be home in four and a half hours." Reaching into the back seat, he rummaged in one of the cardboard boxes and came up with a thick three-ring binder. "Let's go through it again."

Ferman smiled. "Always the perfectionist."

"Damn straight. You can always prepare more than the other side."

Ferman rolled her eyes. "How many times have I heard you say *that*?"

"It's true," Castor said. "It's the key. Okay," he said, flipping open the binder. "I'll do the opening and then we'll move straight to the crime scene."

"In chronological order."

"Yep. My very first witness is going to be Jeffrey Solomon. That oughta make him happy."

"As if you give a damn."

"Exactly! I'd *love* to make him squirm. After him, there's Driscoll and Craig, the medical people. Then it's your turn."

"I get the statement?"

"Right. And all of Rabinowitz's friends who were at the hospital. You still comfortable with that?"

"Absolutely."

Castor flipped a few pages. "Okay. Then I give you a break by taking the people at the pawn shop and you come back with Anne Newman. Set up the background first."

"Right."

"This is where it starts getting delicate. It isn't going to be easy explaining all his loans and how he used money from one to pay the other."

"No problem. I could do it in my sleep."

"It's going to be a long haul. It's going to be, what," he started counting, "nine witnesses?"

"I've got it covered. Don't worry about it."

"I always worry."

Ferman smiled. "Yeah. Well, don't worry this time. It's a piece of cake."

"Okay," Castor replied, hesitating just long enough to cause Ferman to give him a sharp glance.

"Don't worry. Okay?"

"All right," Castor sighed. "If you say so. I'll do the financial records, his credit card debts, the loans and all that. Then I get to what the media has really been waiting for. Ta da! Summer."

"You still planning not to use her?"

"No way am I gonna call her unless I have to. I've got four people from Delilah's. That oughta do it."

"Then I'm up again. Right?"

"Right. The insurance policies. Then I call Zayas for the *coup de grâce*, and we're through."

"Sounds simple enough," Ferman said.

"Look," Castor pointed. "Here comes a McDonald's. Let's grab a cup of coffee."

Castor sipped slowly through the hole in the plastic top. "Damn, that's hot."

Ferman, still behind the wheel, glanced at him out of the corner of her eye. "You have any idea what the defense is going to do?"

Castor shook his head slowly. "None. They've already confirmed they're not going to try to prove Rabinowitz was crazy or that he was somewhere else. The only thing I can figure is some kind of heat-of-passion defense. But I'm damned if I know how they'll do it." He paused, taking another tentative sip of coffee. "What *can* they say? They only have three options. One," he said, raising his index finger, "they can claim that it wasn't a murder; that the pathologists were wrong and Stefanie died a natural death."

"I don't think they're going to do that," interjected Ferman.

"Me, either. So they move to number two," Castor added, raising his middle finger. "They can say, 'Yes, it was a murder, but Craig Rabinowitz didn't do it.' "

"That's definitely out. The defense already promised no alibi defense and there were no signs of a forced entry so they can't say someone broke in."

"Absolutely right," confirmed Castor. "So there's option three. "Rabinowitz can say, 'I killed her, but I have an excuse.' "

"Back to heat-of-passion, eh?"

"I don't know what else it could be. But if Rabinowitz uses that option, he has to admit that he killed her. His best chance, then, is that the jury will convict him of third-degree rather than first-degree and he'd get twenty-to-forty years instead of life." Castor took a deep swallow. "You know what *really* bothers me?" he said slowly.

"Uummm," Ferman grunted, swinging into the left lane and gunning the Caddy to pass a slow-moving 18-wheeler. "This really has pickup," she grinned.

"A truck," Castor said solemnly.

"Huh?" Ferman asked quizzically, turning to face him. "What truck? That one we just passed?"

"No," Castor chuckled. "The defense truck. You know what Mike always says, 'Where's the truck?' What's going to come out of nowhere and hit us? I can't see anything wrong with our case. Nothing. My instincts tell me we can't lose. But I can't quit asking myself what we've forgotten. What are we missing?"

"Nothing that I can see," said Ferman.

"Me, either," sighed Castor. Putting his head back, he closed his eyes. "Let me think about it some more."

Castor looked up from the legal pad he had been scribbling on. "How close are we?"

Ferman shrugged. "Hour. Hour and fifteen, depending on the traffic. How's it coming?"

"Not bad," Castor said, turning back a few pages. "Let me double-check. What was that total that Rabinowitz would be able to collect after his wife's death? A million . . ."

"*Exactly*," Ferman interrupted, rattling the figure off the top of her head, "$1,883,500."

"That's what I thought," Castor said, making a few notes. "Okay. This is how I'm planning to start out: 'Ask most men what their wives mean to them. . . .' I pause. 'Then ask Craig Rabinowitz what his wife, Stefanie, meant to him. He would say, "One million, eight hundred and eighty-three thousand, five hundred dollars." ' I pause again. 'Ask him what the term *forsaking all others* signified, and he'd answer, "One million, eight hundred and eighty-three thousand, five hundred dollars." ' Another pause. 'To Craig Rabinowitz, his wife was a walking pile of money, not a human being. She was just something that was worth more dead than alive. She was his meal ticket.' "

"I like it," Ferman nodded. "Gets right to the heart of the matter."

"Yeah. I think we need to make it very clear right from the beginning that this is a case about money. Money is the only reason that Stefanie Rabinowitz is dead. The jury needs to understand that up front."

"You won't get any argument from me."

"I wasn't expecting any." Castor laughed. "Okay," he said, glancing at his pad. "A little background goes in here,

'In October 1995, he panicked. That's when Stefanie learned she was pregnant. It rocked him. He had no money . . . no job . . . no skills . . . no nothing. That's when he started his pyramid scheme. By May 1996, he was sixty thousand dollars in debt. Four months later, that debt had risen to seventy thousand dollars, plus what he owed on his credit cards. . . .' ''

Castor stopped to meditate, staring out the window. "I think here is where I'm going to tell them about Delilah's. Something like this: ' . . . In the meantime, he had started patronizing Delilah's Den, and in October he met Summer. Within weeks, his debt more than doubled to a hundred and seventy-one thousand dollars . . .' I don't want to load them down with too many figures. You think that's too much?"

Ferman shook her head.

"Me, either," Castor replied. "They have to understand the money. Once they can see what drives Rabinowitz, everything else will fall into place."

"I agree," Ferman said.

"I think then I'll get into the life insurance and about how he saw it as his only way to get out of debt. Something like this: ' . . . He had been trying to raise more money with loans from his friends but he had pumped that well dry. By the end of February, some of them were starting to push him to get paid. By then, he had two hundred and fifty thousand dollars in investor debt and his options had run out . . .' ''

"This is where you tell 'em about the ledger?"

"Right. I tell 'em how, by April thirteenth, Rabinowitz was totally focused on killing his wife. That's when he took a scrap of paper and covered it with figures that showed who he owed, how much was due, and how much could be recovered if he could collect on the insurance. Listen," he added, looking at his notes, '' 'Before killing her, though, he wanted to squeeze every last penny he could get. On April twenty-eighth, he talked her into cashing in the stock portfolio her parents had been building for her for all her life. How much was it? Seven thousand, seven hundred and eleven dollars. For her—for Stefanie—it may have been the last straw. In her mother's presence, when she handed him the check, she said, somewhat harshly, *This is my money and I want it back.'* "

"Which we can get Anne Newman to confirm."

"Right," said Castor. "Then I look at the jury and I ask: 'What did he do with this money? He paid a quick visit to Summer and gave her six hundred dollars. Then he went to his family doctor and complained of having trouble sleeping, talking the doctor into prescribing a mild sedative, a drug called Ambien. He probably used her money to buy the sleeping pills.' "

"Go on," Ferman urged.

"That's as far as I've gotten. But the rest is easy. It's just a chronological recitation."

"You're going to tell 'em how she was killed, aren't you?"

Castor nodded. "Have to. Has to be graphic, too. How he had tried to knock her out with Ambien. How she goes to sleep and he puts her in the tub, planning to drown her. Then she starts waking up and he has to strangle her. How much she suffered in those four minutes it took her to die, but how he kept squeezing until she quit breathing. I'm gonna tell them how he chose drowning because it was critical to him that he make the murder look like an accident, not a murder committed by someone else. His whole plan was based on the premise of accidental death, because anything else would have touched off an investigation."

"But we're really just making that up. How he killed her, that is."

"Of course we're making it up." Castor laughed. "But it's based on solid fact. What's he going to do, jump up and say, 'No, that isn't the way I did it?' "

Ferman laughed, then turned sober. "Poor Anne Newman. That's going to be really tough for her to have to listen to."

"I know," said Castor. "But the jury has to hear it if we want 'em to sock him for first-degree. After I tell 'em how she died, I'm gonna tell 'em how he almost got by with it, but how he made little mistakes, like leaving her jewelry on . . . how he didn't count on her mother telling investigators how much Stefanie disliked taking baths , . . all the little things. You know," he said thoughtfully, "I think when he was released after giving his statement, he thought he had gotten away with it."

"He came awful close."

"Yeah," Castor nodded. "Too close."

Norristown
Late afternoon

"You're happy then? With the jury?" Mike Marino asked.

"Couldn't *be* happier," Castor said with a grin. Leaning forward, he added: "Mike, this guy doesn't stand a chance. I don't remember the last time I've felt so good about a case. I swear, I can't see any problems. I can't wait to square off with Miller and DeSimone."

"Don't get over-confident," Marino cautioned.

"Don't worry about that. But it's hard to explain how well things have gone together this time. I can't believe it."

"So what are you going to do? Start celebrating now?"

Castor blushed. "Sort of, now that you mention it. Elizabeth's fixing a roast for dinner and I've got a bottle of Kendall–Jackson red zinfandel I've been saving."

"Okay," Marino smiled. "Go home. Have a good dinner. I'll see you in the morning."

Courtroom B, Montgomery County Courthouse
Thursday, October 30
9:10 a.m.

Anne Newman looked around the courtroom, gratified to see how many of Stefanie's friends had driven to Norristown to show their support. They filled two complete rows of benches behind the prosecution table on the left side of the room. Anne waved to several of them, smiling weakly, then turned, sad-eyed, to wait for her former son-in-law's arrival. Staring at the empty seats at the defense table, where Craig would be sitting in a few minutes, tears began to roll down her cheeks. "Today was Lou's birthday," she said softly, speaking to no one in particular.

Not surprisingly, the room was jammed with reporters: the tv people with their blow-dried, sprayed-stiff hair, dressed like they were on their way to church; the print reporters, more disheveled, needing haircuts. Taking up a large chunk of seats on the right side of the room, behind the defense table, they chatted excitedly among themselves, their eyes bright with anticipation. It had been six months almost to the day since Stefanie had been killed, and interest had not lessened. In an era where most stories have the longevity of a carton of milk, the Craig and Stefanie Rabinowitz saga had been as enduring as a TV soap opera. Judge Salus's gag order had curtailed the flow of information, but it did not stifle the curiosity.

That morning, the *Inquirer* had printed a thirty-four-paragraph front page story zeroing in on Summer and speculating how she might take the stand to testify about her alleged call to Rabinowitz the night his wife was murdered. The story also raised the same question that so puzzled prosecutors: What defense could Rabinowitz offer? In one respect, the gag order had been a blessing for Miller and DeSimone. It kept them from having to explain their stance on a regular basis to curious newspeople. But, because of Salus's decree, it had been four months since the defense floated a new theory about Stefanie's murder, and *no one* had a clue about what the defense was going to do. The only possible route for DeSimone and Miller, the newspaper conjectured, was to try for an O.J.–type verdict, one in which the jury would find reasonable doubt and acquit, or at least convict on a lesser charge if they had the option.

The *Daily News*, at a severe disadvantage because its late publishing time made it impossible to get the jump on the broadcast media or even its print competitor, had little more than a token presentation in Thursday's early edition, mentioning Summer only in passing. The bulk of its story was devoted to individual descriptions of the jurors and speculation that the defense might ask for a postponement because of a dispute between prosecutors and defense attorneys over two after-death photos of Stefanie Rabinowitz.

Bruce Castor, who had been worried because he didn't have anything to worry about, was not overly concerned about the photo controversy. Earlier, he had promised DeSimone and Miller that he would not show the jury any after-death pictures of Stefanie. However, during lunch with Ferman in Greensburg on Tuesday, he changed his mind. As they questioned potential jurors they became more convinced that during the trial they were going to have to show how close Rabinowitz had come to committing the perfect murder. The best way to do that, they decided, was to show the photos of Stefanie's face, taken some twelve hours after she was pronounced dead, to demonstrate how, even then, the marks of strangulation—the dots of petechia around the eyes—were so faint that they might have gone unnoticed by a pathologist less experienced than Dr. Hood. There would be a debate, Castor figured, over whether the prosecutors would be allowed to change their minds and offer the pictures, but in the long run he was confident that Judge Salus would see the wisdom of his argument. The prosecutor did not expect it to be a major sticking point; arguments might delay the start of the trial for a half-hour at most.

Walking briskly to the chair he always took when he was prosecuting a case, the one closest to the jury box that stretched down the front left side of the room, Castor smiled at Ferman. "You look nice," he said.

"You like it?" she asked, brushing a spot of lint off her sleeve. "I bought it for the trial."

"We could be twins," Castor joked, pointing out that both were dressed in conservative navy blue suits. "Did you sleep okay last night?"

Ferman shrugged. "Yeah, I guess so. Considering. You?"

"Like a rock," Castor smiled. "We're going to steamroll this guy."

There was a murmur in the courtroom, causing Castor and Ferman to turn. Through a door on the right came Miller, DeSimone, and the local counsel, Bill Honig. They were followed almost immediately by a uniformed officer and a handcuffed Craig Rabinowitz. Immediately behind the defense table, Castor noticed, were Detectives Craig and Peffall, also looking spiffy in their best suits.

"Right on time," Ferman whispered.

9:25 a.m.

While waiting for the judge to appear, Castor made a quick visual check of the prosecution's documents. At his elbow was a gurney, not unlike a supermarket shopping cart, loaded with exhibits and eight fat binders. In the binders, all carefully labeled, was everything pertaining to each witness the prosecution planned to call, right down to a neatly typed list of questions they would be asked. In addition, he and Ferman had prepared sixty exhibits they planned to show the jury. One of the most dramatic was a two-foot-tall color photo of Summer showing the dancer wearing only multi-colored bikini panties, a long-sleeved man's shirt splayed open with a single button fastened, and a garter halfway up her left thigh. More important was a five-foot-tall reproduction of Rabinowitz's hand-scribbled ledger. When a reporter saw the volume of prosecution material, he leaned over the rail separating the spectators from the lawyers and chided Castor about being obsessive. "I

have a phobia about not being ready,'' the prosecutor replied with a smile. "Besides, the jury needs to see that
we're organized and ready to go."

Castor looked at his watch and the empty bench. "Let's
get this thing started," he said half-aloud, drumming his
yellow #2 pencil on the tabletop, which was bare except
for the legal pad that contained his notes for the opening
statement, neatly laid out in outline form, complete with
Roman numerals and block capital letters. He was re-
reading his notes when he felt a tap on his left shoulder.
Half turning, he could see Frank DeSimone crouching behind him.

"This is going to be a short proceeding today," the defense lawyer whispered, breaking the tradition that the two
men had of never speaking directly to each other.

"Oh?" Castor said curiously. "And why is that?"

DeSimone paused dramatically. "He's going to plead
guilty."

Castor and Ferman exchanged shocked glances. "Marino
was right!" Castor blurted.

"The judge wants to see us all in his robing room,"
DeSimone continued, still speaking softly.

A small, spartan chamber with barely enough space for an
institutional desk and a few chairs, the robing room was
not designed to accommodate more than four people com-
fortably. With the four lawyers and Salus crammed inside,
it seemed to shrink to the size of a telephone booth.

"Well?" Salus said when the lawyers entered.

DeSimone got immediately to the point. "It's going to
be a plea," he said without elaboration.

Salus, still in his suit coat, accepted the news with equa-
nimity.

"Very well. What's your position?" he asked, looking
at the prosecutors.

"We'd like a colloquium," Castor replied quickly, referring to a detailed document in which Rabinowitz would

have to confirm that he understood what he was doing by initialing a number of points, then signing it. It would have to be co-signed by his lawyers.

"It'll take a few minutes to get one drawn up," Salus pointed out.

"That's all right," said Castor, who was finding it difficult to hide his disappointment at not being able to go to trial after so much preparation. "Let's just make sure there aren't any mistakes."

Rich Peffall and Charlie Craig looked quizzically at each other when the prosecutors and defense lawyers, except for Honig, who remained at the table with a now-unshackled Rabinowitz, trooped out of the courtroom, heading determinedly through a side door.

"What's going on?" Charlie Craig asked.

Peffall sighed. Earlier he had noticed that DeSimone had been carrying only a single, thin file folder when he walked into the room. That was strange, Peffall said to himself, because he had never yet seen a lawyer show up for the start of a trial with only one folder. "I'll bet the defense is going to ask for a continuance," he whispered, noting the hum behind him as the reporters and spectators, still ignorant about Rabinowitz's intention, speculated excitedly about the unexpected departure of the attorneys.

The investigators, who knew no more than the others, also were discussing the possibilities when Tim Woodward slipped into an empty chair next to Detective Craig.

"What's happening, Tim?"

"I think he's going to plead guilty," Woodward whispered.

Detectives Peffall and Craig stared disbelievingly at each other, then simultaneously exhaled deeply in relief. Although they felt the evidence against Rabinowitz was overwhelming, and they never doubted that he would be convicted, neither was looking forward to testifying and being subjected to long, brutal cross-examination. Charlie

Craig, particularly, felt as if a huge burden had been lifted, because he had been unexpectedly subpoenaed by the defense a few days earlier to appear as a witness for Miller and DeSimone. Since he was scheduled as the third witness for the prosecution, it meant he would have to appear on the stand twice, and twice be subjected to cross.

"Come on," Woodward said, rising. "Bruce and Risa want to see you."

Following Woodward into the hallway, they joined Ferman and Castor, both of whom were grinning broadly. "It's true," Castor said. "He's pleading guilty to first-degree murder. I just wanted to thank you guys," he said offering his hand. "You did a hell of a job. We'll talk more later, but right now I have to go in and announce what's happened. Be careful that you don't get trampled by the reporters."

"Why do you think he did it?" Charlie Craig asked Peffall as they watched the prosecutors go back into the courtroom. "Change his plea?"

Peffall took his time in replying. "I don't think he would have been able to sit there and listen to all the evidence against him. After everything came out, he would have looked like such a shit that even his own mother would have disowned him."

SEVENTEEN

Craig Rabinowitz twisted nervously in the witness box, his hands tightly clasped in his lap, his eyes bouncing around the room, never staying long in one place. Dressed in a tailored, gray pin-stripe suit, a striped tie, and a light blue shirt with a white collar, he looked slimmer than he had when he surrendered. Appearing ready to break into tears at any moment, Rabinowitz glanced nervously at his mother, who was sitting behind the defense table, her head down, and then at Frank DeSimone. In Pennsylvania, when a defendant changes his plea, he has to explain his decision in open court, a process designed to protect the defendant, by insuring that he made the choice freely, and the commonwealth, in case there is a later appeal.

"For the record," DeSimone said kindly, "what's your name?"

Rabinowitz rolled his shoulders and breathed through his mouth in short, sharp gasps, like a runner who was hyperventilating. "Ca ... Ca ... Craig ... Adam ... Rabinowitz," he stuttered, blinking rapidly.

"And why are you here?"

"I want to say that I'm guilty of these charges and accept and take full responsibility for my wife's death."

DeSimone cleared his throat. "Why did you plead guilty?" he asked.

"I have brought enough hurt and detestation to all of you," Rabinowitz replied gravely. "This has to come to an end. I realize it will never end, but this has to end now. Enough is enough. I am so deeply sorry for what I have done," he continued, starting to sob. "It would take me a thousand lifetimes to express the remorse I feel. I broke so many people's hearts, including my own; hearts that will never be repaired. There will always be a hole in everyone's heart because of what I have done."

Charlie Craig listened carefully, nodding slowly to himself. This, he thought, is what Rabinowitz must have sounded like when he was sitting with his friends watching the Flyers, bragging about how well his latex glove business was doing, and asking them to invest more money, sounding so earnest, so trustworthy. He nudged Rich Peffall. "I can see how he conned everybody," he said softly. "He sounds sincere as hell to me."

Rabinowitz, wiping his eyes, began talking about his daughter. "Right now, Haley is thankfully unaware of what has happened. But every day she grows up, and there will come a time when she knows what happened." His lawyers, he added, had explained to him that he would not be able to appeal his sentence. That, in itself, would be a kindness to his daughter. "An appeal down the road would bring all this out in the open," he said, adding that he was unwilling for that to happen. "I have already done the worst thing I could do to her, and I would never do anything again that I thought would cause her more pain."

"Sounds rehearsed to me," Castor mumbled grumpily from his seat at the prosecution table.

"What was it that led you to this decision?" DeSimone asked.

Rabinowitz took a deep breath. "Two nights ago, while I was asleep in my cell in Westmoreland County, I had a dream." In the dream, he continued, he was back in the house he had grown up in on Edgeville Road in Penn Wynne, "a place where nothing bad ever happened." He was standing in the hallway, he said, getting his bearings, when he heard someone calling his name. It was Stefanie.

"Come here," she beckoned. "We want to talk to you."

Peffall leaned over and whispered in Charlie Craig's ear. "Do you think anybody is buying one word of this bullshit?"

Following the sound of her voice, Rabinowitz said, he dream-walked into the breakfast room, where Stefanie was sitting at the table with his father, Henry, who had died four years before, and his father-in-law, Lou Newman, who had died on September 28, which was Rabinowitz's thirty-fourth birthday. "Usually," he told the court, "my dreams are not that vivid, but this was *so* vivid . . ."

Stefanie spoke directly to him. "Craig, sit down. We want to talk to you."

Stunned, he collapsed into a chair and pulled himself forward, resting his hands on the tabletop. "They put their hands on my hand and," Rabinowitz groaned, "and they said, 'Craig, it's time to do what's right. It's time for you to do the right thing.' "

Rabinowitz looked soulfully at DeSimone. "And I hope today, I think today, that I have done the right thing. And that's why I've done this."

Castor rolled his eyes and mumbled under his breath. "What fucking nonsense."

DeSimone nodded at the prosecutor and returned to his seat at the defense table.

Castor glared at Rabinowitz, silently cursing him for being such a coward. "Why did you do it?" he growled. "Why did you kill your wife?"

"Mr. Castor," Rabinowitz said ardently, appearing on the verge of tears, "that's something that I think about and wonder about every moment of every day."

Apparently unable to contain his emotions, he again broke into sobs. "There's no simple or easy or direct answer," he said, his voice breaking. His life, he continued, muttering semi-coherently, had become a "sham," a "fraud." Finally, he realized that he was only getting deeper into a hole he had dug for himself. "And the hole became so, so deep . . ." he cried, his voice trailing off.

He paused to dab at his eyes. "I've spoken to my lawyers about it," he began again, after recovering his composure. ". . . we've had numerous discussions about it and they asked me the same question. Somewhere along the line in my life—and these are Mr. DeSimone's words—I must have suffered a moral disconnect. I lost my ability to know right from wrong. Right became wrong and wrong became right.

"There are no excuses," he continued. "I would not sit here and try to fool anybody by making an excuse to try and legitimize what I've done or make an excuse to try to garner sympathy. I believe that my mind just was not able to know what the right thing to do was. Whether I didn't want to know what the right thing to do was, or whether I didn't want to do the right thing, I don't know."

Rambling, frequently repeating himself, Rabinowitz struggled to regain his chain of thought. "In my entire life, as I stand sworn on this stand today, I've never been involved in any fight or a physical confrontation or hurt anybody. And the one person who I shared my life with for thirteen years . . . the one person who loved me and who I loved so dearly, I hurt the most and did the most damage to. What I did to Steffi is beyond reprehensible and horrible. And the fact that I took my child from her is worse—a child whom I love more than I could describe, a child who brought so much to her mother and I for way too short a period of time. When I think of these things it makes me ask the same question you asked me: How and why could I do this?"

Realizing that he wasn't going to get a direct, straightforward answer from Rabinowitz—that the defendant had not said a word about how he had strangled Stefanie, watching her face as she struggled to breathe; that he had not mentioned cheating his friends, or the Newmans, or his own mother, and was not going to—Castor threw him one more hate-filled glance and returned to take a seat next to Ferman. "It's all part of his act," he said angrily. "It's nonsense. I don't believe a word of what he's said."

"I swear," Peffall said to his partner, "if it hadn't been so serious, when he started talking about his so-called dream, I would have laughed."

11 a.m.

Judge Salus, as stone-faced as he had been when he was told that Rabinowitz was changing his plea, read Rabinowitz the sentence required by law for a guilty plea to first-degree murder: Life in prison without parole. The only hope Rabinowitz could hold for ever again being free was that some future governor would grant him clemency, a highly unlikely circumstance. Salus also imposed additional prison time for the theft charges, but it was meaningless because what really mattered was the sentence for first-degree murder.

After the sentencing, Rabinowitz was shackled and hustled out of the room by uniformed deputies. At the doorway, he paused and turned back. Catching his mother's eye, he silently formed the words, "I love you." A tearful Joyce Rabinowitz blew him a kiss.

11:45 a.m.

Bruce Castor, still seething, held an impromptu news conference on the courthouse steps, sharply criticizing Rabinowitz as "a swindler . . . a faker . . . a liar." Squinting into the sun and the glare of portable tv lights, the prosecutor accused Rabinowitz of trying another con. "I think he was playing to the family, to Mrs. Newman, to his mother, and to other people in the courtroom to try and give them some feeling that maybe he isn't the monster that the commonwealth intended to portray that he is. But I didn't believe a word he said," Castor added. "I didn't think for a moment that Rabinowitz cares about the family or anyone else."

Castor spent the next thirty minutes going through the evidence that he and Ferman had been preparing to present at the trial, explaining in detail their theory that Rabinowitz had gotten into such debt that the only way he could pay off the loans was by collecting on his wife's life insurance. Waving the blown-up copy of the ledger, Castor told reporters it was one of two major pieces of evidence that he and Ferman would have used to try to persuade the jury about motive. The other major piece of evidence—one which clearly showed premeditation—was the laboratory report showing the Ambien in Stefanie's system, a drug that Rabinowitz, not his wife, had obtained a prescription for.

In response to reporters' questions, Castor explained that he had not planned to call Summer as a prosecution witness because he didn't want his case muddied by the possibility that her statement was not entirely candid. The telephone message that she had admitted leaving on Rabinowitz's machine, he added, was innocuous and had nothing to do with Stefanie's murder.

Talking separately to reporters, Miller and DeSimone elaborated on the process that led Rabinowitz to change his plea. It began, the defense lawyers said, when Lou Newman died, an event that caused Rabinowitz considerable anguish.

Beginning about the middle of October, some two weeks after his father-in-law's death, DeSimone and Miller began discussing with Rabinowitz the possibility that he might plead guilty. Rabinowitz, in turn, talked it over with his mother, his sister in Florida, and her husband. What finally convinced him, however, was the dream that he had on Tuesday night. Less than twenty-four hours later, at about nine p.m. on Wednesday, the night before the trial was scheduled to begin, Rabinowitz made his final decision.

"He came into the visiting room and he started to cry,"
DeSimone said, sobbing that it was the six-month anniver-
sary of Stefanie's death. "He said he felt the right thing to
do was go into the courtroom and end the suffering."

DeSimone nodded when a reporter asked if he and Miller
had supported Rabinowitz's decision. "We told him, We're
with you either way. We told him we were suited up and
ready to go."

The defense lawyer paused, adding that he and Miller
had explained to Rabinowitz that the evidence against him
was massive and he was probably going to prison no matter
what. "It was as much evidence as I've ever seen in a
homicide case," interjected Miller.

Despite questions from reporters, the defense lawyers refused to discuss anything that Rabinowitz may have told
them about what happened at 526 Winding Way on the
night that Stefanie was killed.

Norristown
Friday, October 31

While the radio and tv stations filled the airwaves all Thursday afternoon and evening with the news of Rabinowitz's
guilty plea, the city's two large daily newspapers had to
wait until the next day to tell their readers about his change
of heart.

"Rabinowitz Admits to Killing Wife," the *Inquirer*
screamed in a headline that crossed all eight columns of
the front page, "A dream urged him to 'do the right
thing.' "

Relegated to second place in importance was a story
about a visit to Philadelphia by Chinese President Jiang
Zemin, who had arrived fresh from a contentious meeting
in Washington with some of the country's top lawmakers,
and a controversial speech he had made, in which he compared China's 1950 invasion of Tibet with President Lin-

coln's order freeing the slaves during the Civil War.

The plea-change story covered the top half of the front page, plus two full pages inside, and included a statement from Summer expressing her sympathy to Stefanie's family. "I have kept quiet out of respect . . . I consider myself very lucky because I still have my son and my family, unlike Stefanie's family, who lost a daughter and a father." Accompanying the story was a four-column picture of a blank-looking Rabinowitz being led away in handcuffs, as well as a picture of Stefanie and the infant Haley, side-by-side with a photo of a smiling Summer wearing a revealing blouse cut off at the midriff.

In the *Daily News*, the story was not just *on* the front page; it *was* the front page. Under the bright yellow headline "Craig's Ghosts . . . Rabinowitz says shocking guilty plea followed dream—prosecution sneers," was a tightly cropped headshot of Rabinowitz and a smaller picture of a smiling Stefanie. The *News* also devoted two and a half inside pages to the story.

Even after Rabinowitz's plea, the story refused to die. In the following weeks, the media continued to belabor the issue, rapidly switching focus from the role Jeffrey Miller and Frank DeSimone played in the case (they were as much counselors as attorneys, DeSimone said, delving into Rabinowitz's past while philosophically debating guilt and morality), to Rabinowitz's life behind bars (he has cable tv in his cell in the medium-security prison to which he was assigned and, according to Miller, is determined to finish his undergraduate studies through an inmates' study program and go on to earn a Ph.D.).

Amazingly, less than a week after dramatically making his admission of guilt, Rabinowitz contacted Miller and complained about how his image was being trashed in the media.

"He's being portrayed as some kind of diabolical murderer who used some kind of angle or spin or subterfuge to enter a plea or better his situation," Miller told the *Daily News*. "And while he acknowledges that what he did in connection with the homicide was reprehensible, he denies emphatically that his change of pleas was done for any reason other than to save his family from some sort of agony and avoid a horrendous ordeal. He loves his mother, he loves his mother-in-law, and he loves his baby," Miller concluded. "All the other issues are secondary."

On Wednesday, November 5, the same day that Rabinowitz's gripes were articulated by Miller in the *Daily News*, the admitted killer placed a collect call to Bruce Castor. Whatever he intended to say to the prosecutor—perhaps he wanted to appeal to him to ease off on his criticism as well—remains unknown.

"There's a *what*?" the surprised Castor asked when his secretary rang through to tell him about the call.

He tightened his grip on the phone, staring straight ahead. "Hell, no, I won't accept it," he said crisply. "I don't have anything to say to him."

EPILOGUE

True crime books are difficult for some people to read. There are those who dislike being faced with the realities of evil; they prefer their murders taking place in the hypothetical. There are others who have little patience for slogging through the details of what really happens in a courtroom; *Perry Mason* endings don't happen in true crime. And then there are readers who are distinctly uncomfortable with not knowing precisely who did what and why. In crime fiction everything is tidily wrapped up in the final chapter. In true crime, this is never the case. There always are a number of ends hanging loose: questions never satisfactorily answered; events never fully explained. The Craig Rabinowitz case was no exception.

At what point did Rabinowitz decide to kill his wife? What was it that drove him over the edge? Why did he think he could get away with it? How did he get Stefanie to ingest the sedative? Had there been a quarrel? At what point did she regain consciousness? Did Craig have her in the bathtub at the time? Or did she awaken on the couch, surrounded by baby Haley's toys? What was he doing during the two or more hours following the time she died, before he dialed 911? Did Summer truly get the answering machine when she called Rabinowitz at 11:30 that night? What *really* motivated him to change his plea?

Charlie Craig and Rich Peffall, who are as competent and conscientious as any investigators I've met in the course of writing eight previous true crime books, don't know the answer to these questions. And it is highly unlikely that they ever will. Peffall makes an effort to contact many of the criminals he helps convict, asking them if they will help him—for his own satisfaction—clear up some of the details that continue to nag. Often he gets no response. Sometimes they write back with obscene suggestions, recommending imaginative but impossible-to-perform activities. Occasionally, they actually answer some of his questions. Only rarely are the responses complete. And even when they are, who can tell for sure if the writer is being truthful, delusional, or simply self-serving?

Peffall says he intends to drop a letter to Craig Rabinowitz. He is curious about the Ambien: how he gave it to Stefanie and how it affected her. He would like to know at what point Rabinowitz quit thinking of his wife's murder as a possible alternative and definitely made up his mind to kill her. And he's inquisitive, in a less intense way, about where Rabinowitz was going with the Runaway-brand suitcase they found in the trunk of his car stuffed with summer clothes. "Wherever it was," the detective says, recalling Jeffrey Miller's comment that Rabinowitz had been planning to visit his mother at the New Jersey shore, "it sure as hell wasn't Atlantic City."

Charlie Craig would like to know precisely how, when, and where the murder was committed and how long Rabinowitz had been planning it. When he bolted, was he going to take Haley with him, or was he just going to abandon her with one of her grandmothers? He also wonders what Rabinowitz contemplated doing with the insurance money, provided he got it. Was he looking at a future with Summer?

Peffall is highly doubtful that the exotic dancer would have played much more than a peripheral role in Rabinowitz's life even if he had gotten away with the murder and collected on the insurance. She would not have been well-

accepted in Rabinowitz's Main Line lifestyle, which ultimately was more important to Rabinowitz.

Although Rabinowitz failed to list Summer among his
communicative ghosts, her presence continues to hover
over the case.

One of the detectives' major regrets is that they did not
have an opportunity to conduct a second interview with the
dancer. If they had, they would have pushed her further in
order to learn whether she knew more than she had originally told them about Rabinowitz's plans for the murder.
Peffall, particularly, would like to know more about the
conversation that she and Rabinowitz had in the parking
lot at Delilah's Den on May 2. The investigator's well-
honed instincts made him wonder whether she was totally
candid about the encounter. "I don't believe he told her he
killed his wife; I don't believe she knew he was going to
do it. But I sure would like to know what they said."

Summer continued to make headlines in the Philadelphia
newspapers long after Rabinowitz was shuffled off to his
permanent prison in Houtzdale, a community of fewer than
2,000 people located almost in the center of the state. On
December 4, the *Inquirer* had a story about Summer's de-
but as an actress—a role in a legitimate stage play entitled
Porno Stars at Home, which was opening in a local dinner
theater the day after Christmas.

The more colorful *Daily News* put a slightly different
slant on the same story. Splashed over the entire front page
was a close-up picture of the dancer with her tongue pro-
truding between her front teeth. The headline read: "Summer Gets a Tongue Lashing . . . Stefanie's mom: My
daughter's dead—and dancer is promoting her career." Despite the headline, most of the story was devoted to Summer, who used the opportunity to slam the media for
describing her as a "stripper."

"I hate that word," she said at a news conference called
to introduce the play's performers. "I am a woman of many

talents and I don't want to be stereotyped as a stripper.''

On January 7, 1998, two weeks after the show opened, she was back on the *News*'s front page. This time the headline read: ''Summer's Over . . . she's fired from 'Porno Stars' show.'' The illustration featured another large close-up of Summer's face, with a small insert photo showing four other performers and only a white, ghost-like image where Summer's likeness should have been.

The story, by *News* theater critic Stu Bykofsky, began, ''It was a very brief Summer,'' and went on to quote producer Robert Barretta as saying that she had been fired because she was unwilling to do publicity for the production. Her excuse was that she had signed a contract with a tabloid tv show, *American Journal*, that prohibited her from talking to the media until after the show aired. Apparently Barretta was not upset about the turn of events. He claimed that her presence had drawn more hate mail than ticket orders.

When *American Journal* aired the Summer segment early in February, the *Daily News* story was hardly a rave review. Summer appeared at the studio for the taping with her lawyer, with whom she consulted during the filming, the newspaper said. Quoting ''people familiar with the taping,'' the *News*'s Jim Nolan added, ''. . . [she] used a stripper's charm to try to control the interview, but off camera dropped the sweet facade to yell about questions she did not want to answer,'' such as whether she and Rabinowitz had ever had a sexual affair.

During the show, she claimed that she ''missed'' Rabinowitz and thought about him ''every day.'' According to her, Rabinowitz was ''the perfect man . . . the perfect man in an unhappy marriage.''

Summer also told the tv audience that she had first met Rabinowitz ''a couple of months'' before Haley was born. That meant that she had known him since about March 1996, which was considerably earlier than had been previously believed. Contrary to what the media had implied, she said that she had danced for Rabinowitz only on the day she met him when she filled in for another performer. After that, she said, they just "talked." Almost as an aside, she mentioned that Rabinowitz had been "hysterical" when she saw him in the parking lot on May 2. This contradicted what she told Keenan, Peffall, and Charlie Craig when they interviewed her at her house four days later. At that time, she said *she* had been the one who "lost it," running screaming into Delilah's to seek comfort from SherylAnn Bernhardt, the club's day manager.

Unanswered questions remain as well about what Rabinowitz was telling his lawyers, Jeffrey Miller and Frank DeSimone.

Both Miller and DeSimone ignored repeated requests to be interviewed for this book. But it is doubtful that they would have said anything meaningful anyway. Because they would be bound by lawyer/client privilege, they would have been unable to talk about the conversations they had had with Rabinowitz without his approval.

Still, their statements to the local media, especially after the plea change, perhaps raised more questions than they answered.

In a November 2 interview with the *Inquirer*, DeSimone said he "knew" in June, "almost exactly what [Rabinowitz] had done." How and what did he *know*?

As early as the time of the second autopsy on May 4, DeSimone said he "knew" there was no "intruder." If that was the case, why did the defense keep floating the rumor that someone may have broken in and strangled Stefanie? And why did Miller make repeated references to a "mysterious stranger" and "muddy footprints" in the bathroom?

While DeSimone said that he and Miller went over a dozen different defenses, they did not say what those may have been. Neither did they comment on what Rabinowitz may have been telling them about the materials found in the closet storage space.

The alleged Rabinowitz suicide note was never brought

up after it was mentioned by Miller and DeSimone on May 15, the day of the bail hearing. *Was* there a note? What did it say? What happened to it?

According to DeSimone, by late August or early September—a precise date was never mentioned—even while they were fighting for separate trials for Rabinowitz, the defense lawyers' conversations with him had shifted from the case to Rabinowitz's past and a philosophical debate about guilt. From that point on, were the lawyers trying to convince Rabinowitz to plead guilty? DeSimone denied it, saying that he never "lobbied" Rabinowitz to change his plea.

The lawyers also declined to say whether Rabinowitz ever shared details about the murder with them, or, if he did, just what they were.

Detectives Craig and Peffall were never able to determine specifically what gifts Rabinowitz had given and to whom. Although his credit card statements showed that he purchased a number of items that did *not* go to Stefanie, they were never able to say with certainty that they went to Summer, either. One item in particular was enticing. On Valentine's Day in 1997 Rabinowitz purchased from Tiffany & Co.'s Center City store a necklace composed of pearls strung on a sixteen-inch-long eighteen-karat yellow gold chain. The detectives knew that he bought it because they found the sales receipt ($1,979.50, including tax) and a letter on Tiffany letterhead confirming its replacement value ($1,850) in the shopping bag that was recovered from the storage space above Stefanie's closet. They don't know for sure who Rabinowitz gave it to, but they do know that it did not go to Stefanie. Interestingly, *Daily News* reporter Jim Nolan, in his story about Summer's appearance on *American Journal*, noted that she was wearing a necklace that looked remarkably like the one described in the documents.

Equally intriguing were Rabinowitz's mysterious visits to local hotels. Detectives Craig and Peffall were never able to determine who, if anyone, had been with him. If he had been alone, what was he doing there? If there had been someone with him, who? Those are questions that will remain unanswered until—and if—Rabinowitz decides to talk.

On January 6, 1998, Bruce Castor, Risa Ferman, and Judge Salus made a two-hour appearance before the Philadelphia Bar Association to discuss the Rabinowitz case. Among the more interesting comments were the different opinions about what drove Craig Rabinowitz.

Judge Salus, whose attendance raised some eyebrows, because it is very unusual—though totally proper—for the judge in a case to take part in such displays, opined that Rabinowitz had an inferiority complex. "He was a wannabe; a failure with very loyal friends." Because he was surrounded with more successful people, Salus said, he may have decided to obtain the same goals "at any cost."

Ferman reckoned that much of Rabinowitz's problem was that he was living in his wife's shadow. "Stefanie impressed people, not Craig," and Craig used that to his advantage. "People would give him money because they respected his wife," she contended. In the prosecutor's eyes, Rabinowitz was a "lazy" man with an overdeveloped love of money. "Before Stefanie became pregnant, he was borrowing from his family. But after she became pregnant, his borrowing really spiraled." When he could no longer keep up the pretense and was faced with huge debts, Ferman said, he had a choice: "He could have said that he had screwed up and tried to make it right. But, instead, he did the cowardly thing. He killed her."

Castor said the root of Rabinowitz's problems was hormonal. "I think sexual obsession played a more important role in his life. My argument was going to be that he was driven largely by sexual urges. We know he frequented prostitutes both before and after he was married. My suspicion is his wife was paying more attention to the baby than to him." This caused him to seek satisfaction outside the home, and ultimately led to his decision to commit murder.

In response to a question from the audience, Castor said that he had never seriously considered trying to seek a death sentence against Rabinowitz because his crime did not meet any of the sixteen conditions, called aggravating factors, outlined in Pennsylvania law. "A prosecutor can't go for the death sentence just because it's a nasty crime," Castor explained. "To ask for the death penalty, the killing has to meet one of the aggravating factors, which include the killing of a child . . . a killing in furtherance of a drug deal . . . a case where there are multiple murders . . . a case where the defendant has a history of violence . . ." and so forth. "Rabinowitz didn't fit any of these criteria," Castor pointed out. "The closest we could get would be that it was a killing committed in furtherance of a felony, but that wasn't close enough. If it had been available, we would have gone for it."

Less than two weeks later, the Pennsylvania Senate approved, by a 41–7 vote, a bill adding to the list of aggravating factors a killing committed with the intent of collecting on a life insurance policy. The bill still had to pass the house and be signed by the governor. If it eventually makes it into law, it will be the second aggravating factor adopted by the legislature as a result of a case in Montgomery County. Earlier, the legislature added as a factor a killing committed while the victim was under a protective order from the court, the result of one of Ferman's convictions.

Frank DeSimone and Jeffrey Miller did not participate in the January bar association program because DeSimone had appeared before the group earlier. However, after the Salus–Castor–Ferman presentation, Miller told the *Philadelphia Inquirer* that the prosecutors may have misjudged the degree of Craig's calculation. While the defense attorney failed to elaborate, he was quoted in the newspaper as saying that he "understood" that Craig and Stefanie had had "some kind of argument" before she was murdered, and that Rabinowitz was not as "diabolical" as the prosecutors had portrayed him.

This was essentially the same thing that DeSimone had told the bar association in a solo appearance on June 26, a little less than two months after Craig had been arrested. Appearing at a seminar entitled "TV News: Reporter, Judge and Jury," the defense attorney had also raised the possibility—speaking hypothetically, he stressed—that Craig and Stefanie had had a "fight" on the night she was killed. *If*, he underlined, that had been the case, the excessive coverage given the case by the media would have made it difficult for him to bargain for a reduced charge. According to DeSimone's statements after Rabinowitz changed his plea, the lawyer "knew what Rabinowitz had done" by the time he talked to the city's other lawyers, which raises questions about how hypothetical his statement really was.

Also, there is a problem with the "fight" argument: It does not explain the Ambien in Stefanie's system. Did Rabinowitz get her to ingest the drug *before* they had an argument? If so, he apparently was already planning to kill her. If it was *after* they had a tiff, the murder wasn't committed in the heat of passion. If they had been arguing, how did he convince Stefanie to take the drug?

Members of Rabinowitz's once-loyal circle of friends say that he has been trying to re-establish contact, writing letters offering to try to patch the shattered circle. The offers have been rejected out of hand. "There's no shot in hell we're ever going to have any contact with him," said Mark Hirtz, who had remained faithful to Rabinowitz longer than any of the others.

Some of them are still furious with Craig for using Stefanie *and* them so shamelessly. Even the one who had known him the longest—Elaine Miller—has considerable difficulty reconciling her thoughts about the man she thought she knew like a brother with the man who killed his wife, one of her best friends.

She said that a letter she received from Rabinowitz in early June was, in essence, a confession. "It was very intense; very heart-wrenching. He said his life had gotten out of control and he didn't deny anything. Craig always cared what other people thought about him. He said he hoped I wouldn't hate him and [that] one day I might forgive him."

Rabinowitz had been very close to the Millers' children, especially their son, who was then six. "At one point, Todd and I talked about naming Craig and Stef as the children's legal guardians," Elaine said. "That's how close we were. I knew a part of him very well for eleven years, but it wasn't the whole part of him."

Like almost everyone else, Elaine Miller still wonders why Craig turned to murder. "In the letter, he spoke about Stef," she said, "but it was really about him. He said he loved her . . . that he always would love her. But I don't think so. I don't think he ever *really* loved her. He saw her as a vehicle; he had a very powerful need for her. And at the end, he needed her death."

As for his change of plea, she, like many, remained skeptical. "I don't believe he really had this dream, but it was his way of preserving his status. His mind knew it would break under the stress of a trial, so his mind protected him. I think he's been as honest as he'll ever be; I think *he* believes his intentions were honest."

Where the Millers were once united in their affection toward Stefanie and Craig, they now are equally determined to remain attached to Haley, vowing to be a part of her life as long as she will let them.

Anne Newman and her son, Ira, are attending to Haley day-to-day. Craig's mother, Joyce, visits often and the two women remain friendly. Each has suffered huge losses, both personally and financially.

One of the concerns has been how to make sure there would be sufficient funds to provide for Haley until she became an adult. It is a complicated legal question that is still being resolved, but there has been good news in the wake of the bad.

On October 14, 1997, more than two weeks before Rabinowitz changed his plea, the Winding Way house was sold for $225,000. Although that was $5,000 less than they had paid for it, and $45,000 less than Rabinowitz had estimated it would bring after Stefanie's death, it more than paid off the two mortgages Rabinowitz had taken on the property. What was left went toward the $88,000 loan Rabinowitz had negotiated with Allied Mortgage of Villanova in February 1997, two and a half months before he killed his wife. While the Newmans had put up their house as collateral for the loan, an agreement was later worked out with Allied allowing Anne, Ira, and Haley to keep the Newman house.

A trust fund set up for Haley had, by mid-October, grown to more than $10,000.

More good news came from the two insurance companies that wrote policies on Stefanie beginning in late January. In November, the Provident Mutual Life Insurance Co. gave Anne a check for $500,000, declaring that the policy Craig and Stefanie took out on Stefanie's life had been negotiated in good faith. And in February, Neil Epstein said that an agreement had been reached with First Colony, the company that had finalized a $1 million policy on Stefanie only days before she was killed. While declining to reveal the amount of the settlement, Epstein said the family was satisfied. The money from the policies was set aside for Haley.

In addition, Anne Newman's legal advisers did not anticipate any problems in collecting on the other two policies: the one for $10,000 that she held through her employer, and the one for $360,000 that she had through the bar association. Both considerably pre-dated Rabinowitz's murder plot.

Despite the way things seem to be working out financially, Anne Newman understandably remained extremely bitter toward her former son-in-law. "Craig used my daughter from the time he met her," she said. "When he couldn't use her anymore, he got rid of her. Now he's doing what he's always done: sitting on his butt and eating off someone else."

Joyce Rabinowitz's financial status is not so clear. Although her son had been slowly repaying the $85,000 he had borrowed from her, his payments, according to the report from Ricardo Zayas, totaled only a little more than $23,000.

It appears unlikely that Rabinowitz's friends and the others who invested in his business will ever recoup their money, not to mention the credit card companies and the banks from which Rabinowitz had been drawing against a line of credit.

Unless Rabinowitz himself decides one day to fully bare his soul, no one is likely to know exactly what happened in the plain little house in Merion on the night of April 29, 1997.

For six terror-filled years, he couldn't be stopped—until one journalist ingeniously cracked his twisted code...

SLEEP MY LITTLE DEAD

The True Story of the Zodiac Killer

Kieran Crowley

The award-winning *New York Post* reporter whose brilliant work helped crack the Zodiac Killer's secret code reveals the inside story—as only he can tell it—of the man who terrorized the streets of New York City for six years, stalking, savagely attacking, and often killing his unsuspecting victims in cold blood.

SLEEP MY LITTLE DEAD
Kieran Crowley
____96339-4 $5.99 U.S./$7.99 CAN.